Evolutionary Economics and Social Complexity Science

Volume 10

The Japanese Association for Evolutionary Economics (JAFEE) always has adhered to its original aim of taking an explicit "integrated" approach. This path has been followed steadfastly since the Association's establishment in 1997 and, as well, since the inauguration of our international journal in 2004. We have deployed an agenda encompassing a contemporary array of subjects including but not limited to: foundations of institutional and evolutionary economics, criticism of mainstream views in the social sciences, knowledge and learning in socio-economic life, development and innovation of technologies, transformation of industrial organizations and economic systems, experimental studies in economics, agent-based modeling of socio-economic systems, evolution of the governance structure of firms and other organizations, comparison of dynamically changing institutions of the world, and policy proposals in the transformational process of economic life. In short, our starting point is an "integrative science" of evolutionary and institutional views. Furthermore, we always endeavor to stay abreast of newly established methods such as agent-based modeling, socio/econo-physics, and network analysis as part of our integrative links.

More fundamentally, "evolution" in social science is interpreted as an essential key word, i.e., an integrative and /or communicative link to understand and re-domain various preceding dichotomies in the sciences: ontological or epistemological, subjective or objective, homogeneous or heterogeneous, natural or artificial, selfish or altruistic, individualistic or collective, rational or irrational, axiomatic or psychological-based, causal nexus or cyclic networked, optimal or adaptive, micro- or macroscopic, deterministic or stochastic, historical or theoretical, mathematical or computational, experimental or empirical, agent-based or socio/econo-physical, institutional or evolutionary, regional or global, and so on. The conventional meanings adhering to various traditional dichotomies may be more or less obsolete, to be replaced with more current ones vis-à-vis contemporary academic trends. Thus we are strongly encouraged to integrate some of the conventional dichotomies.

These attempts are not limited to the field of economic sciences, including management sciences, but also include social science in general. In that way, understanding the social profiles of complex science may then be within our reach. In the meantime, contemporary society appears to be evolving into a newly emerging phase, chiefly characterized by an information and communication technology (ICT) mode of production and a service network system replacing the earlier established factory system with a new one that is suited to actual observations. In the face of these changes we are urgently compelled to explore a set of new properties for a new socio/economic system by implementing new ideas. We thus are keen to look for "integrated principles" common to the above-mentioned dichotomies throughout our serial compilation of publications. We are also encouraged to create a new, broader spectrum for establishing a specific method positively integrated in our own original way.

More information about this series at http://www.springer.com/series/11930

Masayuki Tadokoro • Susumu Egashira
Kazuya Yamamoto
Editors

Emerging Risks in a World of Heterogeneity

Interactions Among Countries with Different Sizes, Polities and Societies

Springer

Editors
Masayuki Tadokoro
Keio University
Tokyo, Japan

Susumu Egashira
Otaru University of Commerce
Hokkaido, Japan

Kazuya Yamamoto
Kyoto Sangyo University
Kyoto, Japan

ISSN 2198-4204 ISSN 2198-4212 (electronic)
Evolutionary Economics and Social Complexity Science
ISBN 978-981-10-7967-2 ISBN 978-981-10-7968-9 (eBook)
https://doi.org/10.1007/978-981-10-7968-9

Library of Congress Control Number: 2018931407

Printed on acid-free paper

This Springer imprint is published by the registered company Springer Nature Singapore Pte Ltd. part of Springer Nature
The registered company address is: 152 Beach Road, #21-01/04 Gateway East, Singapore 189721, Singapore

Preface

Heterogeneous World

It is even difficult to remember now that in the early 1990s when the Soviet Union collapsed, many believed that the "one world," where everybody on this planet would be linked by liberal values, was emerging at last. In fact, it seemed inevitable then that the world was converging politically to liberal democracy and economically to market capitalism. It was almost unthinkable to imagine any geopolitical challenger to the USA, whose military primacy looked invincible. While the Japanese economic challenge had been widely debated only a few years before, the American economy made an impressive recovery in the 1990s, and its economic and cultural impacts were transmitted through the rapidly globalizing market economy. Now the American way of life seemed irresistible and there seemed to be no alternative.

After nearly a generation, however, it is hard to believe that we live in a world where "history has ended." In retrospect, the biggest winners in the era of globalization were not liberal democracies, but China, ruled by the Communist Party. While China made a brave try at the marketization of its economy, the Communist Party firmly retained its monopoly of power and never yielded to criticism or pressure from the West on human rights issues. Russia, on the other hand, embarked on the radical privatization of its economy, as well as the rapid democratization of its political institutions. Gorbachev's bold initiatives were widely hailed by the Western intellectuals, and Russia was even invited to G7 summits as a major member of liberal democracy. Gorbachev, however, was much less popular among Russians, as the latter experienced severe economic disruption and corruption during the economic transition, as well as political humiliation resulting from the disintegration of the Soviet Empire. Soon Russia's democracy turned into authoritarianism rule by Vladimir Putin. Helped by rapid rises of oil prices, Russian under the Putin regime managed to recover considerably its economic condition as well as its presence as an independent geopolitical player in the world, as we witnessed in its intervention in Ukraine and Syria.

While the former communist camp has recovered its presence without turning into liberal democracies, the advantages of the major liberal democracies, which was supposed to be the model for the rest of the world, have become increasingly questioned by their own people. The overwhelming predominance of the USA, which was even compared to the ancient Roman Empire, was badly damaged by its reckless invasion into Iraq in 2003 and the Lehman Crisis in 2008. Above all, Donald Trump, with his explicit hostility toward postwar multilateral institutions, was elected the US president in 2016. At the time of writing, it is the US president that is the most serious destabilizing factor to the postwar liberal politico-economic order that the USA built and nurtured.

Europe, as the most important pillar of the liberal international order led by the USA, substantially strengthened its international presence since its geopolitical environment dramatically improved as a result of the end of the Cold War. As European integration became wider and deeper, Europeans recovered their confidence as a major independent player in the global affairs. But discord within the EU intensified as the financial crisis in Greece in 2010 and the Syrian refugee crisis in 2015 continued. In addition, the British referendum in 2016 resulted in the UK's decision to leave the EU and delivered a serious blow to the future of EU. Underneath these events, there was unmistakable disillusionment on the part of people in the street over the liberal projects largely led by political and intellectual elites. Voices expressing concerns about a weakening sense of belonging to familiar national and local identities and rising migration and refugees who are not fully integrated into the existing society are no longer limited to marginal radical right wingers but shared widely by the masses. This has resulted in the rising power of "populist" political parties across Europe.

It seems clear by now that the world emerging 30 years after the end of the Cold War is not the one united by the liberal solidarism. It is rather a world where forces opposing the liberal West led by the USA are increasing their influence or a heterogeneous global system which contains many differences that are highly difficult, if not impossible, to be accommodated and subsumed by liberal institutions and values. It is therefore exploring ways for better coexistence in a heterogeneous world, rather than promoting progress based upon liberal values, that is the challenge we are facing today.

The Intertwined World

A heterogeneous world is nothing new in itself. History clearly shows that the world has been full of a variety of civilizations that had norms and worldviews which were mutually incompatible. Ancient civilizations were somewhat like isolated microcosmoses with only limited mutual exchanges. Although it is well known that the Ancient Roman Empire had cultural exchanges with the Han Empire in

China through the Silk Road, the relations were highly selective and sporadic in nature.

If we turn to Japan's experiences, it is undeniable Japan had long been a minor cultural entity located at the margins of Chinese civilization. Thanks to its relative geographical isolation, separated from the continent by the sea, it could maintain political independence. Japan actually had two encounters with the West. When Western merchants and Christian missionaries visited Japan after a Portuguese wrecked ship was first washed ashore to the Southern part of Japan in the sixteenth century, the Japanese showed enormous interest in Western civilization. They quickly mastered how to make a musket and soon became one of the mass producers of the time. The Christian population also increased substantially, and it is estimated that at its peak it numbered as much as 700,000, which considering the total size of the Japanese population at the time (about 10% of today) represents a much higher proportion than today. Nevertheless, the shogunate government of the day placed international trade under monopoly and imposed a complete ban of Christianity by the mid-seventeenth century.

In contrast, at the time of the second encounter when an American Navy fleet armed with newly developed technologies visited Japan in 1853, the Japanese did not have any luxury to repel the Western impact. Geopolitical conditions no longer gave Japan an effective shield against pressure from the outside to protect its own institutions and the value system. Like many non-Western nations in the world, they did not have effective means to counter modern Western pressure. This forced Japan to face difficult challenges to modernize itself to defend its independence.

In the world in the twenty-first century characterized by globalization, neither geographical distance nor national borders allow different players to coexist by territorially segregating themselves. Now, it is just a fact of life that an enormous number of people with different and often incompatible set of worldviews and value systems are forced to interact constantly with each other. In the world of the Internet and ballistic missiles, geographical segregation propped by institutions such as sovereignty is an even more unreliable way to accommodate players with potentially conflicting goals and views of the world.

Today, non-Western modernity with illiberal regimes is just as commonplace. As modern technologies and innovative energies are no longer monopolized by the West, the cross-border flows of influences cannot take place on a one-way street, but they flow both ways between the West and the non-West, sometimes clashing and interfering the others. China, for example, is increasingly aggressive in its claim of territorial irredentism. It has also started using its economic leverage to challenge the postwar Western international institutional arrangements by setting up parallel institutions such as AIIB. The One Belt One Road Initiative may not be as peaceful and apolitical way of communications as was the ancient Silk Road.

The Purpose and Design of This Volume

This volume is a product of a research group with a variety of different expertise with shared interests. As our specialties differ, our academic assumptions, methodologies, and even our terminologies are not the same. We, ourselves, are a highly "heterogeneous" group. While we try to overcome our intellectual barriers by repeating workshops, dining together, and enjoying *sake* together, we came to the shared view that one of major features of the emerging world is the management of the heterogeneous and intertwined system and agreed to undertake analyses of risks to such a system. Needless to say, we never claim that we have comprehensive views on this vast question. While academic disciplines are increasingly narrowly specialized, the challenges today's world is facing are—conversely—in need of multidisciplinary approaches. We hope that our attempt is worth sharing with readers.

Part I focuses on the sizes of countries. One of the striking features of the emerging powers is they are all countries with large populations. China and India in particular are mega-states with population sizes of a different order. The two chapters in this part were written by a political scientist and economists, respectively. In Chap. 1, Tadokoro, after reviewing classical arguments of political thoughts on the optimum sizes of countries, tries to point out potential sources of political disorder resulting from a system consisting of players with vastly different sizes. Yuki and Cen approach the question of the optimum country size from an economic perspective. According to the statistical (regression) analysis they conducted, there is a modest advantage of largeness in terms of economic performances of countries, but the advantage becomes smaller as the economic size of the county concerned gets bigger and when the country becomes more open to international trade and financial transactions.

Part II deals with potential risks resulting from the interactions of players with different regimes and internal structures. In his chapter, Sejima discusses the relation between trade and warfare among heterogeneous states. The chapter points out several provisional hypotheses by employing multi-agent simulation. Chapter 4 focuses on the global foreign aid regime. Ogawa looks into the impact of the expanding roles of non-OECD donors and emphasizes learning by the traditional DAC countries. The traditional DAC donors learned the approaches of non-DAC donors to change their own approaches and participate in the new regime that non-DAC donors established. It is now largely forgotten that Japan was portrayed by Western intellectuals as a unique economic power posing a threat to the order dominated by the "West." Suzuki, by drawing Japan's experiences in the early 1990s, demonstrates how different politico-economic structures of countries can result in frictions, even under conditions of interdependence.

The two chapters in Part III try to analyze dynamic links between states' internal structures and external conditions. By doing so, the authors try to show that a variety of domestic social structures can result in different consequences. In Chap. 6, Komiya, Miyagawa, and Tago demonstrate how Japanese public support for international development assistance and international peace operations sharply differs and how the contrasting public attitudes entail foreign policy choices for the government of Japan. Chapter 7 is an attempt to assess the impact of international intervention in civil war. Conflicting parties decide on their behavior by taking the possibility of intervention into consideration, but intervention is always uncertain. Ishiguro and Yamamoto show the different consequences that result from the players' estimates on uncertainties.

One of the project's notable contributions lies in its interdisciplinary nature. The two chapters in Part IV are an attempt to apply methodologies of different fields to the study of international politics. Egashira argues how agent-based simulation models can be usefully applied to the field of international politics, which is a very complex system where experiments are practically impossible. By setting up a virtual laboratory in a computer and cultivating agents with different state-like natures, he successfully demonstrates how the system containing different types of agents evolves over time through his virtual experiment. In Chap. 9, Hashimoto and Yamada also employ multi-agent simulation. Their experiments demonstrate the effects of the heterogeneity of agents in the provision of global public goods. In doing so, they found an interesting synergetic effect of agents' self-recognition of their own efficacy and agents' normative commitment to the provision of GPG.

Nobody knows the limits of the attempts made here in addressing the vast question we are posing better than the authors of this volume. We still have a long way to go before we can give more relevant and convincing arguments. Nevertheless, we are hoping that our efforts here will stimulate readers to further develop our intellectual exploration in their own ways and improve our understanding of the emerging world.

Tokyo, Japan — Masayuki Tadokoro
Hokkaido, Japan — Susumu Egashira
Kyoto, Japan — Kazuya Yamamoto

Contents

Part I
Size

Chapter 1
Mega-states vs. Compact Powers: Risks in the Emerging International System

Masayuki Tadokoro

Abstract One of the most striking features of the emerging world is the rise of countries with vast populations like China and India, while the number of smaller independent states also keeps growing. What kinds of conflicts are likely to take place in the international system consisting of countries with highly different population sizes? After reviewing classical arguments regarding advantages and disadvantage of large population size of countries, this chapter points out three patterns of risks, namely, the implosion of empires, conflicts over sphere of influences, and interimperial conflicts in transnational spaces.

Keywords Population size · Empires · Governance · Innovation · Sphere of influence

1.1 Introduction

About seven billion humans currently living on this planet are organized separately into political units called sovereign states. It has been argued for long that sovereign states are outdated in the age of globalization, nuclear weapons, economic interdependence, and regionalism, and the end of the sovereign state system has been repeatedly predicted. But the number of states has been steadily increasing. In 2016 there are 193 member countries of the United Nations, whereas the League of Nations was started in 1919 by only 42 members. In addition to the UN members, there are unrecognized bounties, or de facto independent countries, such as Taiwan, Somaliland, South Ossetia, Kosova, and Nagorno Karabakh Republic. It seems likely that the number of independent states will further increase, rather than decrease, in view of many active separatist movements in many parts of the world.

This chapter is developed from my earlier article (Tadokoro 2016).

M. Tadokoro (✉)
Faculty of Law, Keio University, Tokyo, Japan
e-mail: tadokoro@law.keio.ac.jp

M. Tadokoro et al. (eds.), *Emerging Risks in a World of Heterogeneity*, Evolutionary Economics and Social Complexity Science 10,
https://doi.org/10.1007/978-981-10-7968-9_1

But as the modern state system has expanded to cover all over the world, the states have become increasingly diverse in many ways. As is well known, while many in developing world are suffering from severe poverty, in the wealthy world, the challenge is obesity rather than hunger. It is even hard to remember now, but at the end of the Cold War, the world was widely expected to converge to liberal democracies. However, this still remains wishful thinking on the part of Western liberal intellectuals, particularly in view of the sorry state of the Middle East after the "Arab Spring," and the (re)rises of authoritarian China and Russia, the two major players of the communist camp under the Cold War.

Heterogeneity of the system, however, can be also found in the vastly different sizes of states. On the one end of the spectrum, there is China, with a population of more than one billion, which is now a major challenger to the US hegemony. There is also India, which is expected to surpass China in total population in the near future. These countries could be even called empires, as they have not only large territories and populations but also highly diverse ethnic groups within their jurisdictions. On the other end of the spectrum, there are ministates, like Tuvalu, whose population is even less than 10,000. In fact, a great majority of today's independent states are small states. The combined population of half of the UN member states adds up to no more than 5% of the global total population (The 21st Century Concert Study Group 2014).

While it is unlikely that those ministates will be a major force in shaping the emerging international system, it is premature to conclude that the coming international system will be dominated by several empires. Zhiwei Cen identified two groups of major countries by his component analysis as is shown in the figures (Cen 2015). One is a group headed by mega-states like China and India, with literally extraordinary population and comparable and rapidly growing total GDP. The other is wealthy G7 countries. They are relatively compact in their sizes but enjoy much higher levels of per capita GDP and better domestic governance. While those countries, with a notable exception of the USA, have less than 10% of population than China or India, they are wealthier and technologically more advanced and attract immigrants for better life from the emerging empires rather than the other way around.

In Fig. 1.1, the "power element" consisting of population and total GDP is set as one axis and the "governance element" consisting of variables representing social stability and the level of governance is expressed in the other axis. In Fig. 1.2, the "power element" consisting of total GDP and military spending is plotted in one axis, and the "maturity element" consisting of per capita GDP and other governance index is expressed in the other axis. In either figure, BRICS (though Brazil is somewhat exceptional) are comparable to G7 countries in terms of power, but they are located in a contrasting space to G7 in terms of their level of governance and social maturity.

Thus, major players in the emerging international system can be divided into two types of countries. One is the group whose comparative advantage lies in total size, the other in quality of governance, or (at the risk of oversimplification) it is a competition between quantity and quality.

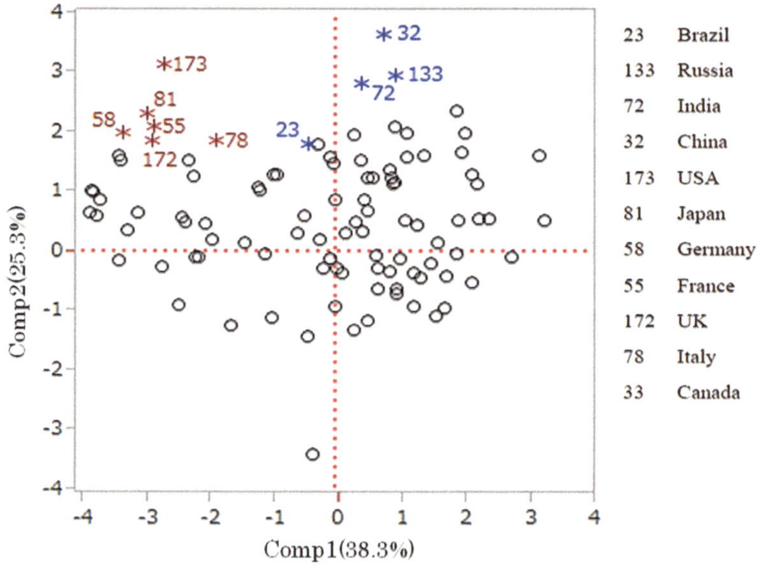

Fig. 1.1 Principal component analysis (Comp1 = Governance, Comp2 = Power)

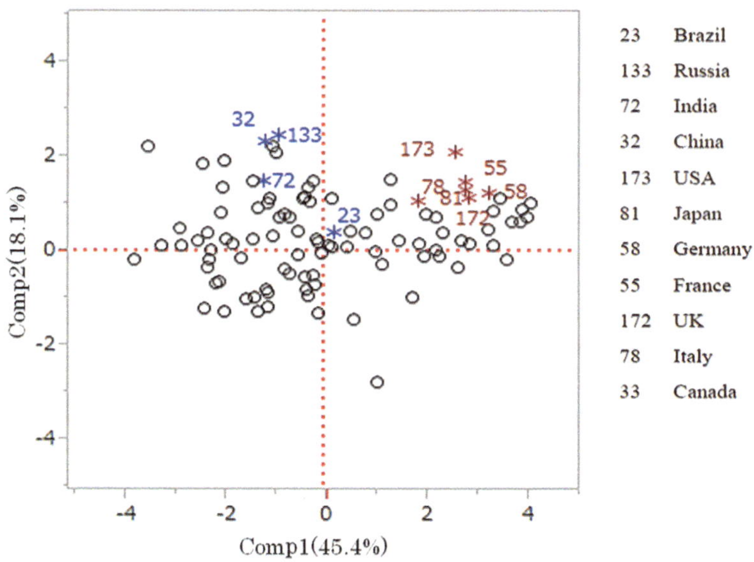

Fig. 1.2 Principal component analysis (2): (Comp1 = Maturity, Comp2 = Power) (*Source*: Cen, op. cit)

1.2 Power and Population Sizes

There is rich stock of insights by great thinkers in the past on the optimum size of the state.[1] There are two contrasting schools of thoughts. One of them emphasizes problems resulting from overpopulation. A classic example of this school is a population theory put forward by Robert Malthus. As is well known, he argued that while increase in food production can increase only arithmetically, population increases geometrically. Thus even if some improvement of productivity takes place, the fruits of improvement would be consumed by the increased population. Therefore, people are doomed to stay at the subsistence level unless population increase is controlled. This dismal view is still relevant enough when one sees poverty in the underdeveloped part of the world. Thus population control has been always a serious agenda for development, and this is exactly why the Chinese government, as is well known, started the "one-child policy" in 1979. What is less well known is even in China there were voices of concern about depopulation. Sun Yat-sen, a prominent Chinese nationalist leader, argued as follows:

> The population of China has not increased during the past hundred years, and it will hardly increase during the next hundred years unless we some way to stimulate the growth. In the last century, the United States has grown tenfold; Russia, fourfold; England and Japan, threefold; Germany, two and a half fold; and -France, least of all; has, however, added one fourth to her population. While their populations are daily growing, ours is at a standstill, or, what is worse, is becoming smaller. Study our own history: as the Han (Chinese) race multiplied, the aboriginal races of China – Miaos, Yaos, Laos, Tungs, and others-disappeared; if we, instead, had been under pressure of population increase on their part, anyone can see that we would have been the ones to disappear. (Sun 1927)

The Malthusian idea focuses on the finiteness of available resources. The major concern is poverty created by population pressure and the miserable condition of welfare of individuals reproduced by the mechanism. This may also have foreign policy implications as well, because expansionism and imperialism could be driven by population. In other words, population pressure would affect goals of states in a way which makes interstate relations more confrontational with each other by provoking competition over limited resources. In addition, a series of sociological instabilities have been also pointed out. When the population is growing, the proportion of younger generation will become larger. The rapid inflows of the younger people into urban areas would encourage social instability, political radicalism, and even revolutionary movements, including terrorism.[2] Today's many of Malthusians arguments take the form environmentalism stressing the limits of environmental capacity of this planet rather than limited availability of farmland.

Sun, however, was concerned about the power of a state, or the capacity of a state to compete in international environments, rather than the welfare of individuals.

---

[1]On discourses on population in studies of international politics in Japan, see Haruna (2015). Regarding changed discourse on population size in modern Japan, see Tadokoro (2014).

[2]For instance, see Heinsohn (2003).

From this perspective, the more population a state has, the more powerful it is. This logic applies particularly well when agriculture is the main industry of the nation and the number of soldiers a state can deploy is a satisfactory indicator of national power.

The realist school of international politics is generally supportive to the position. H. J. Morgenthau sees populations as an element of power though he makes cautious reservations. He argues as follows in his well-known textbook:

> Though one is not justified in considering a country to be very powerful because its population is greater than that of most other countries, it is true that no country can remain or become a first-rate power which does not belong to the more populous nations of the earth. Without a large population it is impossible to establish and keep going the industrial plant necessary for the successful conduct of modern war; to put into the field the large number of combat groups to fight on land, on the sea, and in the air; and, finally, to fill the cadres of the troops, considerably more numerous than the combat troops, which must supply the latter with food, means of transportation and communication, ammunition, and weapons. It is for this reason that imperialistic countries stimulate population growth with all kinds of incentives, as did Nazi Germany and Fascist Italy, and then use of that growth as an ideological pretext for imperialistic expansion. (Morgenthau 1967)

In reality, industrial revolution clearly reduced the link between population and power by dramatically improving productivity, which allowed European powers with relatively small population to dominate the whole world. But does this mean that once the waves of industrialization cover all across the world, we will go back to the world where populous empires are predominant in international politics? Raymond Aron asked in 1962, "Is it conceivable, beyond the phase of industrialization, once every nation has achieved a comparable productivity, that the relation may depend exclusively on the number of men?" (Aron 1966).

About a half century later, Akihiko Tanaka answered, "yes," to the question Aron posed:

> Once technology for improving productivity spread across the world, productivity of a territory concerned is determined by the size of its population. Modern history has come full circle in this way. In the modern period, European countries got powerful by getting magic wands, but the wands can be obtained by anybody today. Once everybody gained these wands, there was nothing magical left in them. Once modernity is completed, distribution of power will revert to the original pattern. Postmodernity, at the end of the day, is pre-modernity. (Tanaka 2009)

1.3 Small But Rich States

The link between power and population size may not be as simple as Tanaka mentions even in the premodern era because sources of power were not limited to agricultural production.

In mediaeval Europe, a variety of polities coexisted side by side. One of the most powerful polities was city-state such as Hanseatic towns, Venice, and the Dutch Republic headed by Amsterdam. Venice, which was "the great power with the least area and population in history" (Kōsaka 1999), enjoyed the hegemony in the East

Mediterranean for more than 200 years since the thirteenth century. Venice's source of power was international commerce between Northern Europe and the Orient, as well as service industries like finance associated with the commerce. In addition to taking advantage of huge profits out of long-distance trade by controlling the vital commercial routes between Europe and the Orient, its innovative capacity such as double-entry bookkeeping and the standardization of ship-building methods made it one of the most powerful players in European politics of the time.

The Dutch Republic was also a small but powerful state in the seventeenth century. As noted by Paul Kennedy:

> The Habsburg-owned Netherlands, a mere part of a part of a vast dynastic empire, restricted in population and territorial extent, which swiftly became a great power inside and outside Europe for almost a century. It differed from the other states – although not from its Italian forerunner, Venice – in possessing a republican, oligarchic form of government; but its most distinctive characteristic was that the foundation of its strength were firmly anchored in the world of trade, industry, and finance. It was, to be sure, a formidable until eclipsed by England in the later seventeenth century. (Kennedy 1987)

England, which took over naval hegemony from the Netherlands by the end of the seventeenth century, had a smaller population and territory than its continental rivals like France or the Habsburg Empire. The country was relatively marginal in the European civilization for long, but it could become a hegemon in the eighteenth century, even before industrial revolution, primarily because of its success in international trade, including the slave trade.

In contrast to large agrarian empires whose power is based on control of land through the mobilization of large-scale ground forces, these small states focused on the control of sea lanes of commerce to take advantage of profitable long-distance trades. Even on land, great empires in the past were not necessarily dependent upon agrarian production. The Mongolian Empire, the largest ever empire, ruled almost all major parts of the Eurasian continent in the thirteenth century. Initially it was its military superiority deriving from highly mobile cavalry forces that allowed the nomads to exploit agrarian economies. But because of its unified rule over the whole Eurasian continent, overland commerce was greatly facilitated. This allowed the empire to mobilize resources necessary to reproduce its rule by taxing on commerce. Under the rule of Kublai Khan, "80% of revenue of the central authority came from state monopoly of salt trades and the remaining 10–15% came from other forms of commercial taxation (Sugiyama 1992)." In other words, this empire was also based on commercial profits.

1.4 Dynamic Effects of Innovation

In the industrial world, it is neither agriculture nor commerce but technology that has been driving economic growth. Populous countries are evidently advantageous for ample availability of labor. Capital may be introduced through international financial markets, and existing technology can also be acquired from abroad. But for growth, what matters is improvement of productivity through continuous innovations. Thus, distribution of power among states is also very much dependent on dynamism created by innovation rather than static distribution of labor and capital.

An illustrative example is the collapse of the Soviet Union. The great power that ruled a vast territory and a huge population was one of the two main players of the Cold War competing with the USA for nearly 50 years. It was never successful in achieving a wealthy society, but it successfully matched militarily the USA and even enjoyed quantitative superiority. The Soviet science and technology were far from backward. On the contrary, it launched the first satellite in the world and could produce weapons that allowed it to be one of the superpowers. But as is well known, it simply could not keep up with rapid innovation in electronic and information technology, which in the end caused its defeat in the Cold War.

By definition innovation is new and thus cannot be predicted by existing conditions. But several points can be made with reasonable certainty. Since it is only human beings that can create new ideas, it is safe to assume that the bigger the size of population is, the more brain power is available for the state. On the other hand, however, for intellectual creativity, freedom is a critical condition, but huge empires with vast and powerful central governments tend to be a threat for the freedom.

Classical thinkers in eighteenth-century Europe are generally negative toward the great empires, because the vast empire can easily damage intellectual and spiritual vitality. In order to rule the vast population, formidable power is needed to maintain its cohesion. But the powerful and vast bureaucracy can oppress free and innovative intellectual challenges. J. J. Rousseau argued as follows:

> Talents are hidden, virtues unknown, vices unpunished in this multitude of men who do not know one another, and whom the seat of the supreme administration has brought together in one place. The Chiefs, overwhelmed by public affairs, see nothing by themselves, clerks govern the State. In the end the measures which have to be taken to maintain the general authority, an authority which so many distant Officials want either to elude or take advantage of, absorb all public attention, there is none left for the people's happiness, and scarcely any left for its defense in an emergency, and that is how a body too large for its constitution collapses and perishes, crushed under its own weight. (Rousseau 1997)

He then concludes, "one should rely more on the vigor born of a good government, than on the resources provided by a large territory (Ibid.)."

It is only humans that can carry out innovation but human resources can be developed only by education. For individual access to education, a level of per capita GDP as opposed to total GDP is more relevant to total size of resources available for a state. If the above arguments are correct, smaller and better-governed countries must be more innovative than huge mega-states with large population (Table 1.1).

According to the 2015 report of the World Intellectual Property Organization, among the most innovative ten countries, only the USA has a population of more than 100 million (Dutta et al. 2015). It is of no surprise that countries like the USA and the UK are ranked very high: the two states can attract ambitious and excellent talent from all over the world with their top universities, educate students, and disseminate their outputs in their own language, English. But at the same time, it is impressive that small and wealthy countries like Switzerland, Sweden, the

Table 1.1 Top 10 innovators in the world

Rank	Country	Score
1	Switzerland	66.8
2	UK	62.42
3	Sweden	62.4
4	Netherlands	61.58
5	USA	60.1
6	Finland	59.97
7	Singapore	59.36
8	Ireland	59.13
9	Luxembourg	59.02
10	Denmark	57.7

Source: Global Innovation Index 2015

Netherlands, and Finland are highly evaluated. In addition, all the countries from the top through 28th are high-income countries, which suggests per capita income is correlated to innovative capacity. Although both China and India are outperforming than the level predicted by the level of per capita GDP (China is ranked 29th and India 81st), their innovative power is still far behind smaller but wealthier countries (Fig. 1.3).

1.5 Cohesion vs. Scales

One of the chronicle difficulties in measuring power lies in the fact that while allocations of tangible resource are observable, its effective and efficient mobilization is much harder to estimate. The relation between the sizes of nations and effective governance was a major theme for classical thinkers.

Plato argued the ideal number of citizens of a city-state should be 5040. He even suggested means to control the population size (Plato 1960). Aristotle also thought about the optimum size of a state. If it is too small, the city-state cannot be self-sufficient, but too large population makes it impossible to make collective actions efficiently. In his *Politics*, he argues the optimum standard of population is "the greatest surveyable number required for achieving a life of self-sufficiency" (Aristotle 1995).

Similarly, J. J. Rousseau argues that there is a limit in the size of territory for a state to control. If it is too small, it will be unsustainable, and if too large, effective rule will be impossible. He then argues:

> Just as nature has set limits to the stature of a well-formed man, beyond which it makes only Giants and Dwarfs, so, too, with regard to the best constitution of a State, there are bounds, to the size it can have in order not to be either too large to be well governed, or too small to be self-sustaining. In every body politic there is a maximum of force which it cannot exceed, and from which it often strays by dint of growing too large. The more the social bond stretches, the looser it grows, and in general a small State is proportionately stronger than a large one. (Rousseau 1997)

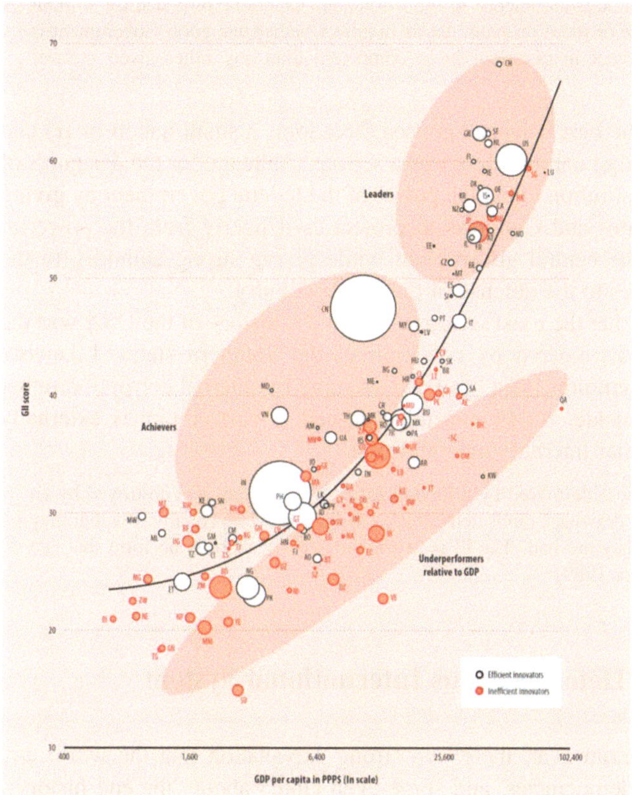

Selected county codes
CH Switzerland
CN China
DE Germany
EE Estonia
ET Ethiopia
FI Finland
GB Great Britain
IN India
JP Japan
KR ROK
LU Luxemburg
MW Malawi
NG Nigeria
NL Netherlands
PH Philippines
PK Pakistan
RU Russia
SD Sudan
SE Sweden
VE Vietnam
VN Venezuela

Fig. 1.3 Innovation and per capita GDP (PPP) (sizes of circles represent population sizes) (*Source*: Global Innovation Index 2015, p. 28)

In addition, a larger state must rule over a more diverse population. Diversity can be a source of vitality and creativity, but at the same time, it can reduce the cohesion of a society and weaken the link between a state and the population it rules. Making sure that those with different ideas, interests, and worldviews live together and work out the common good is the very essence of politics. But in a vast empire, it is hard to rely on the natural social cohesion of inhabitants such as common religions, common ethnicity, common languages, and shared collective memories. Sharing costs and redistributing benefits will be more challenging for empires than states with more compact and cohesive populations.

Needless to say, however, larger countries do still have a decisive advantage. The strategic depth they enjoy out of their territorial and population size and the huge amount of resources they possess are highly valuable assets for competition among states. Thus, John Jay, one of the Founding Fathers of the USA, called for creating a unified military force under the command of a single president instead of military forces of individual states:

> As the safety of the whole is the interest of the whole, and cannot be provided for without Government, either one or more or many, let us inquire whether one good Government is not, relative to the object in question, more competent than any other given number whatever. (Jay 1961)

But how to strike the best balance between "freedom" a small nation offers and "national security" a large nation offers was a serious challenge for the designers of the USA. The US Constitution limits the power of the federal government by giving large power to the states and Congress to protect civil liberty from the powerful executive branch of the central government while giving strong authority to the president when it comes to the defense of the whole country.

Still, it is symbolic that the most serious crisis of the history of the USA was the Civil War, which was triggered by cessation of the Southern states. Likewise, collapses of historical empires have been caused more by internal corruption rather than invasion from outside. As Montesquieu argued, a vast empire is externally powerful but has peculiar internal vulnerabilities:

> If a republic is small, it is destroyed by a foreign force; if it is large, it is destroyed by an internal vice. This dual drawback taints democracies and aristocracies equally, whether they are good or whether they are bad. The ill is in the thing itself; there is no form that can remedy it. (Montesquieu 1989)

1.6 Risks of the Heterogeneous International System

After the end of the Cold War, there was strong expectation that the world will converge into liberal democracies, and some even talked about "the end history." Coupled with democratic peace theorem, which dismisses possibilities of wars among democracies, the world after the collapse of the Communist Soviet was expected to enjoy peace and stability at least among major countries. But in addition to increased intrastate conflicts in many failed states, post-Cold War world was characterized more by remarkable rises of poor but vast mega-states like China and India, rather than substantial democratization. In a world where vast empires and compact powers were interacting, conflicts would not likely be the same as the ones under the traditional European international system, where relatively homogeneous states were constantly interacting with each other.

1.6.1 Imperial Implosion

We could expect that relations among the empires can be stable if they form relatively autarkic systems. Huge and invulnerable empires may have a better chance to coexist in an isolated manner as ancient empires actually did. The Roman Empire and Han China coexisted with practically no regular political, economic, and cultural exchanges, thus no chance for mutual conflicts. Empires had a better chance for self-sufficiency, as resources available within it were very huge. Furthermore, culturally, they had their own value systems and distinctive cultural codes. The traditional empires were all self-contained civilizations. If the intercourses between them were limited, there were only limited dangers of conflict.

Today's empires, however, face more serious challenges in controlling their own huge population and different ethnic groups in their vast territories than in the past. Ancient empires were civilizations with highly open membership and could offer attractive cultural and economic benefits to "barbarians." As the Roman Empire expanded, it constantly Romanized the population of new territories they conquered, and China repeatedly Sinicized invading nomads from the North throughout its history, maintaining an amazing continuity of its civilization. But today, empires are increasingly dependent on nationalism for the source of their political legitimacy. The Soviet Union used to be a multiethnic empire ruled by Marxist universalist ideology, but now it has nowhere else but to turn to nationalism to justify its regime. Postcolonial and post-Maoist China is unmistakably highly nationalistic, talking about the rejuvenation of great "Chinese people." Even the USA, which boasts its origin as an immigrant nation, is now talking about "America First." This is obviously a double-edged sword, as by definition the empire is multiethnic, and fanning nationalism inevitably creates negative reactions from within.

With less coherence in its society, once the empires lose their capacity to offer satisfactory material benefits to its huge number of people, all sorts of centrifugal forces could be discharged. They could be internally weakened or could even start disintegrating at worst. In fact, this is exactly the way many traditional empires collapsed. While ruling a vast population is always a challenge, now it may be even more difficult to control centrifugal forces as today's empires are not immune from modern ideas such as democracy and self-determination. Religious or dynastic authority cannot look as legitimate to the people of more urbanized and modern industrial empires, as was to the subjects of the ancient empires.

Instead, as today's rising empires are highly dependent upon economic success in an open global economy in justifying their regimes, they could be more vulnerable to global economic instability than smaller yet better-governed states. As sharing hardship can be more difficult to manage than compact countries, an economic shock would reduce the state's capacity to co-opt potentially rebellious groups encouraging centrifugal forces. Other transnational challenges such as environmental issues would have the same effects, as the vast size of the empire may not offer better protection, and poorer empires may be less capable of controlling destabilizing effects than smaller but richer countries.

Imperial implosion would be inevitably a matter of serious global concern, because it would inevitably have major destabilizing impacts over the rest of the world. It could destabilize geopolitical balances, stimulate aggressive nationalism, or could cause an uncontrolled massive outflow of the population of an empire. Chaos of empires can be as dangerous as their imperialism to the rest of the world.

1.6.2 Failed Control of Spheres of Influence

Cooperation among great major players may offer the best hope for the coming global order. But detailed institutionalization of relations among empires will be more difficult than among compact powers, as they are more autonomous and less interdependent, thus less willing to adjust their behavior to accommodate interests of others. In fact, China, Russia, India, and the USA all tend to act more unilaterally and are more selective in binding themselves to international institutions.

Thus, a concert among empires is in many cases organized by segmentation of the world: in other words, mutual recognition of spheres of influence. An illustrative example of attempts for this type of concert can be seen in the following remarks made by a high-ranking Chinese navy officer, who was reported to have told a US counterpart in 2009:

> You, the US, take Hawaii East and we, China, will take Hawaii West and the Indian Ocean. Then you will not need to come to the western Pacific and the Indian Ocean and we will not need to go to the Eastern Pacific. If anything happens there, you can let us know and if something happens here, we will let you know. (The Indian Express 2009)

Stabilization through mutual recognition of spheres of influence of powers did work generally well in Europe after the Congress in Vienna. Powers managed European issues largely through diplomacy while mutually recognizing status of other great powers. But it seems that controlling spheres of influence is much more difficult today than it was in the nineteenth century.

First, rising empires today have difficulty in co-opting smaller states within their spheres of influences. As we have seen, the comparative advantage of today's rising empires lies in their large aggregate sizes of power resources, not in their quality of lifestyles or attractive intellectual lives. Unlike ancient empires that could co-opt "barbaric states" with their advanced civilization or attractive religious or political symbols, they cannot cajole lesser powers through the soft power, nor can they bribe wealthier compact powers.

If co-opting is impossible, the empires would need to rely on coercion. Coercion is generally an inefficient way of exercising power, as it invites resistance and drains away resources. Besides, research shows that the odds for winning wars are not as favorable for larger states as the imbalances of power would suggest. This "paradox of power" can be attributable to a variety of factors, but one of the plausible explanations is that smaller states can mobilize limited resources for limited goals more efficiently through better governance and tighter social cohesion.[3]

Moreover, smaller states today have a better chance of resisting imperial coercion than in the past. In the globalized world today, geographical segmentation as was suggested by the Chinese above is less relevant. Smaller states could balance coercive pressure from the regional empires by bringing in powers from outside of the imperial sphere. Cubans successfully resisted American pressure for long by

[3]Regarding "paradox of power," see, for example, Yamamoto (2012).

allying with the USSR, Pakistanis do the same vis-a-vis India through its relations with China, and the Japanese have been reacting to mounting Chinese military pressure by strengthening its security alliance with the USA. Empires today cannot help having much more globalized stakes than in the past. Thus, they would find it difficult to reach effective agreements upon neatly defined geographical spheres of influences, which, in turn, makes it difficult for them to control smaller states within their respective spheres.

1.6.3 Interimperial Confrontation in Transnational Spaces

As was repeatedly discussed, the advantage of empires is the vast territories and population they control, which provide them with large resources as well as their deep strategic depth. As military conquest of the vast empires is practically impossible, relations among invulnerable empires may be more stable than those among smaller states that are constantly exposed to mutual existentialist geopolitical threats. But in the twenty-first century when borders are increasingly porous, control of vast territories does not necessarily guarantee assured and exclusive control of territories. In addition, there are a variety of increasingly important non-territorial spaces where empires confront each other.

Cyberspace, for instance, is one of front lines of interimperial competition today. It is widely known that cyberattacks have been actually conducted by many players (Yamada 2017). In 2009–2010, nuclear facilities in Natanz in Iran were attacked and infiltrated by the Stuxnet worm which broke a number of uranium enriching centrifuges. The attack is widely believed to be conducted by the US government under the code name of Olympic Games (New York Times 2012). The USA certainly is not the only country that is conducting cyberattacks. China is believed to be involved in hacking foreign corporations and organizations to steal confidential information. The Unit 61398 of PLA's General Staff Department is dedicated for the purpose, which, according to an estimate, is staffed by hundreds and perhaps thousands of personnel (Mandiant 2013). According to US intelligence organizations, Russia also was reported to have hacked a variety of American institutions including Democratic Party bodies to influence the result of 2016 US presidential election (DHS and FBI 2016). Russia is also alleged to have been very actively involved in cyberattacks to many other nations (Windrem 2016).

When states compete and confront each other in cyberspace, a large army and many missiles are simply irrelevant. Even vast empires with deep strategic depth can be easily infiltrated, which makes it difficult even for them to coexist peacefully, protected by large territories. Likewise, for security related to the outer space or to the ecosystem, the large sizes of nations are less relevant than conventional geopolitical security. Empires, of course, may be able to mobilize more resources for the advancement of their superiority in these areas. More experts on cybersecurity can be recruited, and more money can be spent for space programs. But when technology keeps developing rapidly, more compact, wealthier, and freer states may well have the advantage in innovative capacity. Besides, there are more relevant players in the game, including non-state actors such as private corporations with technological edges, terrorist organizations, transnational criminal organizations and international NGOs, as well as smaller but technologically advanced countries.

1.7 Conclusion

This chapter has focused on asymmetry of comparative advantages between two groups of major players in the emerging international system, namely, mega-states and compact powers. While mega-states with a vast population can have much larger resources, they have difficulty in mobilizing them for their political purposes. Besides, when technological innovation plays critical roles in determining national power, the link between existing resources allocation and national capability becomes more fluid and less certain. Thus, the advantage of the mega-states in international competition is not as evident as GDP figures and stock of weapons suggest.

Although there is nothing new in that states compete with each other trying to make full use of their advantages while minimizing their vulnerabilities, it is important to remember that the emerging international system is different from the classical European international system in the eighteenth and nineteenth century, where major players interact with each other somewhat like billiard balls. What is new is major players in the emerging international system have highly different structures of vulnerabilities and sensitivities. While vast empires tend to be touchy on the issues related to their domestic instability, compact powers are generally more sensitive to geopolitical pressure put by the empires. If foreign policy-makers fail to take into account of the asymmetry assuming others are the same as they are, and touch sore spots of others too hard, unexpected hard reactions could be caused, triggering the destabilization of order nobody wants. Empathy is all the more difficult in the heterogeneous system.

References

Aristotle (1995) Politics, Oxford world's classics. Oxford University Press, Oxford

Aron R (1966) Peace and war. Widenfield and Nicolson, London

Cen Z (2015) The heterogeneity between nations: an empirical analysis by Macro Data. Mimeo

Dutta S, Lanvin B, Wunsch-Vincent S (2015) The global innovation index 2015: effective innovation policies for development. In: World intellectual property organization. www.wipo.int/edocs/pubdocs/en/wipo_gii_2015.pdf. Accessed 22 Oct 2017

Haruna N (2015) Jinkō, Shigen, Ryōdo: thoughts on diplomacy and international politics in modern Japan. Chikura Shobo, Tokyo

Heinsohn G (2003) Söhne und Weltmacht: Terror im Aufstieg und Fall der Nationen. Orell Füssli, Winterthur

Jay J (1961) The federalist paper 4. In: Cooke JE (ed) The federalist. A Meridian Book, Cleveland
Kennedy P (1987) The rise and fall of the great powers. Random House, New York
Kōsaka M (1999) Bunmei ga Suibōsurutoki [When the civilization declines]. In: Kōsaka M (ed) Collected works, vol 5. Toshi Shuppan, Tokyo
Mandiant (2013) APT1, exposing one of China's cyber espionage units. https://www.fireeye.com/content/dam/fireeye-www/services/pdfs/mandiant-apt1-report.pdf. Accessed 22 Oct 2017
Montesquieu (1989) The spirit of the laws, Cambridge texts in the history of political thought. Cambridge University Press, Cambridge
Morgenthau HJ (1967) Politics among nations, 5th edn. Alfred Knopf, New York
New York Times (2012) Obama order sped up wave of Cyberattacks against Iran. 1 June 2012
Plato (1960) The laws, everyman's library 275, theology & philosophy. JM Dent & Sons, London
Rousseau JJ (1997) The social contract and other later political writings. Cambridge University Press, Cambridge
Sugiyama M (1992) Daimongoru no Sekai [The world of the Great Mongolian Empire]. Kadokawa Shoten, Tokyo
Sun Y-S (1927) San min Chu I [The three principles of the people]. China Committee, Institute of Pacific Relations, Shanghai
Tadokoro M (2014) Changed discourses on demography in Japan. In: Beretta S et al (eds) Italy and Japan: how similar are they? Springer, Heidelberg
Tadokoro M (2016) Population size and power shift: are bigger countries necessarily more powerful? Kokusai Seiji Int Relat 183:15–30
Tanaka A (2009) Posuto Kuraisisu No Sekai [The post crisis world]. Nihon Keizai Shimbun Sha, Tokyo
The 21st Century Conert Study Group (2014) 21st century concert of powers. Peace Research Institute, Frankfurt
The Department of Homeland Security (2016) GRIZZLY STEPPE – Russian malicious cyber activity. JAR-16-20296A, 29 Dec 2016. https://www.us-cert.gov/sites/default/files/publications/JAR_16-20296A_GRIZZLY%20STEPPE-2016-1229.pdf. Accessed 22 Oct 17
The Indian Express (2009) China proposed division of Pacific, Indian Ocean regions, we declined: US Admiral. 15 May 2009 http://archive.indianexpress.com/news/china-proposed-division-of-pacific-indian-ocean-regions-we-declined-us-admiral/459851/. Accessed 22 Oct 2017
Windrem R (2016) Timeline: ten years of Russian cyber attacks on other nations. 18 Dec 2016 http://www.nbcnews.com/storyline/hacking-in-america/timeline-ten-years-russian-cyber-attacks-other-nations-n697111. Accessed 22 Oct 2017
Yamada T (2017) Zero Day: Bei Chū Ro Saibaa Sensō ga Sekai o Hakaisuru. Bungei Shunjū, Tokyo
Yamamoto Y (2012) The paradox of power and the changes in the international system. Waseda J Polit Sci Econ 384:2–22

Chapter 2
Effects of the Size of a Country on Its Economic Performance

Kazuhiro Yuki and Zhiwei Cen

Abstract The world is composed of countries that are heterogeneous in various dimensions. One dimension this chapter focuses on is size, in particular, demographic, economic, and geographic sizes. How does the size of a country affect its level and growth of income (per capita GDP)? Do small countries perform better than large countries because of their smallness, or do they perform worse? Emerging powers in the world, China and India, stand out in population size and have large territory. Is their enormous size advantageous or detrimental to income growth? Answers to this question would provide some clue to the critical issue of whether or not these countries continue to grow rapidly and become economic and political superpowers on par with the USA in the near future. The chapter explores these issues with the assistance of economic theories and statistical (econometric) analysis.

The chapter starts with providing a summary of theoretical arguments of why and how the size of a country matters for the level and growth of income (per capita GDP), drawing mainly on economic theories. Theoretically, country size has both positive and negative effects through various mechanisms; thus whether or not the size is advantageous to economic performance can be answered only empirically. The next section conducts statistical (regression) analysis that relies on the theoretical arguments and improves upon existing works in terms of choices of variables in regression models and data. Finally, based on results of statistical analysis, the above questions regarding economic performance of China and India are explored.

Keywords Country size · Economic development · Economic growth · Regression analysis

---

K. Yuki (✉)
Faculty of Economics, Kyoto University, Kyoto, Japan
e-mail: yuki@econ.kyoto-u.ac.jp

Z. Cen
Faculty of Economics, Kyoto Sangyo University, Kyoto, Japan

M. Tadokoro et al. (eds.), *Emerging Risks in a World of Heterogeneity*, Evolutionary Economics and Social Complexity Science 10,
https://doi.org/10.1007/978-981-10-7968-9_2

2.1 Introduction

The world is composed of countries that are heterogeneous in various dimensions. One dimension this chapter focuses on is size, in particular, demographic, economic, and geographic sizes. How does the size of a country affect its level and growth of income (per capita GDP)? Do small countries perform better than large countries because of their smallness, or do they perform worse? Emerging powers in the world, China and India, stand out in population size and have large territory. Is their enormous size advantageous or detrimental to income growth? Answers to this question might provide some clue to the critical issue of whether or not these countries continue to grow rapidly and become economic and political superpowers on par with the USA in the near future. The chapter explores these issues with the assistance of economic theories and statistical (econometric) analysis.

The chapter starts with presenting a summary of theoretical arguments of why and how the size of a country matters for the level and growth of income (per capita GDP), drawing mainly on economic theories. Theoretically, country size has both positive and negative effects through various mechanisms; thus whether or not the size is advantageous to economic performance can be answered only empirically.

The next section conducts statistical (regression) analysis that relies on the theoretical arguments and improves upon existing works, such as Alesina et al. (2000, 2005), Alcala and Ciccone (2003), Rose (2006), and Desmet et al. (2012), in terms of choices of variables in regression models and data. Unlike the previous studies, this study examines all major theoretical mechanisms, for example, it examines whether effects of country size are different between very large countries such as China and India and smaller countries.

Major findings of statistical analysis are summarized as follows. First, consistent with existing studies, income level and growth are positively associated with the log of population and are negatively associated with its product with the degree of openness in international trade (the ratio of trade to GDP). This implies that the positive impact of demographic size on the income level and growth of a country is very large when it trades little with foreign countries, but the advantage of largeness (or the disadvantage of smallness) becomes smaller when it becomes more open in trade. Still, the marginal effect of demographic size is positive, unless the trade/GDP ratio is very high, which is true only for a limited number of countries with small population in the sample.

Second, income level and growth are positively associated with the log of GDP and are negatively associated not only with its product with the degree of trade openness but also with the square of the log of GDP, which is a new finding. This implies that the positive impact of economic size on the income level and growth of a country is very large when it trades little with foreign countries or when it is very small in economic size, but the advantage of largeness (or the disadvantage of smallness) becomes smaller when it becomes more open in trade or its economic size becomes greater. Still, the marginal effect of economic size is positive, unless the trade/GDP ratio is very high or GDP is very large, which is the case only for a small number of developed countries in the sample.

Third, income level and growth are positively associated with trade openness and are negatively associated with its product with the log of population or the log of GDP, which is consistent with existing studies, but there is some evidence that the degree of openness in financial markets is more important than the degree of trade openness as a determinant of income level and growth, which is a new finding.

Fourth, the log of land area (a measure of geographic size) of a country is not significantly related to its level and growth of income. Further, a theoretical prediction that the effect of ethnic or religious diversity on income level and growth depends on demographic and economic sizes is not confirmed. (Ethnic or religious diversity itself too is not found to be significantly related to income level and growth.)

In the conclusion section, based on results of statistical analysis, questions posed at the beginning regarding economic performance of China and India are explored.

2.2 Theoretical Mechanisms

This section summarizes theoretical mechanisms through which the size of a country may affect its level and growth rate of per capita income (per capita GDP), partially drawing on Alesina and Spolaore (2003) and Alesina et al. (2005).

Positive Effects The first type of mechanisms through which size has a positive effect on the income level and growth is related to the presence of *scale economies in production*, the property that productivity increases and cost decreases with scale of production. First, in markets of goods in which the degree of scale economies is large, the number of producers and thus the degree of competition increase with the size of markets, which depends of the size of population and production/income (GDP) of a country. Prices of these goods are low, and their per capita production levels are high in a large country because of a high degree of competition. Second, the growth of sectors or industries in which scale economies are important, i.e., those requiring a large amount of investment in machines, buildings, or distribution channels to initiate production, depends crucially on the size of markets. Third, demographic and economic sizes of a country increase the variety of goods with scale economies produced and consumed in the country and thus raise its *effective* income level. Finally, the establishment of infrastructure and institutions important for production of goods (such as power plants and road networks) and well-being of people (such as public health institutions) exhibits scale economies and thus depends on the sizes of a country.

Note that, except the last mechanism, the importance of the sizes of a country diminishes with the degree of openness in international trade. This is because, when a country becomes more open and increases trade, the importance of domestic markets to its products falls and that of foreign markets rises.

The second type of mechanism is also linked to scale economies in production. A country with a large population or large GDP receives a disproportionally large amount of foreign direct investment (FDI) aimed at entering the domestic market, because of scale economies in production. FDI raises production and income of the country not only directly but also indirectly through the diffusion of more advanced knowledge and technology. The importance of this mechanism too decreases with the degree of trade openness: a small but open country can attract a large amount of FDI if it has advantages as a production base for exports. By contrast, the importance of this mechanism *increases* with the degree of openness in *financial markets*.

The third type of mechanisms is related to the *resilience to large negative shocks* that could have a sustained impact on the economy. First, a country with a large population or large GDP is relatively resilient to large negative shocks, such as large changes in commodity prices and in economic conditions and policies of major foreign countries, because it does not specialize in production of limited varieties of goods and thus does not rely on international trade heavily. Unlike the above mechanisms, the positive size effect *increases* with the degree of trade openness, because a smaller country specializes in narrower sectors and relies more on trade when it becomes more open by relaxing trade restrictions such as tariffs. Second, a country with large GDP is relatively resilient to these shocks because associated changes in flows of financial assets from and to foreign countries are small relative to its economic size. This mechanism becomes more important when the degree of openness in financial markets *increases*, because a small country becomes more vulnerable to these shocks due to increased flows of financial assets.

The remaining mechanisms are related to *diversity* and *international influences*. First, a large country typically has diverse human resources and culture because of its population size and ethnic (or religious) diversity, which is conductive to the creation of new ideas for businesses, products, and technologies. Thus, both population and ethnic (or religious) diversity have a positive effect on the income level and growth. Further, the positive effect of diversity might increase with population size, if the creation of new ideas exhibits "scale economies." Second, a demographically or economically large country has great influences on other countries in culture and values and thus has advantages in exporting goods with large cultural or values components. Finally, a *very* large country benefits from great influences it can exert on international policies, rules, and institutions.

Negative Effects The first type of mechanisms through which size has a negative effect on the income level and growth of a country is related to *diversity*. First, a country with a large population or large territory is typically diverse in ethnicity, religion, and values and thus incurs a large cost in maintaining social stability through security measures and policies such as income redistribution. Second, policy-making is difficult in such a large country, because heterogeneous people have varying benefits from policies and diverse preferences for them. These mechanisms suggest a negative effect of diversity given the size of a country. Finally, social unity and national identity might be difficult to be achieved in a large country because its population size and diversity make people feel distant from other people and the national government. The lack of unity and national identity has a negative effect on the amount and quality of public goods and institutions and a positive effect on internal armed and non-armed conflict. The importance of the negative effect of diversity might increase with population size, if mobilizing people to participate in conflict exhibits "scale economies."

The second type of mechanisms operates through the *geographic size* of a country. Establishing and maintaining infrastructure (such as roads and railroads) and governmental institutions in a geographically large country is costly. The cost of maintaining law and order too is high.

The third type of mechanism is on *investment* (expenditures on machines and buildings) interacted with the openness of financial markets. By allowing freer transactions with foreign countries in financial markets, a country with smaller GDP can grow more rapidly than an economically larger country, because it can attract greater loans from foreign countries relative to its economic size and thus increase investment more rapidly.

Summary Theoretically, demographic and economic sizes (population and GDP) of a country have both positive and negative effects on its level and growth rate of per capita income (per capita GDP).[1] The importance of the positive effect of these sizes increases with the degree of financial openness, while the degree of trade openness has both positive and negative associations with the importance of the positive size effect. By contrast, the importance of the positive effect of financial market openness decreases with the economic size of a country. Further, theoretical mechanisms suggest both positive and negative effects of ethnic and religious diversities given demographic and economic sizes. The importance of both positive and negative effects of diversity might increase with the sizes of a country. Finally, the geographic size of a country has a negative effect on its income level and growth.

2.3 Regression Analysis

How important are demographic, economic, and geographic sizes of a country on its income (per capita GDP) growth and level in the real economy? Drawing on theoretical mechanism in the last section, this section examines the issue empirically using regression analysis.

[1]According to the discussions above, *given* population size, GDP does not have negative effects on growth and income. In regression analysis below, effects of demographic and economic sizes are examined in different equations because the two sizes are highly correlated. Under such specifications, theoretical mechanisms predict both positive and negative effects of GDP because effects of population size are not controlled for.

2.3.1 Regression Model

Effects of the sizes of a country on its income growth are examined by estimating the following growth regression model.

$$(\text{Average per capita GDP growth})_i = \alpha + \boldsymbol{\beta}\,\mathbf{Size_i} + \boldsymbol{\gamma}\mathbf{X_i} + \epsilon_i$$

In the above equation, the dependent variable is the average growth rate of per capita GDP of country i over the sample period 1960–2010, $\mathbf{Size_i}$ is a vector of variables that capture effects of demographic, economic, or geographic sizes of the country on the income growth, $\mathbf{X_i}$ is a vector of control variables that capture effects of various factors other than the size variables, and ϵ_i is the disturbance (error) term.

In order to examine effects on the level of per capita GDP in the final year 2010, the following income regression model is estimated.

$$\ln(\text{Per capita GDP in 2010})_i = \widetilde{\alpha} + \widetilde{\boldsymbol{\beta}}\,\widetilde{\mathbf{Size}}_{\mathbf{i}} + \widetilde{\boldsymbol{\gamma}}\widetilde{\mathbf{X}}_{\mathbf{i}} + \widetilde{\epsilon}_i$$

In Sect. 2.3.2, specific variables included in the above equations and their data sources are explained.

The above regression models are estimated using the ordinary least square (OLS) method. Choice of the simple cross-sectional estimation rather than panel data estimation (such as the fixed effect estimation, the Arellano–Bond general method of moments (GMM) estimation, and the Blundell–Bond system GMM estimation) and hybrids of panel and cross-sectional estimation (such as the random effect estimation and the seemingly unrelated regression (SUR)) follows the analysis by Hauk and Wacziarg (2009). They investigate the performance of these estimation methods in a standard growth regression model when the presence of realistic magnitudes of measurement errors of variables are assumed and find the smallest biases of estimators of coefficients of most variables when the OLS is used. Their analysis suggests that, under constraints on numbers of countries and sample periods and qualities of data available for the regression analysis, the OLS is a better method than other popular methods.

2.3.2 Variables and Data Sources

2.3.2.1 Dependent Variables

As presented in Sect. 2.3.1, the dependent variable for the growth regression model is the average growth rate of per capita GDP over the sample period 1960–2010, and the one for the income regression model is the natural log of per capita GDP in 2010. Per capita GDP data measured in purchasing power parity (PPP) terms are from *Penn World Tables Version 7.1* (http://www.rug.nl/research/ggdc/data/pwt/pwt-7.1).

2.3.2.2 Size Variables

Based on the theoretical mechanisms explained in Sect. 2.2, a subset of the following variables is included in regression.

Demographic size: ln(Population), $[\ln(\text{Population})]^2$, ln(Population) × (Trade openness), ln(Population) × (Financial openness), ln(Population) × (Ethnic diversity), ln(Population) × (Religious diversity)
Economic size: The same set of variables as demographic size with ln(GDP) in place of ln(Population)
Geographic size: ln(Land area), $[\ln(\text{Land area})]^2$

The squares of the log of population, the log of GDP, and the log of land area are intended to capture the possibility that the marginal effect of the scale variables is more (or less) important in very large countries. The products of the scale variables with openness or diversity measures take into account effects of these measures on the importance of size effects. Theoretical mechanisms are ambiguous about signs of coefficients on the log of population, the log of GDP, and their squares, while they predict a negative coefficient on the log of land area. Signs of coefficients on the products of the scale variables with openness or diversity measures too are ambiguous theoretically.

Unless noted otherwise, average values over the sample period 1960–2010 are used.[2] For example, ln(Population) in regressions is the average of the log of population over the period. Population and land area data are from *World Development Indicators* (*WDI*) of the World Bank. The degree of trade openness is calculated as the sum of nominal exports and imports divided by nominal GDP and is from *Penn World Tables Version 7.1* (*PWT 7.1*). The degree of financial openness is measured by the 2013 update of Financial Openness Index by Chinn and Ito (2006) (http://web.pdx.edu/~ito/Chinn-Ito_website.htm), which is available from 1970. The measure of ethnic diversity is one of measures of ethnolinguistic fractionalization, ELF(15), computed by Desmet et al. (2012), which is found to be more significant than other measures in their growth regression analysis. The measure of religious diversity is the religious fractionalization measure created by Alesina et al. (2003). Both diversity measures are cross-sectional data.

2.3.2.3 Control Variables

According to the standard model of economic growth, the Solow model, control variables of the growth regression model should include the log of per capita GDP in the initial period, population growth rate, variables measuring physical capital

[2] In order to increase the number of countries, countries with a small number of missing values too are included in the sample.

accumulation and human capital accumulation or their causes, and variables capturing productivity level in the initial period and productivity growth in subsequent periods (or their causes).[3]

There exist many variables capturing each of physical and human capital accumulation, initial productivity level, and productivity growth. For example, human capital accumulation can be measured by the average enrollment rate in either primary education, secondary education, or tertiary education during the sample period, or it can be measured by average years of schooling of the working population. Which particular variables are included in regression is determined drawing on the analysis by Doppelhofer et al. (2004) and Eicher et al. (2011). They investigate the robustness of the statistical significance of independent variables to changes in combinations of included variables in the growth regression and find that only a small subset of candidate variables are robust to changes in the specification.

In addition to these variables, the openness measures and the diversity measures explained in Sect. 2.3.2.3 too should be included in the regression model, because theoretical mechanisms in Sect. 2.2, standard theories of international trade and finance, and existing empirical studies suggest that they affect the income level and growth given the sizes of a country.

As for the income regression analysis, there does not exist a theory as standard as the Solow model of economic growth that guides choices of control variables included in regression; thus the same set of variables as the growth regression are used.

Based on the above discussions, a subset of the following variables is included in regression.

Growth regression on:[4]

In(Per capita GDP in 1960), (Population growth), (Investment rate)
Human capital: (Average schooling), (Secondary education enrollment), (Llife expectancy)
Openness measures: (Ttrade openness), (Financial openness)
Diversity measures: (Ethnic diversity), (Religious diversity)
Institutional quality: (Rule of law)
Geographic variables: (Share of shores), (Share of tropics)
Natural resource abundance: (Share of mining)
Regional dummies: (East Asia), (Sub-Saharan Africa), (Latin America), (MENA)
Religious variables: (Buddhist), (Hindu), (Muslim), (Protestant), (No religion)

Unless noted otherwise, average values over the sample period are used. The population growth rate is the average rate over the sample period 1960–2010 from

[3]Physical capital accumulation is investment in equipment (such as machines and tools) and structure (such as buildings and physical infrastructure), while human capital accumulation includes expenditures on education, health, and job training.

[4]For a small numbers of countries that have data starting from 1961, the value in 1961 is used.

WDI; the investment rate is the ratio of investment to GDP from *PWT 7.1*; the average schooling is average years of total schooling of the population of 25 years old and older from Barro and Lee (2013), which is available for every 5 years after 1970; the secondary education enrollment is the gross enrollment rate of both sexes from *WDI*, which is available after 1970; and the life expectancy (at birth) is from *WDI*. The population growth rate, the investment rate, and one of the human capital variables are always included in regression. The rule of law variable is the period (years 1996, 1998, 2000, 2002–2010) average of Rule of Law Index, one of six indices of institutional quality of *Worldwide Governance Indicators* by Daniel Kaufmann and Aart Kraay (http://info.worldbank.org/governance/wgi/index.aspx#home).[5] The share of shores (land area within 100 km of ice-free coast or sea-navigable river) and the share of tropics in land area are from Country Geography Data by John Luke Gallup (https://www.pdx.edu/econ/jlgallup/country-geodata). The share of mining in GDP, available after 1970, is from *WDI*. Regional dummies are constructed based on the classification by the World Bank. (MENA is an abbreviation for Middle East and North Africa.) Finally, the religious variables are the average proportion of individuals with faith in each world religion and without faith in the population for years 1970 and 2000 from Religion Adherence Data by Barro and McCleary (2003).

2.3.3 Relation to Existing Works

Before presenting results of regression analysis, the relation of this work to existing works is explained. Preceding works that examine effects of size of a country on its rate of growth or level of GDP using regression include Alesina et al. (2000, 2005), Alcala and Ciccone (2003), Rose (2006), and Desmet et al. (2012).

There are important differences between these works and the present work. First, the existing works examine only a part of the theoretical mechanisms discussed in Sect. 2.2. In particular, they do not examine effects of geographic size, the possibility that marginal effects of the size variables are more (or less) important in very large countries by including the square terms, and the possibility that effects of demographic and economic sizes change with financial market openness and ethnic or religious diversities by including products of size variables and these variables. Second, many of these works do not include control variables that are considered to be important determinants of income growth or level, such as institutional quality, geography, and ethnic or religious diversities. Not including important size variables and control variables might exacerbate biases of estimators of coefficients of independent variables. Finally, the present work uses data including more recent years.

[5]The other indices are voice and accountability, political stability and absence of violence, government effectiveness, regulatory quality, and control of corruption. Only one index is included in regression because of high (at least greater than 0.8) correlations between the indicators.

2.3.4 *Results*

2.3.4.1 Descriptive Statistics

Table 2.1 presents summary statistics for main variables of interest. As mentioned above, values of per capita GDP growth, the log of population, the log of GDP, the log of land area, trade openness, investment rate, and population growth are averages over the period 1960–2010; values of financial openness, average schooling, and the index of rule of law are averages over years specific to each variable (see Sect. 2.3.2.3 for details); and the remaining variables are cross sectional.

Table 2.2 presents correlation coefficients among major variables. Per capita GDP growth is positively correlated with the log of GDP, trade openness, and financial openness and is negatively correlated with ethnic diversity, while its correlations with the log of per capita GDP in 1960, the log of population, and the log of land area are small and insignificant. Correlations between the log of per capita GDP in 2010 and these variables too are similar, except that the correlation with the log of per capita GDP in 1960 is very high.

Among size variables, the correlation between the log of population and the log of GDP is high, equal to 0.767, while the correlation between the log of land area and the log of population and the one between the log of land area and the log of GDP are smaller, equal to 0.653 and 0.439, respectively. Note that the correlation between trade openness and financial openness is small: the correlation coefficient is just 0.273. Correlations of

Table 2.1 Descriptive statistics

	Number of observations	Mean	Standard deviation	Minimum	Maximum
Per capita GDP growth (%)	112	1.91	1.48	−2.13	6.26
ln(per capita GDP in 2010)	189	8.77	1.33	5.48	11.82
ln(Population)	211	14.78	2.36	9.02	20.74
ln(GDP)	112	10.29	2.05	6.04	15.70
ln(Land area)	214	10.80	3.04	0.69	16.61
Trade openness (%)	113	67.76	43.77	17.85	330.10
Financial openness	114	0.44	0.28	0.01	1.00
Ethnic diversity	227	0.41	0.31	0.00	0.99
ln(per capita GDP in 1960)	112	7.70	1.13	5.65	9.95
Investment rate (%)	113	23.10	8.44	3.97	53.19
Average schooling	145	5.94	2.86	0.74	12.29
Population growth (%)	211	1.88	1.20	−0.06	8.94
Rule of law	199	−0.03	0.98	−2.35	1.94
Share of shores	164	0.47	0.37	0.00	1.00

Table 2.2 Correlation coefficients among major variables

	Per capita GDP growth	ln(per capita GDP in 2010)	ln(per capita GDP in 1960)	ln (Population)	ln(GDP)	ln(Land area)	Trade openness	Financial openness	Ethnic diversity
Per capita GDP growth	1.000								
ln(per capita GDP in 2010)	0.610***	1.000							
ln(per capita GDP in 1960)	0.118	0.858***	1.000						
ln(Population)	0.044	−0.018	−0.050	1.000					
ln(GDP)	0.292**	0.604***	0.569***	0.767***	1.000				
ln(Land area)	−0.171	−0.149	−0.077	0.653***	0.439***	1.000			
Trade openness	0.317**	0.248*	0.105	−0.515***	−0.284**	−0.593***	1.000		
Financial openness	0.260*	0.656***	0.654***	0.036	0.463***	−0.048	0.273**	1.000	
Ethnic diversity	−0.235*	−0.483***	−0.453***	0.110	−0.226*	0.150	0.101	−0.221*	1.000

*$p < 0.05$, **$p < 0.01$, ***$p < 0.001$

the two openness measures with other variables too are different. Trade openness is negatively correlated with the three size variables, while financial openness is positively correlated with the log of GDP and is not significantly correlated with the other variables. Further, correlations between financial openness and the log of per capita GDP in 1960 and in 2010 are positive and large, while correlations between trade openness and the income variables are small or insignificant. These results suggest that the log of land area and financial openness respectively capture aspects of the size of a nation and its openness different from conventional measures used in existing works.

2.3.4.2 Results of Growth Regressions

This section presents results of growth regressions. Effects of demographic and economic sizes are examined in different regressions, because, as noted above, the log of population and the log of GDP are highly correlated.

Table 2.3 shows results of growth regressions when the log of population and its products with other variables are included. All specifications incorporate the log of population, trade openness, their product, the log of per capita GDP in 1960, investment rate, average schooling, and population growth rate. Similar results are obtained when life expectancy or secondary education enrollment is included instead of average schooling. Column (1) presents the result when no other variables are included. Consistent with standard growth theory, coefficients of initial income and population growth are significantly negative, and those of investment rate and average schooling are significantly positive. Coefficients of the log of population and trade openness (the ratio of trade to GDP) are significantly positive, and the coefficient of their product is negative (though slightly insignificant), which are consistent with empirical findings by Alesina et al. (2000, 2005) and Alcala and Ciccone (2003).[6]

Column (2) adds rule of law (a measure of institutional quality) and the share of shores (the share of land area within 100 km of ice-free coast or sea-navigable river). Both variables are significantly and positively associated with income growth. Further, the coefficient of the product of the log of population and trade openness is now significantly negative. Results on other variables are qualitatively same as Column (1). The specification that includes the share of tropics and the share of mining in GDP as additional controls is also estimated, but their coefficients are insignificant. Column (3) adds regional dummies, and Column (4) adds religion variables to the specification of Colum (2), and results on other variables except the share of shores in Column (3), which is insignificant, do not change qualitatively.[7]

[6]Desmet et al. (2012) also obtain similar results in specifications that include ethnolinguistic diversity as an independent variable, but the coefficient of the log of population is not significant at 10% level in all specifications.

[7]In Column (3), the coefficient of the sub-Saharan African dummy is significantly negative, and that of the Latin American dummy is significantly positive. The large and negative coefficient of the African dummy might be a major reason for the coefficient of the share of shores to be insignificant. In Column (4), the coefficient of the proportion of Protestants is significantly negative at 10% level.

Table 2.3 Growth regressions when size = ln(Population)

	(1)	(2)	(3)	(4)	(5)	(6)	(7)	(8)
ln(Population)	0.363***	0.346***	0.252**	0.309***	0.704	0.433**	0.418***	0.307***
	(0.102)	(0.0976)	(0.100)	(0.110)	(1.212)	(0.169)	(0.127)	(0.109)
$[\ln(\text{Population})]^2$					−0.0102			
					(0.0344)			
Trade openness	0.0425*	0.0471**	0.0492**	0.0451*	0.0542	0.0546	0.0459**	0.0478**
	(0.0233)	(0.0222)	(0.0208)	(0.0234)	(0.0328)	(0.0361)	(0.0223)	(0.0223)
ln(Population) × Trade openness	−0.00217	−0.00295**	−0.00304**	−0.00284*	−0.00342	−0.00343	−0.00275*	−0.00298**
	(0.00154)	(0.00148)	(0.00139)	(0.00155)	(0.00217)	(0.00225)	(0.00149)	(0.00148)
Financial openness						3.293		
						(4.246)		
ln(Population) × Financial openness						−0.189		
						(0.248)		
Ethnic diversity							1.381	
							(2.761)	
ln(Population) × Ethnic diversity							−0.109	
							(0.171)	
ln(Land area)								0.0671
								(0.0835)
ln(Per capita GDP in 1960)	−0.750***	−0.879***	−1.027***	−0.850***	−0.884***	−0.895***	−0.895***	−0.906***
	(0.135)	(0.128)	(0.134)	(0.137)	(0.129)	(0.154)	(0.129)	(0.132)
Investment rate	0.0646***	0.0694***	0.0534***	0.0644***	0.0702***	0.0665***	0.0668***	0.0680***
	(0.0122)	(0.0115)	(0.0121)	(0.0122)	(0.0119)	(0.0140)	(0.0117)	(0.0117)

(continued)

Table 2.3 (continued)

	(1)	(2)	(3)	(4)	(5)	(6)	(7)	(8)
Average schooling	0.230***	0.147**	0.107*	0.155**	0.146**	0.164**	0.134**	0.144**
	(0.0578)	(0.0598)	(0.0569)	(0.0687)	(0.0603)	(0.0696)	(0.0607)	(0.0600)
Population growth	−0.562***	−0.254*	−0.256*	−0.301*	−0.252*	−0.274*	−0.223	−0.280*
	(0.142)	(0.147)	(0.150)	(0.163)	(0.148)	(0.158)	(0.149)	(0.151)
Rule of law		0.503***	0.754***	0.560***	0.508***	0.465***	0.539***	0.504***
		(0.144)	(0.164)	(0.166)	(0.146)	(0.162)	(0.147)	(0.145)
Share of shores		0.964***	0.338	0.792***	0.980***	0.855***	0.878***	1.124***
		(0.276)	(0.299)	(0.295)	(0.283)	(0.310)	(0.290)	(0.341)
Regional dummies			○					
Religion variables				○				
Constant	−0.378	0.681	4.198**	1.433	−2.393	−0.616	−0.209	0.686
	(1.992)	(1.947)	(2.053)	(2.074)	(10.57)	(3.042)	(2.265)	(1.952)
Observations	99	94	94	94	94	85	94	94
R-squared	0.642	0.692	0.753	0.707	0.693	0.671	0.699	0.695

Standard errors in parentheses ***$p < 0.01$, **$p < 0.05$, *$p < 0.1$

Column (5) adds the square of the log of population to the specification of Column (2). Not only the square term but also the log of population, trade openness, and their product become insignificant, suggesting that the marginal effect of the log of population on income growth does not change with the scale variable. Column (6) adds financial openness and its product with the log of population to the specification of Column (2), but coefficients of these variables are highly insignificant. Trade openness and its product with the log of population become marginally insignificant, although signs are same as before. Results on other variables do not change qualitatively. Column (7) adds ethnic diversity and its product with the log of population to the specification of Column (2). Their coefficients are highly insignificant, and results on other variables are qualitatively same as Column (2). The coefficient of ethnic diversity remains insignificant when the product term is excluded. Similar results are obtained when religious diversity and its product with the log of population are included instead. By contrast, Desmet et al. (2012) find that, in a similar specification without the product term, the coefficient of the same measure of ethnic diversity is highly significant under OLS using data for 1970–2004. The result suggests that their finding is not robust to small changes in sample periods and control variables. Finally, Column (8) adds the log of land area to the specification of Column (2). The coefficient of the geographic size is highly insignificant, and results on other variables are qualitatively same as before. Results are similar when the square of the log of land area too is included.

Because coefficients of the log of population and trade openness are significantly positive and the coefficient of their product is significantly negative, the effect of the demographic variable on income growth decreases with trade openness, and that of trade openness on income growth decreases with the log of population.[8] According to estimates of Column (2), when the average population of a country over the sample period is 1% greater, per capita GDP growth is higher by $0.346-0.00295\times$(trade openness) % point, and when its average trade openness (the ratio of trade to GDP) is 1% point higher, income growth is higher by $0.0471-0.00295\times\ln$(Population) % point.[9] The threshold degree of trade openness above which population size negatively affects income growth is 117.288. Only a limited number of countries with small population such as Belgium and Hong Kong have the higher degrees of trade openness. Thus, the effect of demographic size on income growth is positive, unless the trade/GDP ratio is very high, which is true only for a limited number of countries with small population in the sample. By contrast, the threshold value of the log of population above which the effect of trade openness becomes negative is 15.966, which is higher than but not very far from the average value for all countries in the sample, 14.812. Sweden is the last country with a positive effect, and Ecuador is the first country with a negative effect, so the effect of trade openness is *negative* for most major countries in the world.

[8]Although casual effects of independent variables are not assured, words such as "affect" and "effect" are used for ease of explanation.

[9]Since the log of population in regressions is an arithmetic average of values over the sample period, the average population is a geometric average.

Table 2.4 shows results of growth regressions when the log of GDP and its product with other variables are included. Like Table 2.3, all specifications incorporate the log of population, trade openness, their product, the log of per capita GDP in 1960, investment rate, average schooling, and population growth rate. Column (1) presents the result when no other variables are included. As before, coefficients of these variables have expected signs, but coefficients of trade openness and its product with the log of GDP are insignificant. Column (2) adds rule of law and the share of shores. Both variables are significantly and positively associated with income growth as before, but coefficients of trade openness and its product with the log of GDP remain insignificant. Alesina et al. (2000, 2005) find that coefficients of these variables are significant under several estimation methods including OLS. Different results are obtained probably because of differences in time periods or included control variables.

Column (3) adds the square of the log of GDP to the specification of Column (2). The coefficient of the square term is significantly negative, which is a new finding. Further, coefficients of trade openness and its product with the log of GDP are now significant. (Results on other variables are qualitatively same as before.) This result suggests that the effect of the log of GDP on income growth decreases with the size variable. Column (4) adds regional dummies, and Column (5) adds religion variables to the specification of Colum (3). Results of Column (5) are qualitatively same as Colum (3) except that the coefficient of average schooling is insignificant, while in Column (4), coefficients of the log of GDP, its square, the product of trade openness and the log of GDP, and the share of shores too become (for most coefficients, not highly) insignificant.

Column (6) adds financial openness and its product with the log of GDP to the specification of Column (3). Such specification is not examined in preceding works. The coefficient of financial openness is significantly positive, and that of the product is significantly negative, while coefficients of trade openness and its product with the log of GDP become *insignificant*. The result is different from Column (6) of Table 2.3, in which coefficients of financial openness and its product with the log of population are highly insignificant (and coefficients of trade openness and its product with the log of GDP are slightly insignificant). Hence, there is some evidence that the degree of openness in financial markets is more important than the degree of trade openness as a determinant of income level and growth, which is a new finding. Coefficients of both the log of GDP and its square are insignificant, while in Column (7), which removes the square term from the specification of Column (6), the coefficient of the log of GDP is highly significant. Thus, with financial openness and its product with the log of GDP, the specification without the square term might be better.

Column (8) adds ethnic diversity and its product with the log of GDP, and Column (9) adds the log of land area into the specification of Column (3), respectively. As before, coefficients of these variables are highly insignificant, and results on other variables are qualitatively same as Column (3).

Because coefficients of the log of GDP and trade openness are significantly positive and coefficients of their product and the square of the log of GDP are

Table 2.4 Growth regressions when size = ln(GDP)

	(1)	(2)	(3)	(4)	(5)	(6)	(7)	(8)	(9)
ln(GDP)	0.342***	0.361***	1.566***	0.876	1.646***	0.712	0.547***	1.490**	1.619***
	(0.100)	(0.0934)	(0.574)	(0.619)	(0.595)	(0.781)	(0.128)	(0.581)	(0.584)
$[\ln(GDP)]^2$			−0.0501**	−0.0232	−0.0546**	−0.00749		−0.0470**	−0.0509**
			(0.0235)	(0.0252)	(0.0244)	(0.0349)		(0.0236)	(0.0237)
Trade openness	0.0139	0.0184	0.0406**	0.0300*	0.0421**	0.0186	0.0153	0.0396**	0.0422**
	(0.0147)	(0.0145)	(0.0176)	(0.0178)	(0.0180)	(0.0227)	(0.0162)	(0.0177)	(0.0179)
ln(GDP) × Trade openness	−0.000282	−0.00119	−0.00341*	−0.00224	−0.00361**	−0.00142	−0.00109	−0.00310*	−0.00360**
	(0.00135)	(0.00141)	(0.00173)	(0.00177)	(0.00177)	(0.00216)	(0.00150)	(0.00176)	(0.00177)
Financial openness						5.376**	5.716***		
						(2.651)	(2.111)		
ln(GDP) × Financial openness						−0.468**	−0.501***		
						(0.234)	(0.175)		
Ethnic diversity								−0.943	
								(1.382)	
ln(GDP) × Ethnic diversity								0.0483	
								(0.134)	
ln(Land area)									−0.0452
									(0.0797)
ln(Per capita GDP in 1960)	−0.967***	−1.055***	−1.105***	−1.192***	−1.071***	−1.113***	−1.111***	−1.130***	−1.108***
	(0.127)	(0.122)	(0.122)	(0.141)	(0.137)	(0.139)	(0.138)	(0.125)	(0.123)
Investment rate	0.0551***	0.0583***	0.0527***	0.0465***	0.0497***	0.0524***	0.0527***	0.0491***	0.0528***
	(0.0120)	(0.0115)	(0.0115)	(0.0123)	(0.0121)	(0.0134)	(0.0132)	(0.0117)	(0.0116)
Average schooling	0.191***	0.105*	0.0991*	0.0702	0.0943	0.148**	0.152**	0.0852	0.0995*
	(0.0553)	(0.0577)	(0.0566)	(0.0557)	(0.0657)	(0.0673)	(0.0640)	(0.0570)	(0.0569)

(continued)

Table 2.4 (continued)

	(1)	(2)	(3)	(4)	(5)	(6)	(7)	(8)	(9)
Population growth	−0.528***	−0.239*	−0.279**	−0.275*	−0.300*	−0.294**	−0.293**	−0.237*	−0.261*
	(0.134)	(0.141)	(0.139)	(0.150)	(0.154)	(0.146)	(0.145)	(0.141)	(0.143)
Rule of law		0.502***	0.567***	0.805***	0.660***	0.514***	0.506***	0.587***	0.566***
		(0.138)	(0.138)	(0.158)	(0.160)	(0.152)	(0.147)	(0.138)	(0.139)
Share of shores		0.857***	0.780***	0.393	0.664**	0.587*	0.583*	0.650**	0.668**
		(0.266)	(0.263)	(0.288)	(0.280)	(0.296)	(0.293)	(0.275)	(0.329)
Regional dummies				○					
Religion variables					○				
Constant	3.762***	3.989***	−2.272	2.898	−2.499	1.767	2.605*	−1.431	−2.120
	(1.326)	(1.245)	(3.185)	(3.675)	(3.304)	(4.194)	(1.519)	(3.272)	(3.209)
Observations	99	94	94	94	94	85	85	94	94
R-squared	0.684	0.720	0.734	0.770	0.746	0.729	0.729	0.743	0.735

Standard errors in parentheses $^{***}p < 0.01$, $^{**}p < 0.05$, $^{*}p < 0.1$

significantly negative in most specifications, the effect of the log of GDP on income growth decreases with trade openness and the log of GDP, and that of trade openness on income growth decreases with the size variable. According to estimates of Column (3), when the average GDP of a country over the sample period is 1% greater, per capita GDP growth is higher by $1.566-0.102 \times \ln(\text{GDP})-0.00341\times$ (trade openness) % point, and when its average trade openness is 1% point higher, income growth is $0.0406-0.00341\times\ln(\text{GDP})$ % point higher. The marginal effect of economic size is positive in all developing countries in the sample, where values of economically large countries such as China (0.04) tend to be much smaller than those of economically small countries such as Bangladesh (0.359). The marginal effect is generally smaller in developed countries because of greater GDP, and a small number of countries, those with very high trade/GDP ratio such as Hong Kong and Singapore and the county with the biggest GDP (USA), exhibit *negative* effects. By contrast, the threshold value of the log of GDP above which the effect of trade openness becomes negative is 11.906, which is higher than the average value for all countries in the sample, 10.325. The marginal effect of trade openness is positive for developing countries except a small number of economically large countries such as China, India, and Brazil, while the effect is negative for many high-income countries: Norway is the last country with a positive effect, and Greece is the first country with a negative effect.

2.3.4.3 Results of Income Regressions

This section presents results of income regressions in which the dependent variable is the log of GDP per capita in 2010.

Table 2.5 shows results of income regressions when the log of population and its products with other variables are included. All specifications incorporate the log of population, trade openness, their product, the log of per capita GDP in 1960, investment rate, average schooling, and population growth rate. Specifications without the initial per capita GDP too are estimated, but estimated coefficients of major variables of interest, the log of population, its products with other variables, and trade openness often change greatly when a set of independent variables is changed and some of them become insignificant in many specifications. Such results are found in Alesina et al. (2000) that perform income regressions without the log of initial per capita GDP. Inclusion of the log of initial income in income regressions might be justified by that it captures time-invariant determinants of income not captured by other control variables.

Results are qualitatively same as results of growth regressions presented in Table 2.3 except that the coefficient of the log of per capita GDP in 1960 is significantly positive. In particular, coefficients of the log of population and trade openness are significantly positive, and the coefficient of their product is

Table 2.5 Income regressions when size = ln(Population)

	(1)	(2)	(3)	(4)	(5)	(6)	(7)	(8)
ln(Population)	0.181***	0.173***	0.126**	0.154***	0.352	0.216**	0.209***	0.154***
	(0.0511)	(0.0488)	(0.0502)	(0.0552)	(0.606)	(0.0845)	(0.0637)	(0.0546)
$[\ln(\text{Population})]^2$					−0.00509			
					(0.0172)			
Trade openness	0.0213*	0.0235**	0.0246**	0.0226*	0.0271	0.0273	0.0230**	0.0239**
	(0.0116)	(0.0111)	(0.0104)	(0.0117)	(0.0164)	(0.0180)	(0.0111)	(0.0111)
ln(Population) × Trade openness	−0.00109	−0.00148**	−0.00152**	−0.00142*	−0.00171	−0.00172	−0.00137*	−0.00149**
	(0.000771)	(0.000739)	(0.000694)	(0.000777)	(0.00108)	(0.00112)	(0.000744)	(0.000741)
Financial openness						1.646		
						(2.123)		
ln(Population) × Financial openness						−0.0946		
						(0.124)		
Ethnic diversity							0.690	
							(1.381)	
ln(Population) × Ethnic diversity							−0.0543	
							(0.0857)	
ln(Land area)								0.0335
								(0.0417)
ln(Per capita GDP in 1960)	0.625***	0.560***	0.486***	0.575***	0.558***	0.553***	0.553***	0.547***
	(0.0674)	(0.0638)	(0.0670)	(0.0685)	(0.0646)	(0.0770)	(0.0646)	(0.0661)

Investment rate	0.0323***	0.0347***	0.0267***	0.0322***	0.0351***	0.0332***	0.0334***	0.0340***
	(0.00610)	(0.00576)	(0.00604)	(0.00608)	(0.00593)	(0.00699)	(0.00587)	(0.00583)
Average schooling	0.115***	0.0734**	0.0534*	0.0773**	0.0729**	0.0819**	0.0670**	0.0720**
	(0.0289)	(0.0299)	(0.0285)	(0.0343)	(0.0301)	(0.0348)	(0.0304)	(0.0300)
Population growth	−0.281***	−0.127*	−0.128*	−0.151*	−0.126*	−0.137*	−0.111	−0.140*
	(0.0712)	(0.0735)	(0.0752)	(0.0815)	(0.0740)	(0.0790)	(0.0747)	(0.0754)
Rule of law		0.252***	0.377***	0.280***	0.254***	0.233***	0.269***	0.252***
		(0.0721)	(0.0820)	(0.0828)	(0.0730)	(0.0809)	(0.0736)	(0.0723)
Share of shores		0.482***	0.169	0.396***	0.490***	0.428***	0.439***	0.562***
		(0.138)	(0.149)	(0.147)	(0.141)	(0.155)	(0.145)	(0.170)
Regional dummies			○					
Religion variables				○				
Constant	−0.189	0.340	2.099**	0.716	−1.197	−0.308	−0.105	0.343
	(0.996)	(0.974)	(1.027)	(1.037)	(5.283)	(1.521)	(1.132)	(0.976)
Observations	99	94	94	94	94	85	94	94
R-squared	0.915	0.932	0.945	0.935	0.932	0.923	0.933	0.932

Standard errors in parentheses ***$p < 0.01$, **$p < 0.05$, *$p < 0.1$

significantly negative in a vast majority of specifications, while coefficients of the square of the log of population, financial openness and its product with the log of population, ethnic diversity and its product with the log of population, and the log of land area are all insignificant.

According to estimates of Column (2), when the average population of a country is 1% greater, per capita GDP in 2010 is greater by 0.173−0.00148×(trade openness) %, and when its average trade openness is 1% point higher, income level in 2010 is greater by 0.0235−0.00148×ln(Population) %. The threshold degree of trade openness above which population size negatively affects income level is 116.89, very close to the number obtained in growth regressions. Thus, the effect of demographic size on income level is positive, unless the trade/GDP ratio is very high, which is true only for a limited number of countries with small population in the sample. The threshold value of the log of population above which the effect of trade openness becomes negative is 15.878, also very close to the number obtained in growth regressions. Thus, the effect of trade openness is *negative* for most major countries in the world.

Table 2.6 shows results of income regressions when the log of GDP and its products with other variables are included. (Specifications without the initial per capita GDP too are estimated, but estimated coefficients of major variables of interest are unstable.) Results are qualitatively same as results of growth regressions presented in Table 2.4, except that the coefficient of the log of per capita GDP in 1960 is significantly positive. In particular, coefficients of the log of GDP and trade openness are significantly positive, and coefficients of their product and the square of the log of GDP are significantly negative in most specifications; when financial openness and its product with the log of GDP are included, their coefficients are significantly positive and negative, respectively, and coefficients of trade openness and its product with the log of GDP become insignificant; and ethnic diversity and its product with the log of GDP and the log of land area are insignificant.

According to estimates of Column (3), when the average GDP of a country is 1% greater, per capita GDP in 2010 is greater by 0.783−0.05 × ln (GDP)−0.00171×(trade openness) %, and when its trade openness is 1% point higher, income level in 2010 is higher by 0.0203−0.00171×ln(GDP) %. Results are qualitatively same as growth regressions: the marginal effect of economic size is positive in all developing countries in the sample, while the marginal effect is generally smaller in developed countries and a small number of them exhibit negative effects; the marginal effect of trade openness is positive in developing countries except a small number of economically large countries, while the effect is negative in many high-income countries.

Table 2.6 Income regressions when size = ln(GDP)

	(1)	(2)	(3)	(4)	(5)	(6)	(7)	(8)	(9)
ln(GDP)	0.171***	0.180***	0.783***	0.438	0.823***	0.356	0.273***	0.745**	0.809***
	(0.0501)	(0.0467)	(0.287)	(0.310)	(0.298)	(0.390)	(0.0639)	(0.290)	(0.292)
[ln(GDP)]^2			−0.0250**	−0.0116	−0.0273**	−0.00375		−0.0235**	−0.0254**
			(0.0118)	(0.0126)	(0.0122)	(0.0175)		(0.0118)	(0.0118)
Trade openness	0.00696	0.00919	0.0203**	0.0150*	0.0210**	0.00932	0.00763	0.0198**	0.0211**
	(0.00736)	(0.00724)	(0.00881)	(0.00891)	(0.00902)	(0.0113)	(0.00810)	(0.00884)	(0.00895)
ln(GDP) × Trade openness	−0.000141	−0.000597	−0.00171*	−0.00112	−0.00180**	−0.000710	−0.000544	−0.00155*	−0.00180**
	(0.000676)	(0.000707)	(0.000867)	(0.000884)	(0.000887)	(0.00108)	(0.000748)	(0.000881)	(0.000885)
Financial openness						2.688**	2.858***		
						(1.325)	(1.056)		
ln(GDP) × Financial openness						−0.234**	−0.250***		
						(0.117)	(0.0875)		
Ethnic diversity								−0.471	
								(0.691)	
ln(GDP) × Ethnic diversity								0.0241	
								(0.0672)	
ln(Land area)									−0.0226
									(0.0399)
ln(Per capita GDP in 1960)	0.516***	0.472***	0.447***	0.404***	0.465***	0.443***	0.445***	0.435***	0.446***
	(0.0634)	(0.0612)	(0.0611)	(0.0705)	(0.0685)	(0.0695)	(0.0688)	(0.0625)	(0.0614)
Investment rate	0.0275***	0.0292***	0.0264***	0.0232***	0.0249***	0.0262***	0.0264***	0.0245***	0.0264***
	(0.00599)	(0.00573)	(0.00577)	(0.00613)	(0.00604)	(0.00669)	(0.00659)	(0.00585)	(0.00579)
Average schooling	0.0954***	0.0527*	0.0496*	0.0351	0.0472	0.0741**	0.0761**	0.0426	0.0498*
	(0.0276)	(0.0289)	(0.0283)	(0.0278)	(0.0328)	(0.0336)	(0.0320)	(0.0285)	(0.0284)

(continued)

Table 2.6 (continued)

	(1)	(2)	(3)	(4)	(5)	(6)	(7)	(8)	(9)
Population growth	−0.264***	−0.120*	−0.140**	−0.137*	−0.150*	−0.147**	−0.147**	−0.118*	−0.130*
	(0.0670)	(0.0704)	(0.0696)	(0.0749)	(0.0770)	(0.0730)	(0.0725)	(0.0706)	(0.0717)
Rule of law		0.251***	0.284***	0.402***	0.330***	0.257***	0.253***	0.293***	0.283***
		(0.0689)	(0.0692)	(0.0790)	(0.0800)	(0.0760)	(0.0735)	(0.0692)	(0.0695)
Share of shores		0.428***	0.390***	0.197	0.332**	0.294*	0.291*	0.325**	0.334**
		(0.133)	(0.132)	(0.144)	(0.140)	(0.148)	(0.147)	(0.137)	(0.165)
Regional dummies				○					
Religion variables					○				
Constant	1.881***	1.995***	−1.136	1.449	−1.249	0.884	1.303*	−0.716	−1.060
	(0.663)	(0.623)	(1.593)	(1.838)	(1.652)	(2.097)	(0.759)	(1.636)	(1.605)
Observations	99	94	94	94	94	85	85	94	94
R-squared	0.925	0.938	0.941	0.949	0.944	0.936	0.936	0.943	0.941

Standard errors in parentheses ***$p < 0.01$, **$p < 0.05$, *$p < 0.1$

2.4 Conclusion

This chapter has provided a summary of theoretical arguments of why and how the size of a country matters for its level and growth of income (per capita GDP), then has conducted regression analysis that relies on the theoretical arguments and improves upon existing works in terms of choices of variables in regression models and data.

According to results of regression analysis, given other things equal, countries that are large in population size or economic size generally grow faster and have higher per capita income than smaller countries, but the advantage of largeness (or the disadvantage of smallness) becomes smaller when it becomes more open in international trade or financial transactions and when its economic size becomes greater. The marginal effect of demographic size is positive, unless the ratio of trade to GDP is very high, which is true only for a limited number of countries with small population in the sample. The marginal effect of economic size is positive, unless the trade/GDP ratio is very high or economic size is very large, which is true only for a small number of developed countries in the sample. By contrast, geographically large countries do not differ from smaller countries in income growth and level.

Finally, using results of regression analysis, questions posed in the introduction regarding economic performance of emerging powers in the world, China and India, are explored. Are their enormous sizes advantageous or detrimental to income growth? According to estimates of Column (2) of Table 2.3, the marginal effect of the log of population on per capita GDP growth, which does not depend on the demographic variable, is 0.267 for China and is 0.292 for India. The marginal effect of the log of GDP on per capita GDP growth, which decreases with the log of GDP, is 0.04 for China and is 0.126 for India from Colum (3) of Table 2.5. Thus, for given trade openness, their demographic and economic sizes have been advantageous to income growth. How much does their largeness contribute to closing the income gap with the USA? The difference in per capita GDP growth from the USA attributable to the difference in population size, with its interaction with trade openness taken into account, is *−0.088* for China and 0.331 for India. The negative number for China is because of its much higher trade/GDP ratio than the USA. The difference in per capita GDP growth from the USA attributable to the difference in economic size, with its interaction with trade openness taken into account, is *−0.412* for China and *−0.056* for India. The number is negative in both countries because they are smaller than the USA in economic size (and, as for China, the trade/GDP ratio is much higher). Hence, it would be safe to say that contributions of demographic and economic sizes of China and India in closing the income gap with the USA have been small or negative.

References

Alcala F, Ciccone A (2003) Trade, the extent of the market and economic growth 1960–1996. Unpublished manuscript. Universitat Pompeu Fabra

Alesina A, Spolaore E (2003) The size of nations. MIT Press, Cambridge, MA

Alesina A, Spolaore E, Wacziarg R (2000) Economic integration and political disintegration. Am Econ Rev 90(5):1276–1296

Alesina A, Devleeschauwer A, Easterly W, Kurlat S, Wacziarg R (2003) Fractionalization. J Econ Growth 8:155–194

Alesina A, Spolaore E, Wacziarg R (2005) Chapter 23: Trade, growth and the size of countries. Handb Econ Growth 1(Part B):1499–1542

Barro R, Lee J-W (2013) A new data set of educational attainment in the world, 1950–2010. J Dev Econ 104:184–198

Barro RJ, McCleary RM (2003) Religion and economic growth. Am Sociol Rev 68:760–781

Chinn MD, Ito H (2006) What matters for financial development? Capital controls, institutions, and interactions. J Dev Econ 81(1):163–192

Desmet K, Ortuño-Ortín I, Wacziarg R (2012) The political economy of linguistic cleavages. J Dev Econ 97:322–338

Doppelhofer G, Miller R, Sala-i-Martin X (2004) Determinants of long-term growth: a Bayesian averaging of classical estimates (BACE) approach. Am Econ Rev 94(4):813–835

Eicher TS, Papageorgiou C, Raftery AE (2011) Default priors and predictive performance in Bayesian model averaging, with application to growth determinants. J Appl Econ 26(1):30–55

Hauk W, Wacziarg R (2009) A Monte Carlo study of growth regressions. J Econ Growth 14 (2):103–147

Rose A (2006) Size really doesn't matter: in search of a national scale effect. J Jpn Int Econ 20 (4):482–507

Part II
Political Regimes and Social Structure

Chapter 3
Analyzing Dependence and Conflict in a Heterogeneous World: Computer Simulation and Evolutionary Dynamics

Makoto Sejima

Abstract One hundred years after the First World War resurrects the debate about the relationship between trade and war. The end of the Cold War witnesses a new world emerging with heterogeneous regime countries enhancing their economic and political presence in the world. New light should be shed upon the relationship between trade and war in this world with more divergent countries. Based upon the existing literature of qualitative and quantitative methods, I use the computer simulation method and the knowledge of evolutionary dynamics to examine the relationship in a heterogeneous world. Apparently, the outcomes of this research fall short of presenting clear-cut conclusions. After all, it is not easy to rebut both liberals and/or realists with one single research chapter. This research endeavor, however, succeeds partially in showing that the regime difference is an important factor in analyzing the relationship.

Keywords Interdependence and war · The heterogeneous world · A computer simulation · Evolutionary dynamics

3.1 Research Problem

The liberal school of international relations argues that interdependence brings peace among countries. Interdependence raises the cost of countries to cut off trade relations with other countries, and thus interdependent countries prefer to maintain cooperative relations with each other.

The realist school, on the other, argues that interdependence does not necessarily lead to peace between countries. Countries are primarily concerned with their security in the anarchical world, and the lack of autonomy in their foreign behaviors threatens their security. Interdependence reduces the autonomy of countries, and in

M. Sejima (✉)
Osaka International University, Osaka, Japan
e-mail: sejima@oiu.jp

M. Tadokoro et al. (eds.), *Emerging Risks in a World of Heterogeneity*, Evolutionary Economics and Social Complexity Science 10,
https://doi.org/10.1007/978-981-10-7968-9_3

this sense it can be a source of threat to the security of countries. Countries seek to enhance their autonomy and this can lead to conflicts among them.

This debate between these two schools of international politics has been lingering so long and has not reached any concrete conclusions yet. Recent works on this research topic, however, direct out attention to two important points about the theoretical framework of interdependence and war (Copeland 2015; Mansfield and Pollins 2003).

One is that the explanatory variables other than interdependence need to be included in the research models. Such variables include the difference in regime types. One of the implicit assumptions of the liberals is that interdependence works for peace among democratic countries. Recent events shed new light upon the importance of this variable. New countries in the ex-Soviet Union and European countries depend upon Russia for its natural gas, and Russia used it as a diplomatic leverage against European countries as well as against Ukraine and Belarus. China almost monopolized the rare-earth supply market in the world and dramatically reduced its rare earth supply to Japan when its relations with Japan turned severed in 2008.

The other point is that the causal relations between dependent and independent variables are more complicated. The causal relations are not lineal from interdependence to peace. Furthermore, there are interactions among independent variables. Using the artificial intelligence technique, Marwala and Lagazio (2011) analyze the correlations between interdependence and war in order to avoid these problems. Yet more is to be done in this direction.

In this chapter, I address myself more to the first recent research direction of third factors. This chapter employs a computer simulation method to examine the relations between trade and war in a heterogeneous political and economic environment. This book as a whole assumes that we witness a new twist of the world order where more and more countries with divergent political and economic regimes play insignificant roles. Such countries include China, Russia, and India. These countries are presumed to follow suit by mimicking the examples and regimes of the USA and West European counties, but it becomes clear that these countries are too stubborn to be merged into the Western political and economic system. China refutes the ideas and rules of the Western world and subscribes to the Chinese original world views. Russia, once thought to transform itself to the Western countries, defies such expectations. India, once regarded as a highly democratic country, suffers from the traditional stratification (the caste system) in its society.

I worked out several simple simulation models among countries in a heterogeneous world by constructing countries using the real-world polity data. In order to make the model dynamic reflecting the changes in the real world, three mechanisms are borrowed from the evolutionary dynamics literature: the selection, the mutation, and the image scoring.

Some words about the key concepts of this chapter are interdependence and war. Dependence, instead of interdependence, is preferred here because of three reasons. First is that the concept of interdependence implies mutual and symmetrical dependence between countries, but in reality trade relations between countries have been

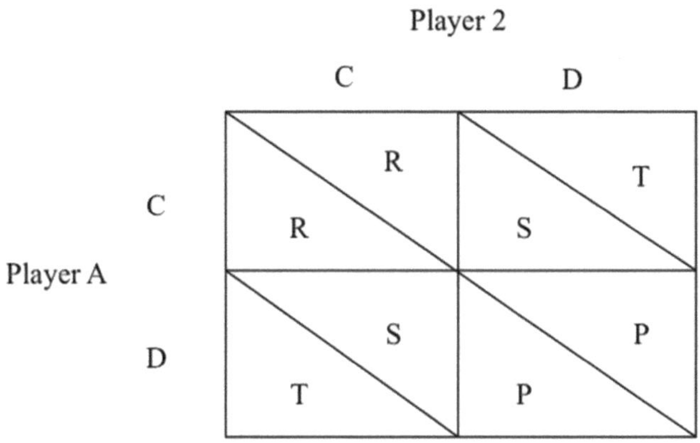

Fig. 3.1 Payoff matrix of the prisoner's dilemma Game

asymmetrical. Second, the main concern of this research is the impact of trade dependence upon how a country chooses its action against another dependent partner, not the nature of interdependence dyadic relations itself. And finally, it is easier to model the dual dependence between two countries than to model the bilateral interdependence in a strict sense. Majority of both qualitative and quantitative literature on this research topic analyzes the behaviors of dependent countries. Interdependence in this chapter is operationalized as mutual dependence between two countries.

I use the word conflict instead of war, because the models of this paper use the famous prisoners' dilemma (PD) game, and the word "conflict" rather than "war" seems more appropriate here. In the PD, the payoff matrix as in Fig. 3.1 qualifies the game results. R represents the reward for mutual cooperation (denoted by C), and T is the temptation to defect (denoted by D) against a cooperative agent, which receives the payoff S as a sucker. P is a kind of penalty for the two players who choose defection against each other. The PD game is differentiated from other games by the following two qualifications: T > R > P > S and 2R > T + S. This chapter follows the typical payoff matrix: $p = 1$, $r = 3$, $s = 0$, and $t - 5$. These payoffs remain the same throughout the turns and throughout all the models in this chapter. War in the PD game is in the right bottom cell of the game matrix, and the defective action of the player is regarded as a conflictual action, observed in the three cells except the top left cell. As the main concern in this research lies in the actions of players and not the bilateral relations between players, conflict instead of war is used here.

The next section describes the research method and data used in this chapter. It is followed by the main parts where, first, a simple basic model (Model 1) is introduced as a kind of benchmark. The model uses the data of trade relations among countries. The following two models become more complicated step-by-step by adding other variables into the model. In the Sect. 3.4, the Model 2 constructs countries using regime-type data from the Polity IV data project (Polity IV Annual time-Series (1800–2013)), and countries use both trade and regime data to determine their actions. This model also examines three dynamic mechanisms widely employed in the literature of evolutionary game theory. As the trade data do not cover before the 1950s, the Sect. 3.4.3 examines the historical treads in the nineteenth and twentieth centuries by using only the Polity IV data that go back to the year of 1800. In the Sect. 3.5, the Model 3 tests another configuration of trade and polity combination, followed by some final remarks.

3.2 Computer Simulation of Dependence and Conflict and Data Source

Contrary to the rich and broad literature on theoretical, statistical, and case studies on this research topic, there are a limited number of researches using the method of computer simulation. Such researches include Bearce and Fisher (2002), who try to construct an agent-based simulation model to examine the relationship between trade and war. They find that the relationship between trade and war depends upon other variables, including geographical distance between agents and the unit-level feature of revisionism. Their research shares at least two common features with others using the method of computer simulation.

The first common feature is that those simulation models are complicated. The agent-based simulation constructs autonomous agents with some endowments (power, natural resources, preference, and others) and then let them interact with each other through simulation runs. Agents choose their actions based upon their endowments, their knowledge of environment around them, and the available information about their interacting agents. Because of this nature of agent-based simulation, the model becomes very complicated and renders it rather difficult to analyze the dynamics of the model. Here it is sufficient to point out two pitfalls Bearce and Fisher suffer from their complicated models.

The first trouble is that their model is too complicated for other researchers to reexamine the validity and robustness of their findings. Simulation models by Bremer and Mihalka (1977), Cusack and Stoll (1990), and Cederman (1997) all simulate war among countries, and their models are sufficiently complicated. The simulation models of trade interdependence and war need to add the aspect of trade relations to the war model, and this inevitably complicates the simulation model. The larger number of both parameters and geographical settings of Bearce and Fischer reflect the complexity of their model. In this chapter, I start with a very simple model and add other variables and algorithms step-by-step into the baseline model, though even that cautious model-building faces some annoying troubles.

The other trouble with Bearce and Fisher is that conflicts and wars are inevitable among countries because the model specification demands countries to engage in conflict with others. Because of this specification, they investigated not the relationship between trade and war per se, but more on the third factors that might influence the relationship.

The second common feature is that they use virtual data instead of historical data. Both case and statistical studies, however, depend highly upon the real data from the real world. The latter studies, as a result, suffer from the problems of data availability and selection bias. The simulation analysis, on the other, can dodge the problem by generating random values as the parameters of the model and thus can examine any hypothetical worlds, free from any limitations posed by the real-world data. Yet, the computer simulation has another problem. In dealing with small N issues, what happened in real history matters significantly, and the relationship between trade and war is such a case. Historical data rather than hypothetical data are more appropriate in this research design. This chapter uses historical data of trade and polities to construct countries and relations among them. Random values are also generated in order to realize some accidental aspects of political life in the model.

Before moving forward to the models explanation and results deliberation, some words about simulation data are in order. The calculation of trade dependence needs imports and exports data and GDP data (hereinafter ExpTradeGdp data), which are available from Kristian Skrede Gleditsh (2004). This data set starts in the 1950s only. Hence the time dimension of this research does not go back before that period. The heterogeneity of countries is realized by using the Polity IV data of the Center for Systemic Peace, which covers the periods of 1800–2013.

It is worthwhile noting that using these two data sets requires a special attention. There is discrepancy of country codes used by the Polity IV and the ExpTradeGdp data. Both data use the same country code system of the Correlates of War project (COW Country Codes (n.d)), but they use different country names in a given year. In 1975, for example, the ExpTradeGdp data uses Russia (its country code is 365), and the Polity IV data used the Soviet Union (its country code is 364). This demands us to examine all the country codes of the years in the analysis.

Below I start with the basic model of homogenous countries with historical trade data to construct relations among them. In addition to the features of the baseline model, the next model, the main part of this research, uses the Polity IV data to construct heterogeneous countries and then tests three additional mechanisms of selection, mutation, and reputation. This model juxtaposes trade relations and polity differences. The final model examines the other way of compounding the two variables. Each model runs for 100 turns each year, starting from 1950 up to 2000, with 5 years interval. One hundred turns consist of one iteration, and in order to examine the robustness of the results, I test 100 iterations and calculate the average value of the 100 iterations.

3.3 A Baseline Model: Model 1

The three models below examine the impact of trade dependence upon the actions of countries in the prisoner's dilemma (PD) game. The Model 1 is a kind of benchmark, which shows that trade dependence among countries are low throughout the periods of this research and the countries choose more defection than cooperation.

The steps of the simulation are as follows. Every country plays the game with all the other countries. The more a country[i] imports from and exports to another country[j], the more cooperative the country[i] becomes toward the country[j]. This means a more dependent country behaves peacefully, as is expected by liberalists. The dependence of a country[i] upon another country[j] is calculated as the share of the country[i]'s imports from plus exports to the country[j] in the GDP of the country[i].

```
dependence[i][j] = (import[i<-j] + export[i->j]) / GDP[i];
```

The results of the Model 1 defy the arguments advanced by the liberals: after 100 turns almost all countries choose defection. The reason for this lies in the fact that the trade dependence of countries throughout the world is very low. The average trade dependence (ranging from 0 to 1.0) is shown in Table 3.1. Trade zero relations are predominant in the world even after the Cold War.

I modify a part of this model by excluding the pair of countries without any trade relations. The result is almost the same with that of the original Model 1, though the share of cooperation slightly increases. The result of the original Model 1 is shown in Fig. 3.2.

This section underlies the argument of Oneal and Russett (1999) that statistical analysis including all dyads weakens the inverse relationship between trade and war. In the following sections, incorporating regime information and evolutionary dynamics shift this all-defective world into more cooperative one, though leaving some curious puzzles yet to be solved somewhere later.

3.4 The Main Model: The Model 2

3.4.1 *Basic Version of the Model 2*

The next model, the Model 2, uses the trade dependence in a slightly different way. In this model, at the first step, pairs of countries with more trade relations are picked up probabilistically, and only they play the PD game at the next step. Here a pair of countries with no trade does not move on to the game step and only dyads with trade volume are examined. This model can be regarded as modeling many quantitative studies excluding politically irrelevant pairs of countries.

```
if (random < dependence[i][j]) {
     country[i] moves to the game step;
}
else {
     country[i] does not move to the game step;
}
```

Table 3.1 Trade dependence of countries, 1950–2000

Dependence	1950	1955	1960	1965	1970	1975	1980	1985	1990	1995	2000
0.0 -	99.8%	99.8%	99.8%	99.8%	99.8%	99.7%	99.7%	99.7%	99.7%	99.7%	99.7%
0.1 -	0.1%	0.2%	0.1%	0.2%	0.2%	0.2%	0.2%	0.2%	0.2%	0.2%	0.2%
0.2 -	0.0%	0.0%	0.0%	0.0%	0.0%	0.0%	0.1%	0.1%	0.1%	0.1%	0.1%
0.3 -	0.0%	0.0%	0.0%	0.0%	0.0%	0.0%	0.0%	0.0%	0.0%	0.0%	0.0%
0.4 -	0.0%	0.0%	0.0%	0.0%	0.0%	0.0%	0.0%	0.0%	0.0%	0.0%	0.0%
0.5 -	0.0%	0.0%	0.0%	0.0%	0.0%	0.0%	0.0%	0.0%	0.0%	0.0%	0.0%
0.6 -	0.0%	0.0%	0.0%	0.0%	0.0%	0.0%	0.0%	0.0%	0.0%	0.0%	0.0%
0.7 -	0.0%	0.0%	0.0%	0.0%	0.0%	0.0%	0.0%	0.0%	0.0%	0.0%	0.0%
0.8 -	0.0%	0.0%	0.0%	0.0%	0.0%	0.0%	0.0%	0.0%	0.0%	0.0%	0.0%
0.9 -	0.0%	0.0%	0.0%	0.0%	0.0%	0.0%	0.0%	0.0%	0.0%	0.0%	0.0%

Data source: The author calculates the trade dependence using the data from Gleditsh (2004)

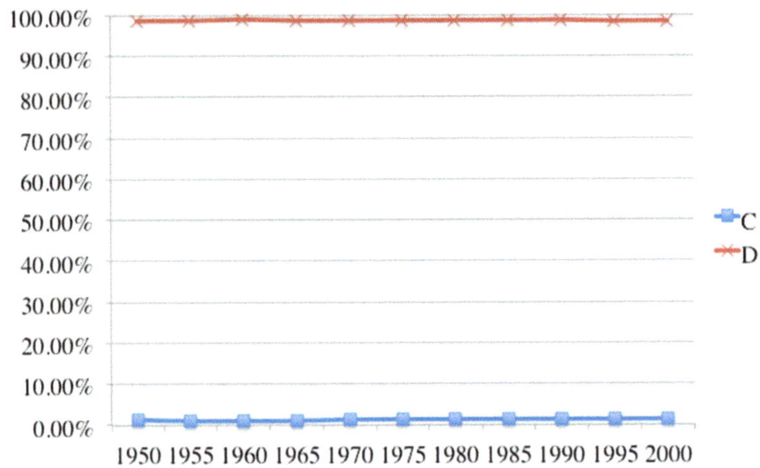

Fig. 3.2 The result of the Model 1

When playing the PD game, heterogeneity comes in. Using the historical data of polities (Polity IV data), each country is endowed with the integer index value of its regime, ranging from −10 (the most autocratic) up to +10 (the most democratic). The idea is that a pair of countries with similar regime index value tends to choose cooperation between them. The similarity of regimes (or "distance") is defined as the difference of regime index values of two countries (i and j), standardized from zero to 1.

```
distance[i][j] = Math.abs(regime[i] - regime[j]);
     if (distance[i][j] < random) {
country[i] chooses cooperation against country[j];
}
else {
     country[i] chooses defection against country[j];
}
```

This formula means the smaller the distance between the two countries, the more chance for them to choose to cooperate. The results are dramatically different from the original Model 1 in that cooperation is the dominant action in the world. Figure 3.3 shows that approximately two-thirds of countries choose cooperation in the world, though the share slightly declines after 1990. This might be because the end of the Cold War promoted globalization and more "distant" countries get involved in trade with each other.

Examining the Polity IV data reveals the static nature of this Model 2. The Polity IV data show how the share of regime types punctuated throughout the period from 1950 to 2000. Figure 3.4 calculates the total regime index values of democracies and autocracies, and Fig. 3.5 counts the number of democratic and autocratic countries.

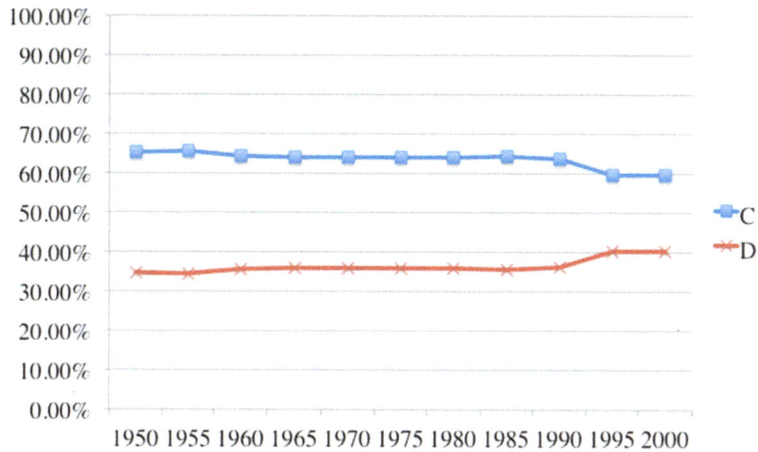

Fig. 3.3 The result of the Model 2

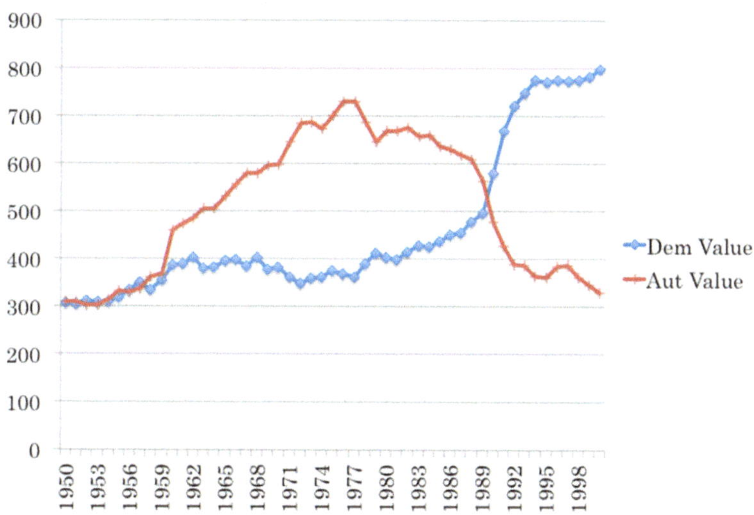

Fig. 3.4 Change of regime-type index values, 1950–2000

In both figures, autocratic countries increased its share until mid-1970s, after which their share declines abruptly especially after the end of the Cold War.

The differences between Fig. 3.3 and Figs. 3.4 and 3.5 appear striking and need to be elaborated further. The Model 2 uses the iterated PD game, but the results of the game (accumulated payoffs accrued by countries) play no roles here. The Model 2 is static and does not reflect any shift of regime heterogeneity in the world. In order to make the model more dynamic and reflect the shift in the world, it is necessary to introduce the ideas of evolutionary dynamics into the model.

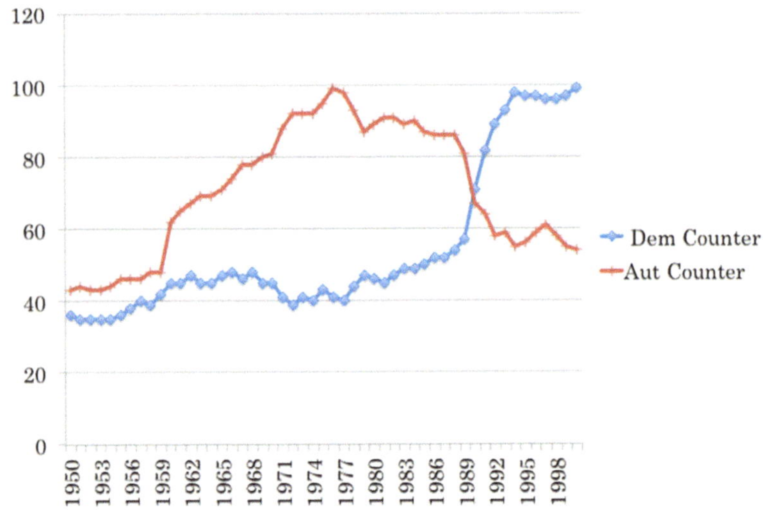

Fig. 3.5 Change of regime-type counter, 1950–2000

3.4.2 The Model 2 and the Three Mechanisms of Evolutionary Dynamics

In order to make the model dynamic and closer to the real world, three mechanisms are introduced to the Model 2. They are the mechanisms of selection, mutation, and image scoring. These mechanisms are widely used in the studies of evolutionary game theory, well surveyed by Lindgren and Nordahl (1994) and others. With the mechanism of selection, lesser countries randomly change their polities to imitate those of the most powerful countries. The power of countries is defined as the accumulated payoffs gained in the iterated PD game. This is a kind of socialization in international politics. Waltz (1979) argues that countries behave almost in the same manner in an anarchical world, because countries failing to imitate other successful countries are doomed to be victims of other predator countries. Mutation is a kind of political revolutions or regime transitions in countries. At the end of each turn, countries might change their polities at the probability of 0.05% into some polity at random (from −10 to +10). The new polity can be democratic as well as autocratic. The third mechanism of image scoring is like the reputation of countries in the world and needs more explanation.

Nowak and Sigmund (1998, 2005) analyze the mechanisms of altruistic behaviors in a huge society where reciprocity does not work. Reciprocity is the essence of the evolution of cooperation deliberated in the tournament game of Axelrod (1984, 1997) and others. Novak and Sigmund succeed in demonstrating that even in the world of no reciprocity, cooperation can evolve. The key concept of their research is the image scoring, and the game using image scoring is called a tag game (Hammond and Axelrod 2006a, b; Laird 2011; Riolo et al. 2001). If an agent chooses cooperation, its image score increases with a given margin, and if defection is the choice of the agent, its image score decreases with the same margin. Even in a random-matching game in a huge society with little chance of playing with the same agents (that is, no reciprocity), a shared knowledge of image scoring makes the society cooperative. The evolutionary game theory presumes a world with uncountable agents, typically the human society and the biological system. If the reputation promotes cooperation among agents in such a large N system, it does much more so in the medium N system, like international system.

In international system, the number of countries is limited to less than 200 at most. It is easy to identify the behaviors of countries. The reputation of other countries plays important roles in the decision-making of political leaders. Though Mercer (1996) presented a highly nuanced argument about reputation in international politics and refutes some conventional assumptions about reputation, he does not negate the importance of reputation in international politics. Putin's Russia, for example, has reputation as more defective in the European system. China is regarded as expanding its influence in the South China Sea at the expense of Vietnam and the Philippines. Reputation of countries, especially of great powers, plays an important role in foreign policy decision-making in international system.

In this model, the image scoring takes the real value from zero to +1.0 (the original score of Nowak and Sigmund ranges between −5 and +6), and each margin of image scoring shifts by 0.1 point. The values of regime type are a common knowledge among agents. When a country[i] decides its action against a country[j], it multiplies the image scoring of country[j] with the random value and compare it to the regime distance[i][j]. If the image scoring of country[j] is bad (or small), the random value becomes smaller and thus reduces the chance of the country[i] to choose cooperation against country[j].

```
if (distance[i][j] < random * image[j]) {
     country[i] chooses cooperation against country[j];
}
else {
     country[i] chooses defection against country[j];
}
```

The results of these modifications present interesting insights as well as puzzles. First, if there is only the mechanism of selection, cooperation occupies about the two-thirds of the world, like the original Model 2, but from 1970s to 1990s, the world was almost 100% cooperative. These periods were the heydays of the liberals advancing the thesis of the peaceful effects of economic interdependence. And with the end of the Cold War, in 1995 and 2000, the share of cooperation declines down to 80%, and the world witnesses the period of international turmoil. Some of the global issues in this current world include regional conflicts in the Third World and in the ex-Soviet Union (Russia versus Ukraine), enduring terrorism, fragile states spreading worldwide, the decline of the US power and the rise of Chinese power, and so on. This result implies that the Model 2 with selection mechanism reflects more the change in the real world (Fig. 3.6).

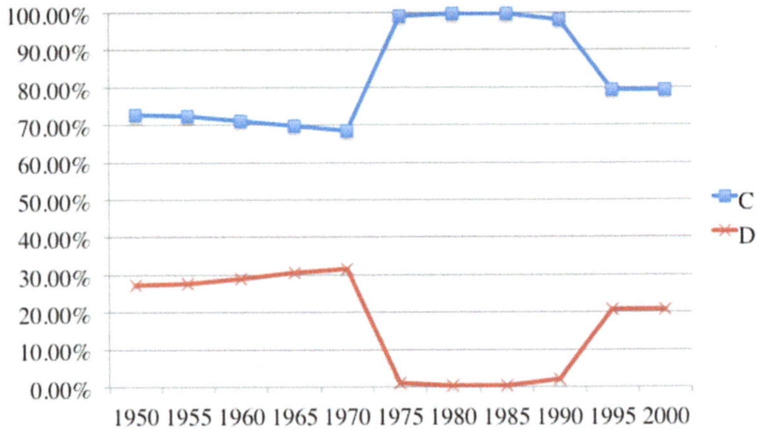

Fig. 3.6 The result of the Model 2 and the selection mechanism

The second mechanism of mutation does not exert any significant impacts upon the distribution of cooperation/defection in the world observed in the original Model 2. Though the mutation mechanism is like a probabilistic earthquake and creates some disturbance of trends, it does not basically change the situation. This is also the case with the Model 2 with the selection and mutation mechanisms combined.

With the single mechanism of reputation added to the Model 2, the result is astonishing: defective actions occupy around 60% before 1970, and after that the share of defection rises up to almost 90% in the world. This result defies any easy interpretation and needs to be elaborated later in other research (Fig. 3.7).

Adding more than one mechanism into the original Model 2 renders interpretation harder again. The mutation mechanism does not transform the basic trajectory of the result of the Model 2, either with selection mechanism or with image scoring mechanism, or with both mechanisms. Combining the mechanisms of selection and image scoring resulted in the distribution pattern of cooperation and defection intuitionally corresponding to the real world. During the Cold War era before 1970, defection was more than 60%, and after 1970 until 1990, cooperation dominated the world. And after 1990 the world witnessed more defection. The result is shown in Fig. 3.8. All three mechanisms simultaneously in the Model 2 produces, as is expected, basically the same results of the tests of selection and image scoring combined.

3.4.3 Heterogeneity and Conflicts

The period covered by the trade data available now is strictly limited after the Second World War and not before that, but the polity data goes back to the nineteenth century. The polity data can shed light on the impact of regime heterogeneity on the behaviors of countries in a longer period of time than the Models 1 and 2. In this

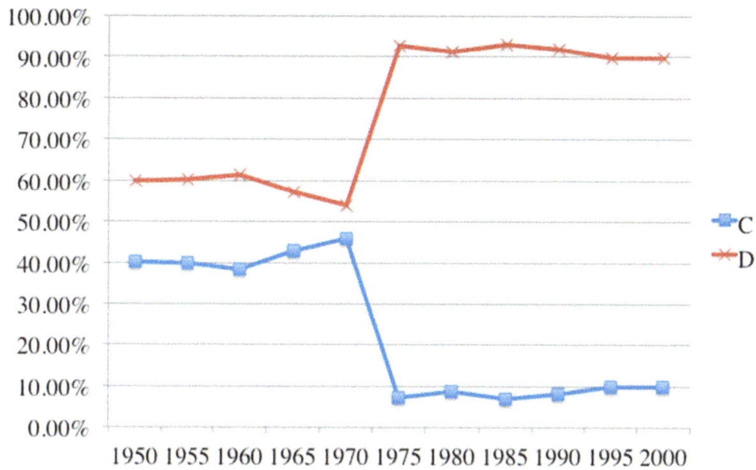

Fig. 3.7 The result of the Model 2 and the image scoring mechanism

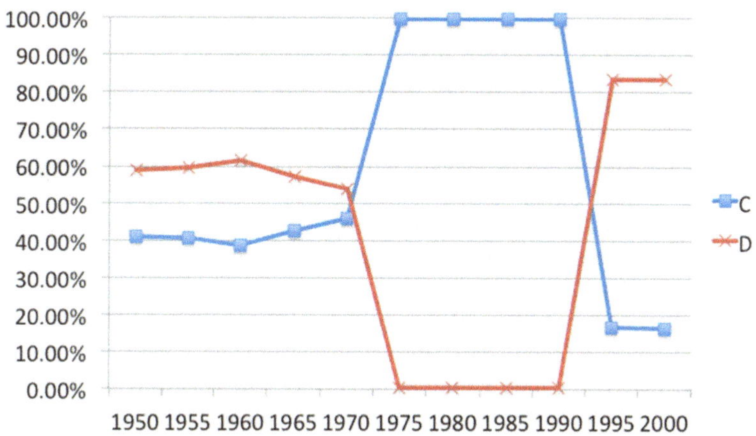

Fig. 3.8 The result of the Model 2 with the two mechanisms of selection and image scoring

Model R1, country[i] chooses between the two actions "cooperate" or "defect," by comparing the two values of distance[i][j] and the random value.

```
if (distance[i][j] < random) {
      country[i] chooses cooperation;
}
else {
      country[i] choose defection;
}
```

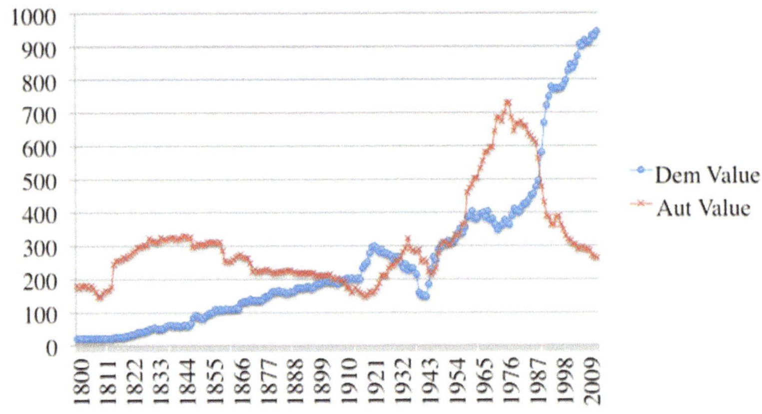

Fig. 3.9 Time-series distribution of autocratic and democratic regime index values

Following the examinations of the Model 2, the Model R2 examines the dynamic mechanism of reputation installed in the Model R1.

Before examining the results of the Model R1, it is necessary to examine the regimes distribution in the world from 1800 to 2013 in order to correctly understand the results of the model. Figure 3.9 depicts the time-series distribution of democratic and autocratic regimes. "Dem Value" summates the all index values of democratic countries, and "Aut Value" is the summation of all index values of autocratic countries. Up until 1910 and from 1926 to 1990, autocratic countries are the majority in the world. The rise of democratic countries above autocratic countries is witnessed between 1914 and 1960 and after 1990.

One issue needs to be examined carefully in this model. Autocrats choose cooperation as often as democrats. This sounds absurd and contrary to our common sense. Democratic peace theory implies that democratic countries are more cooperative with each other than autocratic countries with each other. In the Cold War, however, countries in the Soviet bloc cooperate with each other against the Western bloc of the USA and Western Europe. This means that cooperation among autocratic countries is possible, though this kind of cooperation was more obliged by the stronger country: the Soviet Union against East European satellite countries captured in the Soviet orbit.

I picked up the years of 5-year intervals: 1800, 1805, 1810, 1815, and 2000 in the Polity IV data. Figures 3.10 and 3.11 show the results of models R1 and R2. "Model R1 C" means the average share of cooperation in the world during 100 iterations, and "Model R1 D" is the average share of defection in the world during the same iterations. In the Model R1, cooperation is more frequent than defection, but the share of cooperation decreases gradually until 1990 when cooperation turns upward a little bit. On the contrary, in the Model R2, cooperation is more widespread among

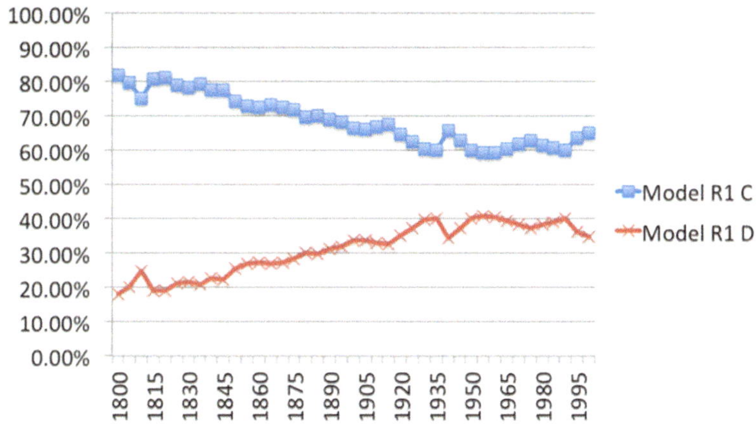

Fig. 3.10 The results of the Model R1, 1800–2000

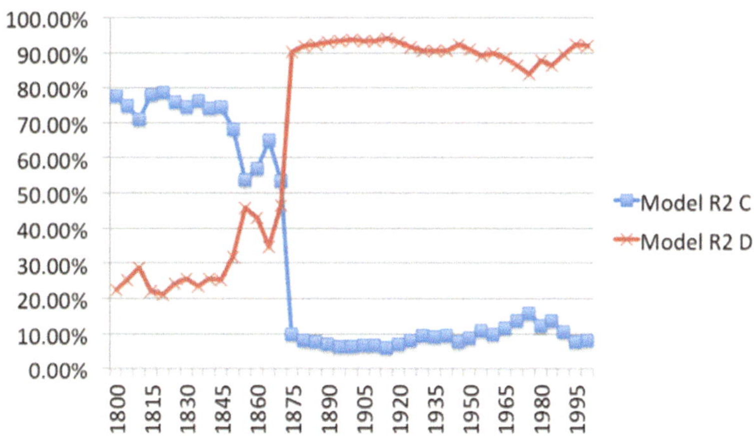

Fig. 3.11 The results of the Model R2, 1800–2000

countries, but after around 1870 defection rules the world, and cooperation decreases its share in the world again after 1980. The results of these two models are quite opposite except in one point. That is, in both models, it is worth noting that around the 1970s cooperation increases its share in the world exactly when the liberal argument of interdependence emerged, typically represented by Keohane and Nye (1977).

It is not easy to tell which model reflects the historical treads of relations among countries, but the Model R2 with image scoring seems to be closer to the real development of international relations in the nineteenth and twentieth centuries. In the first half of the nineteenth century, Europe enjoyed a relatively stable peace among countries under the system of the concert of Europe until the 1860s when the Crimean War (1853–1856) destroyed cooperation among major countries in Europe. After Otto von Bismarck, the Chancellor of Germany, retired in 1890, the world experienced the two world wars and the Cold War.

3.5 The Other Possibility: The Model 3

Going back to the trade and regime model, I pick up the final model. The Model 3 is a variant of the Model 2. The difference between the two models lies in how to combine the two variables. Contrary to the Model 2 where trade dependence precedes the regime distance, the Model 3 combines trade dependence and polity difference. The Model 2 uses the trade dependence as a kind of selection mechanism of countries, excluding the pair of countries with smaller trade relations. In order to simulate the theoretical framework of simultaneous operation of both trade dependence and regime distance, it is absolutely necessary to find a way to combine the values of interdependence and polity difference into one monolithic structure. The trouble is that it is not easy to come up with the idea of how to construct such a simulation model. In fact, this model fails in producing any meaningful insights into the research topic. The idea in this section is first to multiply the trade dependence and regime distance standardized from 0 to 1.0. Then, the value produced by this formula is compared with a random value. If the latter value is smaller than the former, then the country chooses to cooperate. The result is, as is easy to be expected, more defective world than the Model 1, as is shown in Fig. 3.12. Even if all the dyads with no trade are excluded from these data, the result stays almost the same.

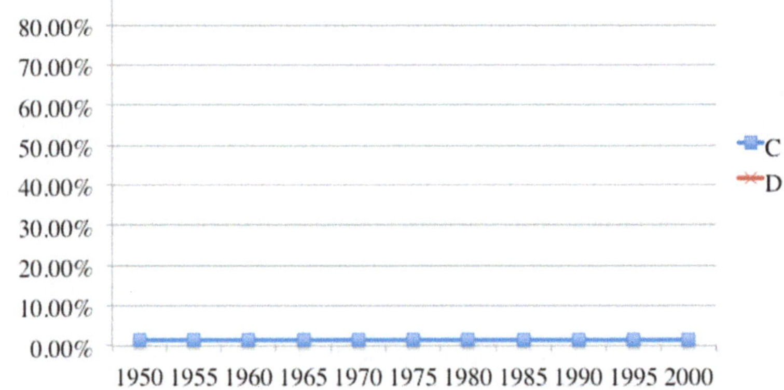

Fig. 3.12 The result of the Model 3

For the sake of research curiosity, each of the three mechanisms of evolutionary game theory is tested separately in this model. These three mechanisms do not alter the result of the Model 3.

3.6 Conclusion

This chapter constructs very simple computer simulation models in order to examine the relationship between economic dependence and conflict. The liberals maintain the argument that trade promotes peace, while the realists' argument is quite contrary: that trade can breed conflict among countries. Recent researches on this topic pay more attention to the third factors other than trade and war.

Extending this research direction, this chapter, however, locates this research theme in a different context. The world observes a new twist of the world order with more divergent regime countries exerting more important economic and political influence in the world scene. This chapter analyzes the relationship in a heterogeneous world.

In the simulation models, each country plays the iterated PD game with each other. The game is repeated for 100 turns, and the robustness of the results is checked by 100 iterations. The result is the average value of the 100 iterations.

The first model reveals that the round robin game of all countries does not support the argument of the liberals of international politics. Action D becomes dominant in the world, and almost all pairs of countries end up with (P, P) situation of the PD game matrix. Even cases excluding no trade dyads cannot alter the basic conflictual nature of the result.

The next model (the Model 2) is the main part of this chapter. It allows the pairs of countries to play the PD game probabilistically in proportion to their trade dependence. This filter leaves pairs of countries with more trade dependence. After this filtering step, countries with similar regime-type (politically less distant pairs of countries) choose to cooperate with each other. This model shows that cooperation is the dominant action in the world as is expected by the liberals. Yet the model remains static and does not reflect the drastic drift of regime-type distribution in the world. Mechanisms of evolutionary dynamics produce quite different picture of the world. The Model 2 with the selection mechanism results in the change of the world corresponding to the one we know. In the 1970s and 1980s, liberals come forth with their argument that interdependence promotes peace among countries, and after the Cold War, the world experiences more troubles in the world. The effects of mutation are negligible, and the image scoring mechanism produces a contrary result from the selection mechanism; the defection becomes dominant especially after 1970. This is a puzzle that needs to be elaborated somewhere later.

The final model, the Model 3, tries another way of combining trade dependence and regime types. The political distance and economic dependence are multiplied, and countries choose C or D stochastically. The result is just like that of the Model 1, and this does not change even with other modifications of trade zero exclusion and the three evolutionary mechanisms added to the Model 3.

This research is different from other existing qualitative and quantitative researches in three points. First is that this analyzes the relationship in a different political context with divergent regime countries. The second is that this uses the computer simulation method instead of historical or statistical methods. The simulation methods enjoy the flexibility in a sense that it can experiment various scenarios integrating various algorisms, like the three evolutionary dynamics. And finally this research, like historical and statistical methods, uses the real historical data rather than artificial random data many simulation analyses often depend upon. This research is located exactly between the historical and statistical methods on the one hand and the simulation method on the other.

Because of these research characteristics, this research suffers from some pitfalls shared by other research methods. The most significant defect is the availability of data, especially the reliable trade data available only after the Second World War. The other lies in the flexibility of the method. Various algorisms produce sometimes quite opposite outcomes, and researchers are at a loss to make theoretical sense of them, like the results of the Model 2 combined with the image scoring selection. Still, this chapter proves to some extent the usefulness of the computer simulation approach in the international politics.

Acknowledgment This work was supported by JSPS KAKENHI Grant Numbers 25245027 and 23530206.

References

Axelrod R (1984) The evolution of cooperation. Basic Books, New York

Axelrod R (1997) The complexity of cooperation. Princeton University Press, Princeton

Bearce DH, Fisher EO'N (2002) Economic geography, trade, and war. J Confl Resolut 46 (3):365–393

Bremer SA, Mihalka M (1977) Machiavelli in Machina: or politics among hexagons. In: Deutsch KW (ed) Problems of world modeling. Ballinger, Boston, pp 303–337

Cederman L (1997) Emergent actors in world politics. Princeton University Press, Princeton

Copeland DC (2015) Economic interdependence and war. Princeton University Press, Princeton

Cusack TR, Stoll R (1990) Exploring realpolitik. Lynnie Rienner, Boulder

Hammond RA, Axelrod RA (2006a) The evolution of ethnocentrism. J Confl Resolut 50:926–936

Hammond RA, Axelrod RA (2006b) Evolution of contingent altruism when cooperation is expensive. Theor Popul Biol 69:333–338

Keohane RS, Nye JS (1977) Power and interdependence. Little, Brown, Boston

Laird RA (2011) Green-beard effect predicts the evolution of traitorousness in the two-tag prisoner's dilemma. J Theor Biol 288:84–91

Lindgren K, Nordahl MG (1994) Cooperation and community structure in artificial ecosystems. Artif Life 1(1_2):15–38

Mansfield ED, Pollins BM (eds) (2003) Economic interdependence and international conflict. The University of Michigan Press, Ann Arbor

Marwala T, Lagazio M (2011) Militarized conflict modeling using computational intelligence. Springer, London
Mercer J (1996) Reputation & International Politics. Cornell University Press, Ithaca
Nowak MA, Sigmund K (1998) Evolution of indirect reciprocity by image scoring. Nature 393:573–577
Nowak MA, Sigmund K (2005) Evolution of indirect reciprocity. Nature 437:1291–1298
Oneal JR, Russett BM (1999) Assessing the liberal peace with alternative specifications: trade still reduces conflict. J Peace Res 36:423–442
Riolo RL, Cohen MD, Axelrod R (2001) Evolution of cooperation without reciprocity. Nature 414:441–443
Waltz K (1979) Theory of international politics. Addison-Wesley, Reading

Data

COW Country Codes (n.d.). The correlates of war project. http://www.correlatesofwar.org/data-sets/cow-country-codes
Gleditsh KS (2004) Expanded trade and GDP data. http://privatewww.essex.ac.uk/~ksg/exptradegdp.html
Polity IV Annual time-Series (1800–2013). Center for systemic peace. http://www.systemicpeace.org/inscrdata.html

Chapter 4
The Superficial Success of the Development Assistance Committee: Emerging Donors and the Revival of Economic Statecraft

Hiroko Ogawa

Abstract This chapter examined how the increasing presence of emerging donors affects the Development Assistance Committee (DAC) regime and the countries in which it is implemented. The DAC, as an Official Development Assistance regime (ODA), has subsumed emerging donors and enlarged the scope of its application to develop itself by keeping its fundamental principles. This means the DAC regime has developed. Meanwhile, many DAC countries are beginning to increase their commercial interests through development assistance as emerging donors. After China announced its plan to establish the Asian Infrastructure Investment Bank (AIIB), most DAC countries, including the UK, successively joined it. The DAC has a long tradition of encouraging its members to provide technical assistance for poverty reduction and cannot easily change its direction. Therefore, the DAC countries have tried to deal with their changing needs individually, and actually, the DAC has been undermined. Recipients welcome this trend of donors to provide the loans for infrastructure construction. The trend of preferring commercial-based activities will continue for a while. Meanwhile, commercial-based activities cannot meet the needs of poverty reduction and cause risks. Where many donors are prioritizing their commercial interests over poverty reduction in the developing countries, we may leave serious poverty problems behind and spread human rights violations and environmental destruction. Thus, global governance of international development cooperation is essential.

Keywords DAC · ODA · Emerging donors · China · AIIB

H. Ogawa (✉)
Tokai University, Kanagawa, Japan
e-mail: ogwhrk@tokai-u.jp

M. Tadokoro et al. (eds.), *Emerging Risks in a World of Heterogeneity*, Evolutionary Economics and Social Complexity Science 10,
https://doi.org/10.1007/978-981-10-7968-9_4

4.1 Introduction

In the 2010s, emerging donors began to increase their presence. Emerging donors provide development assistance based on their own diplomatic policies and aid philosophy, and their development assistance policies do not conform to the basic principles shared by Development Assistance Committee (DAC) countries. What effect will the increasing presence of emerging donors have on the DAC regime formed by Western developed countries during the Cold War period and the DAC countries?

Previous studies present two conflicting views. One is that emerging donors can alter the DAC regime, and the other is that emerging donors cannot alter it. The former takes as evidence the fact that emerging donors altered the fundamental rule of DAC at the Busan High Level Forum (HLF) (Kindornay and Samy 2013). The latter notes that emerging donors have started to comply with DAC rules and to join DAC (Dreher et al. 2013). However, both are mainly looking to the influence of emerging countries on DAC rules.

This article considers not only the impact of emerging countries on DAC rules but also the impact of the rule change on DAC countries. How do DAC countries respond to rule changes? What kind of relationship did they have tried to build with emerging donors? The actions of each DAC country embody its foreign policy itself and better reflect the future of DAC.

In this article, I first describe the formation and development of DAC to clarify what kind of regime the DAC is. Next, I show that DAC has changed its fundamental principles so to reflect the development cooperation of emerging donors. I also argue that some DAC countries followed the new DAC rules after the change. Furthermore, I show that the majority of DAC countries joined the new regime when emerging donors declared its creation. Finally, I present the consequences for the emerging donors and discuss the prospects of international development cooperation governance and the tasks to be faced in the future.

4.2 DAC

4.2.1 Western Donors' Club

After the Second World War, we recognized the needs of development flows to developing countries, from the viewpoint of interdependence and humanity. However, neither the World Bank (WB) nor the United Nations (UN) could provide appropriate flows for developing countries. The WB only provided loans on a commercial basis, which developing countries could use only with difficulty. The UN reflected Soviet influence, so the United States (US) avoided using it as its main development aid organization. The US had to embark on development aid itself, integrating development aid into military aid in 1951, as the tensions in the US–Soviet relationship increased. Naturally, military aid, which was provided from a strategic point of view, had weak effects on economic development. When the Soviet Union and China began development aid in the mid-1950s, the US also realized the need to improve the quality of its development aid. In 1957, the USA established the Development Loan Fund to be responsible for development finance for developing countries. At the same time, however, the US balance of payments turned into a deficit, which caused the US to recognize that it alone could not meet the needs of development flows. Therefore, the US requested that Western countries share the burden of development flows (Hook 1995: 22–25; Wood 1986: 70–72, 1996).

In restructuring the Organization for European Economic Cooperation (OEEC), the US tried to encourage Western countries to use it to increase their flows of development assistance. Originally, in 1948, the OEEC had been established to receive the economic assistance of the Marshall Plan for 16 European countries. After with the economic recovery of the target European countries, the OEEC were reorganized into an organization of Western countries used to adjust their economic policy. European countries had come to believe that new organizations should contribute not only to economic development through the promotion of trade among Western countries but also to economic development in developing countries (US State 1958–1960: VII, Doc 83). The OEEC, which European countries supported, could be a means to encourage European countries to increase their development flows (US State 1958–1960: IV, Doc 188, 189). The International Development Association (IDA) of the WB could not provide all the long-term loans and grants that developing countries needed (US State 1958–1960: VII, Doc 85). Developing countries needed for additional development flows on a bilateral basis rather than on a multilateral basis (US State 1958–1960: VII, Doc 97).

In 1960, US Secretary of State D. Douglas Dillon launched the Development Assistance Group (DAG) as a provisional organization, because it would take time until a successor organization of the OEEC could be established. The DAG was an informal organization designed to increase development flows to developing countries and had no full-time staff. The original member countries were Belgium, Canada, France, Germany, Italy, Portugal, the UK, the US, the EEC Commission, Japan, and the Netherlands. Dillon emphasized that the DAG had a limited scope, dealing with only bilateral development aid to elicit cooperation from European countries (US State 1958–1960: VII, Doc 105). He succeeded in persuading the European countries to accept that the DAG would be a forum that would consider ways to increase development flows and to improve the effectiveness of the flows (US State 1958–1960: VII, Doc 106).

On the initiative of US Secretary of State George Ball, the document "Resolution of the Common Aid Effort" was adopted, whose goal was to improve the quality and quantity of development aid as a common objective. The resolution stated that DAG members agreed to recommend to members that it should be a common objective to secure an expansion of the aggregate volume of resources made available to developing countries and to improve their effectiveness, that, while private and public finance extended on commercial terms is valuable and should be encouraged, the needs of some of the developing countries at the present time were such that the common aid effort should provide for expanded assistance in the form of grants or loans on favorable terms, including long maturities where this is justified, to prevent the burden of external debt from becoming too heavy (OECD 2006: 10). In 1961, when the US and Canada joined the OEEC and it was reorganized into the OECD (the Organization for Economic Co-operation and Development), the DAG was renamed the DAC, and it became affiliated with the OECD and officially encouraged OECD members to increase their development assistance.

However, the DAC was only a forum for conducting survey on the development assistance of its members and making policy recommendations and consultations based on the results of its survey of its members. For this reason, DAC could not easily give directions to member countries on how to expand the amount of development assistance and improve their effectiveness. They considered development assistance as a means of foreign policy and used it to achieve their objectives. For example, the US provided development assistance to the countries that had highly strategic importance and supported infrastructure construction such as roads and dams in developing countries to contribute to the overseas expansion of US companies. The UK and France allocated development assistance to former colonial countries to maintain connection with those countries. Japan intensively provided development loans to infrastructure construction in neighboring Asian countries, to increase their own commercial interests.

4.2.2 *Official Development Assistance Regime*

The DAC, which was established as a forum for Western countries to exchange views of development assistance, gradually began to demonstrate a character as regime. Specifically, the DAC presented targets and principles for high-quality development assistance and evaluated performance to regulate member countries' behaviors and improve the quality and quantity of development assistance.

In 1969, Official Development Assistance (ODA) was defined as indicating good quality development assistance. The DAC adopted the concept of ODA, separating ODA from "Other Official Flows" (OECD 2006: 15). In 1972, the DAC agreed on a firmer definition of ODA, and this definition is still in force today. The DAC defined ODA as flows to developing countries and multilateral institutions provided by official agencies, including state and local governments, or by their executive agencies, each transaction of which meets the following test: a) it is administered with the promotion of the economic development and welfare of developing countries as its main objective, and b) it is concessional in character and contains a grant element of at least 25% (OECD 2006: 16). The definition was based on the idea that grants are more conducive for the long-term economic development of aid recipients. Among the benefits of grants is that they do not incur long-term debt obligations in poor states. Pressure for greater grant aid intensified in the 1990s after many developing countries could not repay the low-interest loans they had received from ODA donors, the WB, and regional banks (Hook and Rumsey 2016: 64).

In 1974, the DAC countries agreed to a "Memorandum of Understanding on Untying of Bilateral Development Loans in Favor of Procurement in Developing Countries" (OECD 2006: 17). The DAC adopted untying as a new measure in the memorandum. This concept measures the extent to which aid transfers are tied to donor goods and services. Whereas donors benefit materially from giving development assistance, tying ODA funds to their own aid agencies and private firms, aid recipients seek autonomy in procuring the products and services afforded by ODA transfers. Recipients are keenly aware that untied aid provides economic efficiencies. "It has been clearly documented that tied aid raises the costs of goods and services by 15–30% and by as much as 40% or more for food aid" (Clay et al. 2008:1; Hook and Rumsey 2016: 65). Agreement to this memorandum means that the DAC had taken a drastic measure to the serious problem of development assistance.

In 1977, the DAC High Level Meeting adopted a "Statement on Development Cooperation for Economic Growth and Meeting Basic Human Needs (BHN)" (OECD 2006: 18). In the 1960s, the DAC member countries worked to encourage economic growth and industrialization in development assistance and did not emphasize the alleviation of poverty nor meeting the BHN of people in developing countries. In the 1970s, many donor countries, UN agencies, the WB, and others, started to recognize the importance of the idea and adopted it as their guiding principle. The DAC also adopted this as a target and encouraged member countries to meet BHN in their development assistance.

In 1996, the DAC High Level Meeting adopted as its new development strategy "Shaping the 21st Century: The Contribution of Development Cooperation." The goals of this strategy are a reduction by one-half in the percentage of people living in extreme poverty by 2015, universal primary education in all countries by 2015, and others (OECD 2006: 26–27). This strategy means that all members should emphasize the sectors of social and administrative infrastructure in ODA.

In 2000, the DAC launched the system Peer Review. This entails periodic reviews of the individual development cooperation efforts of its members. The Secretariat designates members to be reviewed and members to serve as examiners in each given year. The examiners assess the performance of the reviewed to improve the quality and effectiveness of development cooperation policies and systems. The assessment is published in the journal *Peer Review*. The examiners give appreciation of those members who achieved the DAC's targets and comply with the DAC's standards, requiring the members who deviate from the DAC's standards to improve their system and policy. The DAC exerts social pressure on its members to improve the behavior of members who deviate from the DAC's standards (OECD 2006: 30, 2013: 2, 2017a).

In other words, the DAC recognizes that the boundaries of development assistance with commercial activities should be clarified and targets and guidelines should be listed, such as the grant element and the untying status. In addition, the DAC urged its members to improve their development assistance with the main objective of economic growth and increasing the welfare of developing countries. The DAC gradually caused convergence among members in performance.

4.3 Emerging Donors and DAC Standards

4.3.1 Emerging Donors

A large number of states are active as emerging donors. Emerging donors include global giants like China, India, and Brazil; regional powers like South Africa and Saudi Arabia; rapidly industrializing countries like Thailand and Turkey; and former socialist states, such as Russia, Poland, and the Czech Republic. The visibility, presence, and impact of these countries in international development have grown sharply over the last few years (Mawdsley 2012: 1). As a result, they have been the subject of intense interest and analysis as providers of foreign aid and development assistance.

Some emerging donors became members of the DAC. As Table 4.1 shows, Spain, Luxembourg, Portugal, and Greece joined the DAC in the 1990s; Korea joined the DAC in 2010; the Czech Republic, Poland, the Slovak Republic, and Slovenia joined DAC in 2013; the United Arab Emirates joined the DAC in 2014; and Hungary joined the DAC in 2016 (OECD 2016b).

Other emerging donors have not joined the DAC and instead provide development assistance in their own way as non-DAC donors. As Table 4.2 shows, non-DAC donors include 3 OECD non-DAC countries such as Turkey; 15 - non-OECD countries that report to the OECD-DAC, such as Saudi Arabia, Russia, and Bulgaria; and 10 non-OECD countries that do not report to the OECD-DAC, such as Brazil, China, and India. The total amount of development assistance of the 28 non-DAC donors is estimated to reach 34 million dollars. That equals no more

Table 4.1 DAC members (OECD 2016b)

1961	Australia, Belgium, Canada, European Union, France, Germany, Italy, Japan, the Netherlands, Portugal[a], the United Kingdom, the United States
1962	Norway
1963	Denmark
1965	Sweden
1966	Austria
1968	Switzerland
1973	New Zealand
1975	Finland
1985	Ireland
1991	Spain, Portugal[a]
1992	Luxembourg
1999	Greece
2010	Korea
2013	Czech Republic, Iceland, Poland, Slovak Republic, Slovenia
2014	The United Arab Emirates
2016	Hungary

[a]Portugal joined the DAC in 1960, withdrew in 1974, and rejoined in 1991

Table 4.2 Key providers of development cooperation (OECD 2017b Table 33, 33a)

OECD non-DAC	Estonia, Israel, Turkey (3 countries)
Other providers that report to the OECD-DAC	Bulgaria, Croatia, Cyprus, Kazakhstan, Kuwait, Latvia, Liechtenstein, Lithuania, Malta, Romania, Russia, Saudi Arabia, Chinese Taipei, Thailand, Timor Leste (15 countries)
Other providers that do not report to the OECD-DAC	Brazil, Chile, China, Colombia, Costa Rica, India, Indonesia, Mexico, Qatar, South Africa (10 countries)

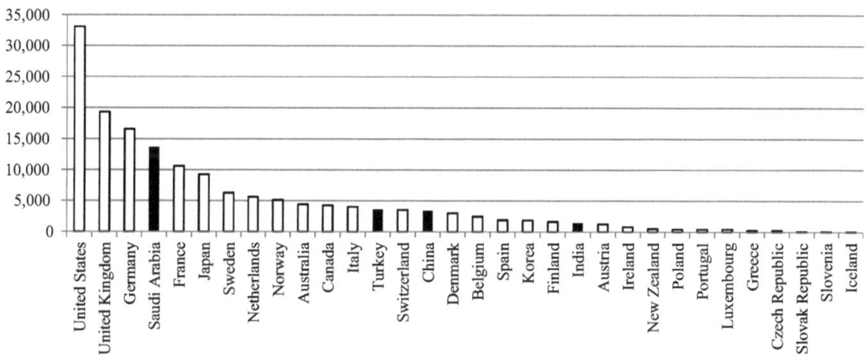

Fig. 4.1 ODA of DAC countries and Concessional Flows of Major non-DAC countries in 2016 (USD million) (OECD 2017b Table 4.1, 33a, 33ae)

than a quarter of the total ODA of DAC countries (OECD 2017b). However, as for country-by-country performance, the presence of individual non-DAC donors cannot be ignored. Figure 4.1 shows that Saudi Arabia comes 4th in the ranking, Turkey 13th, China 15th, and India 21st. The impact of non-DAC donors is obvious at a glance, although we cannot simply compare non-DAC donors with DAC donors because of the different ways of collecting data.

Not surprisingly, most non-DAC donors, especially emerging donors, have tended to keep their distance from the DAC and ignore its rules. This is partly because high administrative costs and hurdles prohibit them from keeping the DAC's rules. It is partly because they doubt DAC rules and hate Western hegemonic ambitions and strategies as well as the dominance of international institutions by Western countries (Mawdsley 2012: 90). This has led to rising concerns among the DAC countries become concerned about the increasing presence of emerging donors.

Among these, concern about China is great. China's aid philosophy contrasts with DAC. The principle of Chinese development cooperation contrasts with that one of the DAC. China bases itself on the principle of equality and mutual benefit in providing development assistance. This principle means that the country providing assistance and the one receiving it are seen as equal partners, with economic development pursued through sharing experience and technology for mutual gain (a "win–win" approach) (Mawdsley 2012: 155; Kobayashi 2007: 131).

On the other hand, DAC supports the aid philosophy of "charity." For DAC countries, wealthy countries should give development assistance to poor countries; lending these countries money and expecting them to repay it is immoral. Thus, development assistance in the form of grants is desirable, and because development assistance is a matter of ethics, the nation providing it cannot expect any reward or compensation (Mawdsley 2012; 152–55; De Haan and Warmerdam 2013: 228). Therefore, the DAC cannot easily accept the principle of equality and mutual benefit, which would lead donors to increase their commercial interest through development assistance.

The DAC also expressed concerns about China's loans for major infrastructure development in Africa and other countries around the world. The DAC is skeptical of development assistance for building infrastructure. China has expanded its loans for large-scale infrastructure to developing countries around the world, especially in Africa. This approach runs counter to the DAC's target for its members of focusing on technical assistance for the social sector. We cannot expect that building infrastructure will improve the standard of living, while it may contribute to the economic growth, of the recipient countries. The DAC prioritizes poverty reduction over economic growth, recommends that its members focus on development assistance for the social sector not economic infrastructure, and has created many rules on principles and the focus areas. China does not provide development assistance on the basis of the DAC's rules.

These preferential loans for building infrastructure have also gathered criticism from DAC countries. The loans are low-interest loans, provided by the Chinese Export-Import Bank, established in 1994. Their interest rates are 2–3% higher than other countries' concessional loans, and repayment periods are short. The grant element of DAC countries' loans is 67.1%, while China's barely exceed 25%, which is extremely low. There are also concerns that preferential loans weaken efforts to provide debt relief to heavily debt-laden countries. In addition, these loans are as a rule "tied" loans, meaning that more than 50% of the materials, equipment, technology, and services for assistance projects must be provided by China. Consequently, labor and materials are not sourced locally, restricting any positive effect on the local economy; this has drawn additional criticism (Watanabe 2013: 104; Zimmerman and Smith 2011: 731–732).

However, it is not only China who is not making poverty reduction a priority like the DAC. Many emerging donors focus on infrastructure, energy provision, and productive capacity intended to enhance growth, rather than working directly on poverty reduction (Mawdsley 2012: 111). They do not draw clear lines between aid, trade, and investment, bringing them together to implement a particular project. These techniques are at odds with mainstream aid norms and practices in which DAC countries separate aid from trade and investment in order not to damage the function of markets nor to pursue self-interest (Mawdsley 2012: 135). Emerging donors can spoil the practices that the DAC has built up over the years.

4.3.2 The DAC's Standards Changed

At the end of 2011, the DAC announced a global relations strategy that aimed to promote participation by non-DAC countries. This strategy's goals were as follows: (1) facilitation of policy discussions and sharing of knowledge, (2) greater awareness and comprehensiveness of DAC's policy-making process and its discussions, and (3) a stronger contributions of the DAC to a more effective development cooperation system. Priority members in this strategy were OECD members that were not DAC countries, OECD accession countries, OECD Key Partners (Brazil, China, India, Indonesia, and South Africa), European Union member states that were not OECD members, and Arab countries and institutions (OECD 2016a).

The DAC has three instruments for the engagement of non-DAC donors, as follows. The first one is policy dialogue with a view to exchanging experience and promoting mutual understanding about shared international goals and how they can be achieved. This was not a simple person-to-person exchange; rather, the DAC allowed non-DAC countries to participate in its policy-making process. Non-DAC OECD member countries were permitted to participate in the DAC's day-to-day affairs, and most are now doing so. Parties with an enhanced agreement with the OECD (Brazil, China, India, Indonesia, and South Africa) and countries that consented to OECD codes (Russia, Columbia, and Latvia) were invited to DAC's annual Senior and High Level Meetings (OECD 2016a, c).

The second instrument is collaboration on management and statistics, to share the DAC's methodologies and guidelines as well as DAC members' experience in these areas. This involved special DAC inspections and seminars, offered by request for countries trying to improve management and statistics. Thus far, Chile, Iceland, Slovenia, the Slovak Republic, Poland, South Korea, and the Czech Republic have undergone these special inspections, while Mexico, Israel, the United Arab Emirates, the Slovak Republic, Turkey, India, and Poland have had seminars. Finally, the third is the analysis of the development cooperation provided by non-DAC countries and related issues (OECD 2016a, d).

These strategies had no small effect. First, as many as 20 non-DAC countries voluntarily began to report information about their development flows to DAC. Second, some emerging donors contacted the DAC office requesting evaluation of their own assistance programs. Third, Mexico and South Africa, contributors to the South–South cooperation, began to participate in the DAC's Peer Review system as observers. Fourth, contributors to the South–South cooperation began to participate in DAC's practical activities such as examining aid for trade and evaluating development (Zimmermann and Smith 2011: 734). Then, in 2013, five countries joined DAC.

The DAC intended to bring non-DAC donors to participation in DAC's political process and daily work, and in doing so, to teach them DAC's models and methods. Consequently, more members came to participate in the DAC.

As emerging donors have increasingly participated in the DAC political process, they have sought to participate in the HLFs, which are the top decision-making body of the DAC. At the 2008 HLF in Accra, the Working Party on Aid Effectiveness (WP-EFF) member categories were expanded to include the following: (1) countries that provide aid, (2) countries that receive aid, (3) countries that both provide and receive aid, (4) international organizations, and (5) civil society organizations (CSOs). The DAC also introduced a North–South joint chairman system; this involves one chairman chosen from a developing country and one from a developed country. The WP-EFF then launched the Advisory Group on Civil Society and Aid Effectiveness, adding CSOs as members, and a working group on South–South cooperation was also established. Consequently, the Accra Agenda was agreed upon by more than 80 developing countries, all OECD countries, approximately 3000 CSOs, emerging donor countries and the UN, as well as international development organizations and private foundations (Kindornay and Samy 2013: 275–276; OECD 2010, 2011: 260).

The DAC cannot help adding the approaches of emerging donors to its basic principles, because the DAC allowed emerging donors to participate in the HLF. In 2011, emerging donors united regionally to demonstrate the superiority of their approaches at the Fourth HLF (HLF4) held in Busan, Korea. Among these movements, the activities of Asian countries deserve special attention. Scholars and experts from China, India, Vietnam, Korea, and Australia discussed important elements of the Asian approach. These Asian countries experienced being simultaneously aid providers and recipients, and they disliked the dichotomy between the two. They focused on sharing their successful experiences with other developing countries and encouraging sustainable development, a sense of ownership among recipient countries and capacity development. Although development cooperation was considered to be related to diplomatic and economic policy goals, they sought almost no conditionality regarding partnerships (OECD 2011: 185). These Asian countries' view that aid is not the sole means of development cooperation is called a result-oriented approach, because it focuses on the results of achieving economic growth.

Then, the Center for Global Development, the UK's Department for International Development (DFID), Norway's Ministry of Foreign Affairs, Sweden's Ministry for Foreign Affairs, Germany's Federal Ministry for Economic Cooperation and Development, and the European Commission held a session aiming to adopt a result-oriented approach to the DAC's principles (OECD 2011: 169). As a result, the DAC included it in the four shared principles—(1) ownership, (2) a focus on results, (3) partnerships, and (4) transparency and shared responsibility—which were proposed at HLF4, located at the core of the agenda (OECD 2012, 2011: 102).

With their participation, the DAC regime was revised to reflect the cooperation of emerging donors in development. We can safely say that the DAC regime has subsumed emerging donors, expanded its scope of application, established new rules, and developed.

4.4 Emerging Donors and the DAC Countries

4.4.1 Changes in ODA

How did DAC countries respond to fundamental changes in the DAC's rules?

Figure 4.2 shows that the total amount of ODA of DAC countries has steadily increased from 1960 to 2015; since 2000, it has drastically increased. The DAC has undoubtedly developed as ODA regime.

Furthermore, Fig. 4.3 shows that the expenditure ratio of social and administrative infrastructure in ODA of total DAC countries has consistently increased. It means that the DAC succeeded in letting the members focus on poverty reduction.

However, regarding charity, the fundamental principle of the DAC, it seems that the DAC countries have tended not to respect it since HLF4 in 2011. Figure 4.4 shows that the grant element, which was created to distinguish ODA from commercial activity, has consistently increased since it was established and reached an average of 97.6% in ODA of DAC countries in 2004–2005, but it decreased to 94.4% in 2014–2015.

In addition, the DAC created untying as a standard for ODA for its members, so that they would not pursue their own commercial interest, but Fig. 4.5 shows that the ratio of untied bilateral ODA to total ODA decreased after the HLF4, in 2011; the ratio was 34.5% in 1985, had steadily increased and reached to 91.8% in 2005, but decreased to 78.1% in 2015.

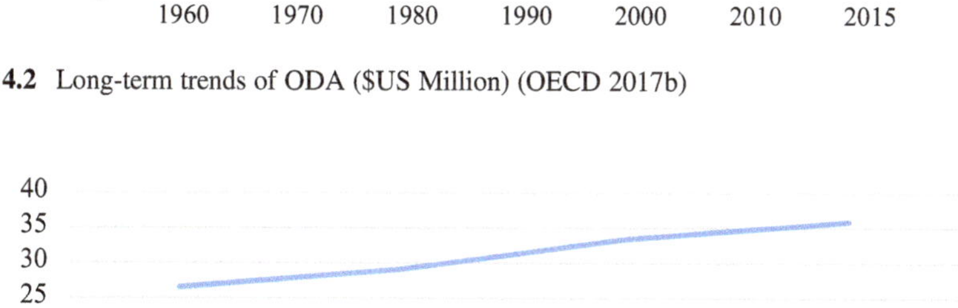

Fig. 4.2 Long-term trends of ODA ($US Million) (OECD 2017b)

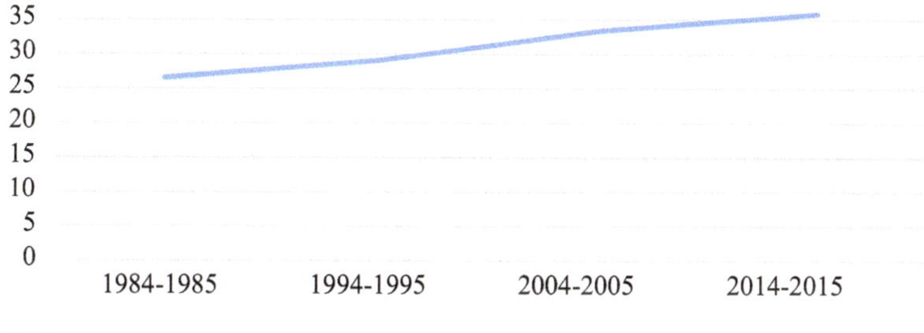

Fig. 4.3 Social and administrative infrastructure of ODA by TOTAL DAC (%) (OECD 2017b)

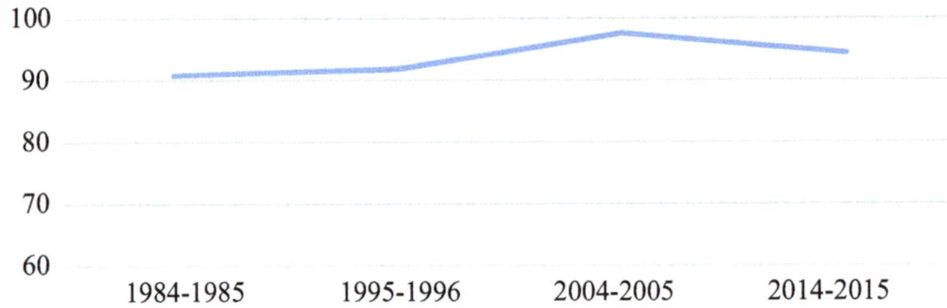

Fig. 4.4 Grant element of total ODA by TOTAL DAC (%) (OECD 2017b)

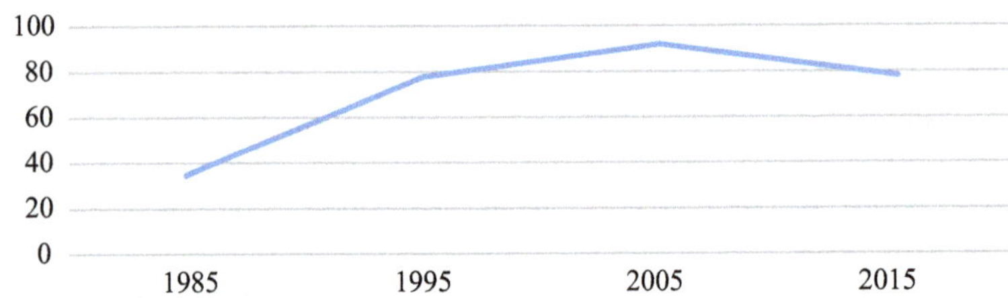

Fig. 4.5 Untied bilateral ODA over total ODA (%) (OECD 2016d)

When we focus on ODA of the individual DAC countries, we can clearly understand that DAC countries have tended to promote commercial interests through ODA in the last few years. Table 4.3 shows to what extent the DAC countries distribute ODA for economic infrastructure: it is clear that the average of total DAC countries decreased from 22.7% in 1994–1995 to 19.0% in 2014–2015. Meanwhile, when we see the expenditure ratio of economic infrastructure of ODA by donor, we find that ten donors—Belgium, Finland, France, Germany, Japan, Luxembourg, Netherlands, New Zealand, Portugal, and Switzerland—increased their ratio by two to three times on average. In particular, Japan, which originally emphasized the development assistance for economic infrastructure, increased from 43.5% in 1994–1995 to 50.9% in 2014–2015. This means that Japan has most clearly embarked on a unique path after emerging donors expanded their presence.

In short, the DAC adopted a result-oriented approach as a fundamental principle to approve the development cooperation of the emerging donors, and furthermore, the DAC countries have also adopted it to their ODA.

4.4.2 Participation in New Regime

In 2013, the Chinese President Xi Jinping declared the establishment of the Asian Infrastructure Investment Bank (AIIB). According to the AIIB's Articles of Agreement, the purpose of the bank is to (1) foster sustainable economic development,

Table 4.3 Economic infrastructure in ODA (%) (OECD 2017b, Table 18)

	1994–1995	2014–2015
Australia	20.9	7.4
Austria	16.0	5.2
Belgium	7.6	8.4
Canada	13.9	4.3
Czech Republic	—	5.2
Denmark	20.6	6.7
Finland	3.8	9.6
France	7.4	24.4
Germany	20.6	31.3
Greece	—	0.0
Iceland	—	12.2
Ireland	8.8	0.9
Italy	11.4	4.1
Japan	43.5	50.9
Korea	60.6	33.1
Luxembourg	5.8	7.5
Netherlands	8.9	11.6
New Zealand	8.6	16.2
Norway	17.0	8.5
Poland	—	2.1
Portugal	6.6	15.0
Slovak Republic	—	1.1
Slovenia	—	0.9
Spain	15.9	2.4
Sweden	11.2	4.3
Switzerland	1.6	5.7
United Kingdom	14.2	10.3
United States	13.2	4.9
Total DAC	22.7	19.0

create wealth, and improve infrastructure connectivity in Asia by investing in infrastructure and other productive sectors and (2) promote regional cooperation and partnership in addressing development challenges by working in close collaboration with other multilateral and bilateral development institutions (AIIB 2017b: 2). In short, the AIIB is a new multilateral financial institution to invest the infrastructure projects in Asia (Weiss 2017: 1).

The AIIB can be expected to alleviate shortages of infrastructure financing in developing countries that will achieve growth. From the early 2000s up to 2030, the world will have to invest US$57–67 trillion in infrastructure, such as roads, ports, power plants, and water facilities. Infrastructure finance requirements in emerging market economies account for 37% of this value (Campanella 2015). Meanwhile, existing multilateral development banks (MDBs) cannot meet the needs of expanding infrastructure financing along with economic growth in developing countries. MDBs initially emphasized infrastructure investment, but, in the 1980s and 1990s, shifted the priority to transferring technology and knowledge. Once the WB directed 70% of its lending to infrastructure in the 1950s and 1960s, but by 1999, infrastructure financing had dwindled to 19% of its lending. The IDB made 70% of its lending to infrastructure projects in 1981, but that figure fell to 10% in 2003. The Asian Development Bank (ADB)'s infrastructure investment declined less dramatically, but until the early 2000s, the trend was downward as well (Humphrey 2015: 3–4; Wang 2017: 114). The AIIB was created to fill the gap between the need and the supply for financing in infrastructure construction of Asian countries (Bai 2017: 102).

However, the existence of the AIIB provokes two main concerns. The first is that it might be a tool of Chinese foreign policy and, in the future, a foothold to establish Chinese hegemony. The AIIB is based in Beijing and headed by Jin Liqun, a former Chinese vice minister of finance, the Chinese sovereign wealth fund chairman, and the vice president of the ADB. China's voting share in the AIIB (28.7%) is substantially larger than that of the second-largest AIIB member country, India (8.3%). The AIIB gives more decision-making authority to regional countries and the largest shareholder, China (Weiss 2017: 1). This can satisfy emerging donors, who expressed dissatisfaction with the executive boards and voting rights of Bretton Woods Institutions not reflecting their growing power and wanted alternative institutions (Huijskens et al. 2017: 1; Strand et al. 2016; Wang 2017: 114). Therefore, it appears that AIIB will increase Chinese influence over international politics and economics (Beeson and Li 2016; Yang 2016; Ren 2016; Peng and Tok 2016).

The second is that AIIB, which provides loans without conditionality, might allow donors to increase their commercial interests and promote human rights violations and environmental destruction by the recipient's governments, which the DAC has carefully prohibited. China is a supreme developing country, with the most consumers and greatest manufacturing capacity of all developing countries, but the Chinese capital market has only had 30 years of development, so it lacks advanced technology and tools (Bai 2017: 102). Therefore, China has been indifferent to the influence of development assistance on environment and society. The AIIB's lending policy, led by China, will enable loans to governments that violate human rights and loans that lead to environmental destruction (Wang 2017: 114; Huijskens et al. 2017: 3). In sum, the AIIB might substantially impair the effects of the existing regime. The DAC countries including the US and Japan have taken a cautious stance toward participation in the AIIB due to these concerns.

However, only the UK recognizes the benefits of strengthening relations with China at an early stage, and it has been secretly deepening cooperation with China. After all, the donors can obtain the great commercial interests by lending for the infrastructure projects that AIIB provides. Intending to collaborate with China in lending for infrastructure projects, joint teams were established in DFID's main office and in African countries (Brautigam 2010: 39–40; Kragelund 2015: 257–58). In 2013, when China launched the One Belt One Road initiative, the UK became one of the most positive supporters of the project. In recent years, due to the joint efforts of these two countries, much remarkable progresses have been made in their financial cooperation. Aside from its active action in the AIIB, the UK has become the second-largest RMB off-shore financial market, and London, the top international financial center, has been playing an irreplaceable role in the globalization of RMB. The mutual investment of China and the UK has also taken great strides (Bai 2017: 102). In 2015, Chinese President Xi visited the UK and was kindly accommodated by the British royal family. During this visit, agreements on several big projects were completed (Bai 2017: 103).

China set the deadline for application of the founding members as of March 31, 2015, and it proactively asked South Korea, Australia, and others to apply to it. The US government, concerned about China's aggressive promotion, directly told the UK not to participate in the AIIB. Nevertheless, shortly thereafter (March 12, 2015), the UK joined the AIIB as first among the DAC countries to do so, which has had a positive effect on the foundation and development of AIIB. As a result, the DAC countries such as France and Germany joined AIIB (Bai 2017: 102; Sun 2015; Sekine 2015: 2; Financial Times 2015).

In December 2015, the AIIB was established with 57 founding members, including six DAC countries (Austria, Germany, Luxembourg, Netherlands, Norway, and the UK). By October 2017, the members of AIIB had grown to 80 countries, including prospective members, which surpassed ADB and the European Bank for Reconstruction and Development, only second to the WB (Weiss 2017: 1; Bai 2017: 102). As Table 4.4 shows, 21 countries (including four prospective AIIB members) among the AIIB members belong to the DAC, which means a majority of all 30 DAC countries have joined AIIB or will join it.

The AIIB has been steadily developing. It approved 21 projects and given loans amounting to $3.49 billion dollars before October 2017 (AIIB 2017a). In the less than 2 years since its official establishment, the AIIB has promoted itself as a serious and consistent alternative to Western-led international financial institutions, most obviously the WB and the ADB. Its growing attractiveness derives in particular from

Table 4.4 AIIB members (AIIB 2017a)

Membership date	Members
December 25, 2015	Austria, Germany, Luxembourg, Netherlands, Norway, the UK
January 7, 2016	Finland
January 15, 2016	Denmark
March 4, 2016	Iceland
April 25, 2016	Switzerland
June 15, 2016	Poland
June 16, 2016	France
July 13, 2016	Italy
June 23, 2016	Sweden
February 8, 2017	Portugal
June 16, 2017	Hungary
October 23, 2017	Ireland
Prospective Members	Belgium, Canada, Greece, Spain

China's intention to present the AIIB as an institution able to reform and complement the post-World War II global economic governance domain promoted by the Bretton Woods institutions (Menegazzi 2017).

In short, the fact that many of the DAC countries joined the AIIB shows that they superficially respect the existing regime but practically seek to promote their own commercial interests, which can impair what the existing regime carefully forbid and hoped to achieve.

4.5 Conclusion

This chapter examined how the increasing presence of emerging donors has affected the DAC regime and its member countries. The DAC understands that, under the principle of charity, donors should not promote their own commercial interests using development assistance and encourages the DAC countries to comply with the concept of ODA and the standards of poverty reduction. As a result, ODA of the DAC countries has converged, and emerging donors who have recently joined the DAC are trying to comply with its standards as well. The ODA regime has subsumed emerging donors and enlarged its scope of application and to develop itself while keeping its fundamental principles.

Meanwhile, many DAC countries are promoting their commercial interests through development assistance, as emerging donors are doing. If we examine ODA of each DAC country, it appears that many DAC countries have increased the allocation of ODA to the economic infrastructure sector, leading to the promotion of their commercial interests. Japan, who has traditionally focused on development assistance for infrastructure construction, emphasized the merits of its ODA again after Chinese development assistance attracted attention. Furthermore, when China announced the plan for the establishment of the AIIB, most of the DAC countries, including the UK, successively joined the AIIB.

The DAC has developed a regime of poverty reduction and cannot be transformed to a regime built on contrasting principles. However, most DAC countries are promoting their own commercial interests without hesitation and have joined AIIB, which will provide loans for infrastructure construction. The value of aid as charity has declined and the aid as economic statecraft, which the DAC regulated for many years, is reviving. This means the DAC regime will be undermined.

It might be considered inevitable that the DAC has been ineffective. Developing countries have achieved economic growth and need major investment for infrastructure construction. The DAC has a long tradition of encouraging its members to provide technical assistance for poverty reduction and cannot easily change its direction. Therefore, the DAC countries have tried to deal with their changing needs individually, and the DAC has been undermined. Recipients welcome this trend of donors to provide the loans for infrastructure construction. The trend of preferring commercial-based activities will continue for a while. Meanwhile, commercial-based activities cannot meet the needs of poverty reduction and cause risks. Where many donors are prioritizing their commercial interests over poverty reduction in the developing countries, we may leave serious poverty problems behind and spread human rights violations and environmental destruction. Thus, global governance of international development cooperation is essential. We keep a very close watch on how far the DAC can play a role in creating global governance of international development cooperation.

References

AIIB (2017a) AIIB: home, https://www.aiib.org/en/index.html. Accessed on 1 Nov 2017

AIIB (2017b) Articles of agreements, https://www.aiib.org/en/about-aiib/basic-documents/_ download/articles-of-agreement/basic_document_english-bank_articles_of_agreement.pdf. Accessed on 14 Nov 2017

Bai Y (2017) Prospect analysis of China-UK financial cooperation under one belt one road initiative. J Chin Econ 5–2:102–104. http://journals.sfu.ca/nwchp/index.php/journal. Accessed on 15 Sept 2017

Beeson M, Li F (2016) China's place in regional and global governance: a new world comes into view. Global Pol 7:4. https://doi.org/10.1111/1758-5899.12348

Brautigam D (2010) China, Africa and the international aid architecture. African Development Bank Group Working Series 107

Campanella M (2015) The AIIB will help fill the infrastructure finance gap. 9 April 2015, East Asia Forum, http://www.eastasiaforum.org/2015/04/09/the-aiib-will-fill-the-infrastructure-finance-gap/. Accessed on 30 Sept 2017

Clay E, et al (2008) The developmental effectiveness of untied aid: evaluation of the implementation of the Paris Declaration and of the 2001 DAC recommendation on untying ODA to the LDCs. Overseas Development Institute, London

De Haan A, Warmerdam W (2013) New donors and old practices: the role of China in the multilateral system. In: Sesada H (ed) Multilateral development cooperation in a changing global order. Palgrave Macmillan, London

Dreher A, et al (2013) New donors. International interactions: empirical and theoretical research in international relations 39(3): 402–415. doi:https://doi.org/10.1080/03050629.2013.784076

Financial Times (2015) UK move to join China-led bank a surprise even to Beijing. http://www.ft.com/intl/cms/s/0/d33fed8a-d3a1-11e4-a9d3-00144feab7de.html#axzz41njdgRaz. Accessed 25 Jan 2016

Grieco J, Gelpi C, Reifler J, Feaver PD (2011) Let's get a second opinion: international institutions and American public support for war. Int Stud Q 55:563–583

Hook S (1995) National interest and foreign aid. Rienner Publishers, Boulder

Hook S, Rumsey J (2016) The development aid regime at fifty: policy challenges inside and out. Int Stud Perspect 17:55–74

Huijskens F, et al (2017) The EU in the AIIB: taming China's influence from within. Security Policy Brief, No. 86

Humphrey C. (2015) 'Developmental revolution or Bretton Woods revisited? The prospects of the BRICS New Development Bank and the Asian Infrastructure Investment Bank.' ODI Working Paper 418. https://www.odi.org/sites/odi.org.uk/files/odi-assets/publications-opinion-files/16pdf. Accessed on 14 Nov 2017

Kindornay S, Samy Y (2013) Establishing a legitimate development cooperation architecture in the post-busan era. In: Sesada H (ed) Multilateral development cooperation in a changing global order. Palgrave Macmillan, London

Kobayashi T (2007) Chugoku no enjo seisaku: taigai enjo kaikaku no tenkai (The Chinese foreign aid policy: the reform of the foreign aid policy). J Res Inst Dev Finan JBIC Inst 35:109–147
Kragelund P (2015) Towards convergence and cooperation in the global development finance regime: closing Africa's policy space? Camb Rev Int Aff 28(2):246–262. https://doi.org/10.1080/09557571.2014.974141
Mawdsley E (2012) From recipients to donors: emerging powers and the changing development landscape. Zed Books, London
Menegazzi S (2017) Why the EU must engage with the AIIB. East Asia Forum, 5 May 2017, http://www.eastasiaforum.org/2017/05/05/why-the-eu-must-engage-with-the-aiib/. Accessed on 3 Sept 2017
Mueller J (2005) The Iraq syndrome. Foreign Aff 84(6):44–54
OECD (2006) DAC in dates: the history of OECD'S development assistance committee. http://www.oecd.org/dac/1896808.pdf. Accessed 1 Feb 2016
OECD (2010) Working party on aid effectiveness. http://www.oecd.org/development/effectiveness/45498646.pdf. Accessed 15 Feb 2016
OECD (2011) Busan high-level forum on aid effectiveness: proceedings. https://www.oecd.org/dac/effectiveness/HLF4%20proceedings%20entire%20doc%20for%20web.pdf. Accessed 15 Feb 2016
OECD (2012) Busan partnership for effective development co-operation fourth high level forum on aid effectiveness. Busan, Republic of Korea, 29 November-1 December 2011. http://www.oecd.org/dac/effectiveness/Busan%20partnership.pdf. Accessed 1 Feb 2016
OECD (2013) Information note on the DAC peer review process. https://www.oecd.org/dac/peer-reviews/DCD%282013%296-ENG.pdf. Accessed 1 Feb 2016
OECD (2016a) DAC global relations strategy. http://www.oecd.org/dac/dac-global-relations/dac-global-relations-strategy.htm. Accessed 1 Feb 2016
OECD (2016b) DAC members. http://www.oecd.org/dac/dacmembers.htm. Accessed 1 Feb 2016
OECD (2016c) Promoting dialogue beyond the DAC. http://www.oecd.org/dac/promotingdialoguebeyondthedac.htm. Accessed 1 Feb 2016
OECD (2016d) Strengthening management of development cooperation. http://www.oecd.org/dac/dac-global-relations/strengthening-management-of-development-co- operation.htm. Accessed 1 Feb 2016
OECD (2017a) Peer reviews of DAC members. http://www.oecd.org/dac/peer-reviews/. Accessed 10 Nov 2017
OECD (2017b) Statistics on resource flows to developing countries. http://www.oecd.org/dac/stats/statisticsonresourceflowstodevelopingcountries.htm, Accessed on 30 Aug 2017
Peng Z, Tok S (2016) The AIIB and China's normative power in international financial governance structure. Chin Polit Sci Rev 1:736–753. https://doi.org/10.1007/s41111-016-0042-y
Ren X (2016) China as an institution-builder: the case of the AIIB. Pac Rev 29(3):435–442. https://doi.org/10.1080/09512748.2016.1154678
Sekine E (2015) Aims and prospects of the asian infrastructure investment bank proposed by china. Nomura J Cap Mark 6(4):1–14
Strand J et al (2016) China's leadership in global economic governance and the creation of the asian infrastructure investment bank. Rising Powers Q 1–1:55–69
Sun Y (2015) The UK signs on to AIIB, East Asia Forum. 19 March 2015. http://www.eastasiaforum.org/2015/03/19/the-uk-signs-on-to-aiib/. Accessed 3 Sept 2017
US Department of State (US State), Foreign Relations of the United States (1958–60), IV
US Department of State (US State), FRUS (1958–60), VII
Wang H (2017) New multilateral development banks: opportunities and challenges for global governance. Global Pol 8(1):113–118. https://doi.org/10.1111/1758-5899.12396
Watanabe S (2013) China's foreign aid diplomacy: challenges and opportunities to the international development assistance regime. Int Relat 172:100–113
Weiss M (2017) Asian infrastructure investment bank (AIIB). Congressional research service report.

Wood R (1986) From Marshall plan to debt crisis: foreign aid and development choices in the World Economy, Berkeley, Los Angeles. University of California Press, London

Wood R (1996) Rethinking economic aid. In: Hook S (ed) Foreign aid toward the millennium. Lynne Rienner Publishers, Boulder

Yang H (2016) The Asian infrastructure investment bank and status-seeking: China's foray into Global Economic Governance. Chin Polit Sci Rev 1:754–778. https://doi.org/10.1007/s41111-016-0043-x

Zimmermann F, Smith K (2011) More actors, more money, more ideas for international development co-operation. J Int Dev 23:722–738. https://doi.org/10.1002/jid.1796

Chapter 5
How Structural Heterogeneities Turned into Political Issues: Lessons from the US–Japan Structural Talks

Kazutoshi Suzuki

Abstract In the midst of growing interdependence among countries, there are an increasing number of cases in which the socioeconomic heterogeneities of nations have given cause for frictions. Currently, such frictions between the USA and China are the subject of much attention. Although each friction is special and contextual to the dyad of nations involved, certain aspects of the increasing risks associated with heterogeneities can be generalized to some extent. For this purpose, this chapter considers the precedent of structural tensions between the USA and Japan and looks at how these structural differences developed into intense diplomatic issues. It also seeks to clarify the precise nature of heterogeneity-related risks by examining the role played by the economic interdependence between two nations. The analysis presented here confirms that, while the problems associated with heterogeneities between the USA and Japan had long existed, the risks were heightened only after the interdependence had been deepened. Nonetheless, these differences and the deepening of interdependence were not, in and of themselves, sufficient to produce a crisis.

Keywords Interdependence · Heterogeneity · Trade negotiation · Structural initiative · Politicization · Risk

5.1 Introduction

The multi-polarization and globalization after the final stages of the twentieth century have brought Western countries, the established leaders of the global economy, into increasingly frequent contact with heterogeneous nations. This applies equally to both the former Eastern bloc and Third World countries. Until the Cold War era, the international system was characterized by the mutual isolation of heterogeneous groups of nations, due to the limits posed by physical distances,

K. Suzuki (✉)
Hiroshima University, Hiroshima, Japan
e-mail: kazutoshis@gmail.com

M. Tadokoro et al. (eds.), *Emerging Risks in a World of Heterogeneity*, Evolutionary Economics and Social Complexity Science 10,
https://doi.org/10.1007/978-981-10-7968-9_5

trade barriers, or ideologically motivated political ruptures. These prerequisites for segregation were now disappearing. Barriers against the flow of goods, money, people, and information have continued to come down owing to technological advances and multilateral trade liberalization advanced under the GATT/WTO framework. Meanwhile, an uninterrupted trend within global politics, marked by the achievement of independence by Asian and African nations, the end of the Cold War, and the rise of emerging nations, has promoted the incorporation of new members into the international economic system. Although all of these changes might be recognized as epiphenomena of the long-term transformation of social structures that occurred after the Industrial Revolution (Buzan and Lawson 2015), the ongoing clashes of heterogeneities over the last 20–30 years would be more directly attributable to these factors.

The enlargement of the GATT/WTO regime and the spread of regional trade agreements (RTAs) such as free-trade areas (FTAs) and customs unions (CUs) provide clear evidence of the expansion of the liberal international economic system in the postwar era. The GATT, begun initially with the UK, the USA, their colonies, and allies, later came to include the various capitalist economies, the Third World, and finally China and Russia, gradually covering the entire globe. The rapid expansion of FTA networks since the 1990s, which follows the wave of liberalization under the GATT and WTO systems, has incorporated even higher degrees of liberalization than under the WTO and has embedded new members more deeply into the international economic system.

Barriers between heterogeneous nations with different degrees of development, socioeconomic structures, and political systems have been removed, resulting in an expansion of economic exchange. In turn, this has created causes for conflict between countries, and such conflicts have indeed emerged from these very differences. At present, the friction between the USA and China, arising from structural differences, might be the example of this dynamic most widely commented upon. The US–China Business Council (USCBC), a group of US companies seeking to expand their business activities in China, has called for a number of social and economic reforms within China, specifically relating to issues such as licensing, labor policy, competition policy, the protection of intellectual property rights, investment regulation, urban and regional issues, bribery, corruption, and certification practices (USCBC 2013, 2014, 2015). Meanwhile, import-competing industries such as the textile industry have focused on trade imbalances between the USA and China, pointing to areas such as the exchange rate of the Chinese yuan, and have demanded that protective measures be put in place. In addition, disputes over security issues have become more pronounced. These are addressed in the Strategic Economic Dialogue (SED, from December 2006) and the Strategic and Economic Dialogue (S&ED, from July 2009). The Trans-Pacific Partnership (TPP) can be regarded as part of an effort by the USA and Japan to encourage domestic structural reforms within Mainland China.[1]

[1]This chapter was submitted on December 3, 2016, before Donald Trump entered office and announced withdrawal from the TPP agreement. Apart from this footnote and some corrections of wording, the original text is not modified.

The US–China case is but one within a wider trend. The specter of structural conflict has arisen elsewhere too. Revisionists during the 1980s, for instance, targeted Japan for these differences, leading to significant conflict. Debates at that time were similar to those now occurring between the USA and China. These concerned not merely governmental policies such as financial and foreign exchange policies, but also the very essence of socioeconomic systems and practices, including transparency of regulations and administrative guidance, the enforcement of rules surrounding intellectual property rights, rule-making around corporate acquisitions and stockholder rights, the complexity of distribution systems, and exclusive trading practices among private firms. The central question asked at that time was whether or not they were (to quote the title of Bergsten and Noland's 1993 work) "reconcilable differences."

As well as such similarities, there are also some significant differences between historical US and Japan friction and that between the USA and China. What could make the relations between the USA and China more difficult is their national security relationship and the disparity of political systems. In the late 1980s, the USA and Japan were allies, and, though the end of the Cold War might have undermined the value of this alliance, the two countries built between them a framework for cooperation based on shared strategies. This is clearly evident from the composition of Japanese armaments, which has been designed to supplement that of the USA in the Far East region. This link in the area of security has served to ease tensions in economic conflicts. Indeed, whenever structural tensions have escalated between the two countries, the US Defense Department has tended to be critical of those in the government who have taken tougher stances against Japan. The American propensity to take a conciliatory approach in trade talks with allied and friendly countries is not limited to this case. In selecting FTA partner countries, the USA has given security interests serious consideration (Oyane 2011). FTAs concluded between the USA and countries such as Israel, Jordan, Singapore, and South Korea can be seen as the strengthening of US security commitments toward its allies and friends.

In contrast, China is showing its intention to challenge the USA and change the status quo by stationing missiles and fighter aircraft in the South China Sea. It is seeking to rapidly enhance its military capabilities, deploying weaponry aimed at warding off US warships. Meanwhile, the framework for TPP negotiations includes countries such as Japan and Vietnam and excludes China and hence is completely in line with the historical trend of US trade policies. Tensions between Japan and the USA reached crisis proportions despite their alliance and despite the fact that both are capitalist and democratic societies. Differences between the USA and China go well beyond that. In addition to their security policies, which seem to be on a collision course, they do not share fundamental values such as capitalism, democracy, and respect for human rights. In this case, heterogeneity could lead to a more emotional and deep-seated political antagonism.

One factor that may prevent the escalation of tensions between the USA and China is the fact that China can learn from the earlier US–Japan tensions. It is much easier to respond to US discontent before it develops into a disaster if one recognizes the need from the beginning. Conciliatory measures such as expansion of domestic investment, appreciation of its own currency, purchasing of US exports (such as airliners), and capital tie-ups with key US industries (such as automobiles) are all on the *carte du jour* with their likely consequences, waiting to be chosen. In addition, such recipes for appeasement can be prepared more quickly in the authoritarian Chinese kitchen because it has to worry less about veto players.[2]

US foreign direct investment to China is another factor that has attracted much attention. Unlike Japan during the 1980s, China proactively sought foreign investment, and there had been an upswing over recent years in the number of companies seeking to access the Chinese market. These companies (typically large corporations) are highly averse to trade wars between the USA and China (Yasui 2005). Moreover, US and Chinese industries are more complementary than those of the USA and Japan. Key industries in China and the USA are thus less likely to come into conflict, in comparison with the high-tech and auto industries in the USA and Japan in 1980s. As a corollary, US industries with comparative advantages are unlikely to agree to hardline trade policies against China for fear of retaliation, making it more difficult for the US government to take tough and credible positions against China (Zeng 2004). Such arguments imply that interdependence works to restrain friction from reaching crisis level. Nevertheless, these very companies also tend to hold the strongest grievances regarding Chinese heterogeneity, and whether the abovementioned interdependence will restrain conflicts or indeed produce new ones is yet to be seen.

The presence of factors that may both increase as well as limit tensions between these two countries makes a comprehensive evaluation difficult. Having said that, we can still safely expect that the range of possible results will be much wider in the US–China case than it was in the US–Japan case and that we have to be ready for the worst consequences under the worst scenario. This is because, firstly, the political, economic, and social differences between China and the USA are greater than those that existed between Japan and the USA, and, secondly, whereas US–Japan relations took place within the framework of a formal alliance, this is not true of US–China relations.

The larger potential risk inherent in this dyad makes the following two questions more important. When does such risk turn into diplomatic crisis? And what is the effect of interdependence on that process? In search for the answers to these questions, this chapter reevaluates the politicization of US–Japan structural heterogeneity. The economic conflict between these two countries is an illustrative case of the politicization of heterogeneity, a valuable precedent in assessing the emerging risks of conflicts with rising economic powers.

Below, we describe a hypothesis that relates "interdependence" and "heterogeneity" and provide some empirical data in support. Subsequently, we explore the process by which US–Japanese heterogeneity grew into a crisis, as well as the role played by their interdependence. While structural disparities have existed between Japan and the USA since they first made contact in modern times, they have been

[2]The possibility that the difference between the two regimes may rather lessen conflict between them is a counterintuitive implication, as kindly pointed out by the editors.

narrowing significantly during the post-WWII period. It was the deepening interdependence that heightened the potential risk of diplomatic conflict. At the same time, nonetheless, the analysis shows that the interdependence did not, in and of itself, provide sufficient cause for crisis.

5.2 Interdependence and the Emergence of Heterogeneity-Based Conflict

The risk produced by the combination of "economic interdependence" and "heterogeneity" is increasing in importance in the age of globalization. However, the same problem was already significant between the USA and Japan from around the 1980s, with extensive theoretical studies conducted on these issues. These studies suggested that domestic heterogeneities become international problems as cross-border activities of individuals and corporations expand. More specifically, deeper interdependence between the two countries tended to broaden the scope of government negotiations to include not only measures implemented at their borders—customs and import procedures—but increasingly the core, fundamental functions carried out within national borders, including domestic policies and institutions such as industrial policy, urban planning, intellectual property rights, consumer credit, distribution systems, and banking systems (Yamakage 1982, 1989).

The correlation of deepening interdependence and the emergence of structural differences as issues is observed in both aspects of international trade diplomacy: trade liberalization and trade disputes. As for the processes of trade liberalization, a quick review of history will suffice. The central pillar of postwar liberalization was the GATT/WTO regime. In the iterated rounds of negotiations, issues were initially limited to "border measures" such as tariffs on industrial goods and quantitative restrictions. With time (and the deepening of interdependence), the scope of negotiations gradually came to encompass "behind-the-border measures." In the Tokyo Round of negotiations, non-tariff barriers became a significant area of discussion, as did agriculture, intellectual property rights, and the service trade in the Uruguay Round. In the Doha Round, investments, government procurement, and the environment were given more emphasis. To get around the impasse of this last Round, the main focus of trade liberalization negotiations has now shifted to regional trade agreements. These RTAs tend to incorporate a range of "WTO-plus" items such as environment, labor standards, and government procurement. In any case, the issues have clearly shifted from the reduction of tariffs toward domestic policies and structures, which are more deeply embedded in domestic societies.

A similar trend can be seen in trade disputes. To provide some empirical evidence, Fig. 5.1 summarizes the main claims of investigations under Section 301 of the US trade law, whose intention is to identify offending countries and demand they change their trade practices. We analyzed 120 investigations that were filed between 1974 and 2000 and classified them into three categories: border measures,

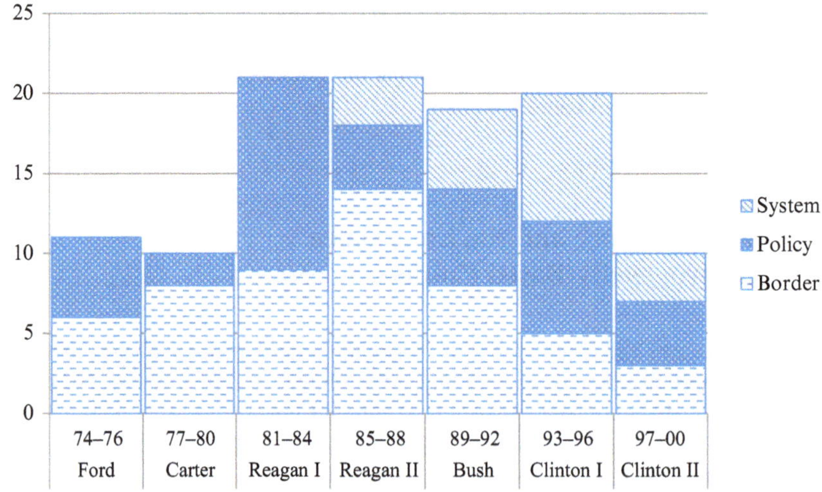

Fig. 5.1 Main targets of 301 cases, sorted by year of initiation. *Border* refers to the investigations on border measures such as tariffs, quotas, and discriminatory treatments (e.g., discriminatory taxes, screen quotas, license requirements applicable only to foreign firms). *Policy* includes government procurements, industrial policies, subsidies, and trade diversion due to arrangements with third countries. *System* refers to nondiscriminatory but allegedly trade-distorting systems such as insufficient patent protection, antitrust laws, construction codes, and safety requirements (Source: *Federal Register*)

domestic policy, and domestic systems. The result indicates that the cases on domestic policies and systems have indeed increased from the mid-1980s. This result supports the above statements concerning interdependence. As the interdependence deepens, domestic structures tend to become more important.

This qualitative change of disputed issues is closely intertwined with the quantitative increase in cross-border interactions. If a country lowers its tariffs, the trade inflows of goods will increase, encouraging foreign firms to make more direct investment in that country. This leads to heightened demands for the freeing up of investment. If deregulation of foreign direct investment occurs, the foreign capital now operating inside the country will develop a stronger interest in that country's industrial policies, financial policies, and business practices, which have been, until then, exclusively domestic concerns of the host country. Increased calls for new policies and systemic reforms will result. The amendment of domestic policies and systems in this way will lead to even further increases in the movement of goods and capital. This circular dynamic ensures that heterogeneities within structures, systems, and practices, formerly considered as purely domestic issues, become, as interdependence intensifies, international in nature.

5.3 Issues Arising from US–Japan Heterogeneity

Issues arising from heterogeneity in policies and systems, as described in the previous section, are more likely to spark serious discord compared to those related to more straightforward border measures. This is because domestic structures, systems, practices, and norms are, in many cases, deeply rooted in a country's social values, culture, and history. Changes to these are more likely to affect not only a country's exporting and import-competing businesses but also a multiplicity of diverse domestic groups that are not normally concerned in international trade (Suzuki 2013). For example, demanding an end to the dumping of Chinese steel is obviously more simple and easy than demanding the privatization of state-owned enterprises and achieving more transparency in policy-making. Structural friction between the USA and Japan provides a good example of precisely these sorts of difficulties, and it is worth reconsidering the process by which latent risks can evolve into a substantial crisis.

Differences between US and Japanese domestic policies and systems, as well as practices within their private sectors, turned into a major political issue in the late 1980s. The "Japan bashing" reached such extreme levels as to engender hate crimes in Detroit. Some Japanese automakers even took down company signboards at their US factories. With the protectionist group gaining strength in the US Congress, additional concerns emerged that it would seek to derail negotiations in the Uruguay Round, negotiations which, as it turned out, would yield one of the most significant advances in the postwar history of trade liberalization. The US–Japan Structural Impediments Initiative (SII), perhaps the most unusual large-scale bilateral trade negotiations in history, was set in motion out of the need to manage these concerns. Below, we look at how structural heterogeneities evolved into such a high-level political issue, pushing two allied countries to the point of a diplomatic crisis.

5.3.1 *Prior to the Structural Impediments Initiative*

US perceptions of Japanese policies, systems, and practices as impediments to trade can be traced back to at least the late 1970s. By the fall of 1977, the USA had already asked Japan to reform its distribution systems.[3] From the 1980s onward, complaints relating to structural problems had become both more diverse and specific. In 1981, a report to then US Treasury Secretary Donald T. Regan stated that, while the number of visible barriers to the Japanese market had reduced, several structural barriers remained that were continuing to hinder imports from the USA. "Japan is still xenophobic, its industrial structure is cartel-like, anti-competitive practices are tolerated, dealing with government officials is time consuming and difficult, the

[3] *Nihon Keizai Shimbun*, November 18, 1977 (Evening edition); November 19 (Morning edition); Destler 1979.

distribution system is impossible, the Japanese language is hard, and the Japanese are truly foreign. It is much like France, only much more so."[4]

These differences became the subjects of joint US–Japan consultations from the middle of the 1980s. Following the Plaza Accord in September 1985, the dollar, which had been trading at around 240 yen, devalued to a low of 140 yen by 1987. Despite this, the US trade deficit with Japan did not improve and indeed continued to worsen up until 1987. Accordingly, exchange rate measures with regard to Japan were deemed insufficient; structural issues were seen as the problem instead.

The need to carry out structural adjustments in order to limit friction with the USA had been highlighted within Japan also. In 1983, the Tokyo Chamber of Commerce and Industry argued that Japan's distribution systems were increasingly seen as a problem abroad and called for a simplification of controls under the Large-Scale Retail Stores Act.[5] The most symbolic and comprehensive statements in this context can be found in the "Maekawa Report"[6] and the "New Maekawa Report,"[7] both of which were submitted by an advisory body for Prime Minister Yasuhiro Nakasone. These addressed issues such as residential and urban redevelopment, the abolition of the tax-exempt savings system, housing tax reductions, changes to zoning and floor area ratios to prevent rising land prices, expediting the adjustment of land rights holders, reductions to working hours and income taxes, construction of social infrastructure in regional areas, implementation of an action program for market liberalization, legislation to create and strengthen the Office of Trade and Investment Ombudsman (OTO), a campaign to promote imports, streamlining of distribution systems, a review of regulations, and strict enforcement of antitrust laws against acts obstructing imports.

Against such a backdrop, the USA proposed starting the US–Japan Structural Dialogue as an arena to discuss structural issues. On July 21, 1986, the two governments held preliminary talks in San Francisco to set an agenda and agree on a schedule. Five meetings were held in total: October 1986, March and October 1987, and April and October 1988. The agenda included the exchange rate, current account balances, US and Japanese savings–investment balances, financial imbalances, consumer credit, investment in housing, food prices, agricultural policy, distribution systems, house and land prices, competition policy, antitrust laws, foreign investment regulations, and issues related to *keiretsu* business conglomerates.[8] Apart from agricultural policy, which was to be discussed in the Uruguay

---

[4]Memorandum, "Japanese Protectionism," from Marc E. Leland to Donald T. Regan, March 18, 1981, Department of Treasury, National Security Archives(NSA), Japan and the U.S., 1977–1992.

[5]The Tokyo Chamber of Commerce and Industry, *1980 nendai no ryutsu bijon to ryutsu seisaku no arikata* [A vision for distribution and distribution policy in the 1980s], September 1983.

[6]Meeting on Economic Structural Adjustments for International Cooperation, April 7, 1986.

[7]Special Subcommittee on Structural Adjustments, Economic Council, April 23, 1987.

[8]From US government preparatory documents and meeting notes, mainly from the NSA.

Round, and the exchange rate issue, which was already heading toward solution because of the rapid appreciation of the yen at the time, most issues were revisited during the SII.

The Structural Dialogue included many domestic issues with ramifications for Japanese sovereignty, and hence the US approach was one of restraint, though of course the principal focus of the USA was in making adjustments to structural problems on the Japanese side. The principal aim of US representatives was "to signal our interest in certain aspects of the Japanese economy and the directions that we would like it to go by the questions and comments we make," with an understanding that "in practice, we (and they) expect most of the discussion to focus on the Japanese economy."[9] However, US representatives also understood that "the dialogue is not a negotiation, and the United States will not have any list of requests or specific desired outcomes to present to the Japanese.... We have told the Japanese that this will be a two-way dialogue...we should not resist a discussion of our own economy if the Japanese raise relevant questions about structural problems on our side." According to the US team, "the dialogue would not be a forum for putting pressure on either side for specific changes, but to understand better sectors and policies in an attempt to identify inefficiencies."[10] These statements imply that the Structural Dialogue was not a negotiation aimed at securing any commitments from Japan, but rather was intended to be a "bidirectional conversation" to encourage the Japanese government to take action voluntarily.

5.3.2 The US–Japan Structural Impediments Initiative and the Crisis

At the time of the Structural Dialogue, political interest in the heterogeneity of structural problems had been heightening, and the related latent risk had already been growing. However, the situation had not reached the point where a failure to reach agreement would lead directly to a serious "crisis." This changed with the beginning of the US–Japan Structural Impediments Initiative.

After the end of the Structural Dialogue, from around the fall of 1988, the US Treasury began to consider the idea of new negotiations concerning structural problems in a different form. In the spring of 1989, preparations were made with other US government departments, and coordination with the Japanese side was

[9]Scope paper, "U.S.–Japan Structural Dialogue," July 1986, Department of State, NSA, Japan and the U.S., 1977–1992.

[10]Cable, "U.S.–Japan Structural Dialogue: Report on the San Francisco Planning Meeting," from George P. Shultz to United States Embassy in Japan, Department of State, NSA, Japan and the U.S., 1977–1992.

also pursued.[11] The plan was brought to fruition as the US–Japan Structural Impediments Initiative, held between July 1989 and June 1990. The SII was made up of six areas: savings/investment balances, distribution systems, land policy, exclusive business practices, *keiretsu* conglomerates, and price mechanisms. These included topics such as public investment planning, abolishing the Large-Scale Retail Stores Act, taxing farmland in areas marked for urbanization similarly to residential lands, establishing a special land-holding tax, reinforcing antitrust laws, regulating mutual stockholding among *keiretsu* conglomerates, deregulation of investment rules, and strengthening shareholder rights. Most of these issues had been included in the Structural Dialogue and were not in themselves new. However, owing to the "Super" 301 of the US Trade Act, there was a significant difference in how these were dealt with in the Structural Dialogue and in the SII.

The original impetus for beginning the SII was the passage in August 1988 of the Omnibus Trade and Competition Act, by which Section 310 was added to the existing rules of the 301 process. This section obliged the USTR (US Trade Representative) to designate priority countries for negotiations and relevant trade barriers for 1989 and 1990 and to begin Section 301 investigations. This obligatory process of Section 301 investigation is called "Super" 301. In May 1989, just prior to the submission of a report by Carla Anderson Hills, the US Trade Representative responsible for designating countries for prioritized negotiations, President Bush issued a statement designating three areas in Japan, two in India, and one in Brazil for priority negotiations. At the same time, he added that the new initiative with Japan relating to structural impediments would take place outside of the Section 301 framework.[12]

In the preparatory meetings held between the USA and Japan on June 28–29, 1989, in the Federal Reserve Building, the Japanese side strongly insisted that structural issues be discussed in the context of a "talk" and not a "negotiation."[13] This was motivated by a fear that where an "agreement," as defined by the US Trade Act, was reached under the SII, Japan would potentially be subject to unilateral measures by the USA under Section 301 in the event it was deemed not to be adhering to such an agreement. As a result, it was clarified that the SII would "take place outside of Section 301 of the U.S. Trade Act." Furthermore, the objective of the SII would be "to identify and solve structural problems *in both countries* that stand as impediments to trade and balance of payments adjustment with the goal of contributing to the reduction of payments imbalances" (italics added).[14]

---

[11]Assistant Secretary to the U.S. Treasury Charles H. Dallara in an interview with an NHK reporter. NHK, *Nichibei no shototsu* [The U.S.-Japan Clash], (NHK Publishing 1990), pp. 65–71.

[12]George Bush, "Statement by President Bush on United States Action Against Foreign Trade Barriers," May 26, 1989.

[13]Briefing Book, U.S.–Japan Talks on Structural Impediments Initiative, New York City, June 28–29, 1989, SII Preliminary Meeting, New York, 6/28–29/89, [OA/ID CF00502], (1 of 3), George Bush Presidential Library.

[14]"Joint Statement by President Bush and Prime Minister Uno on Economic Issues," July 14, 1989.

As such, the SII would, as with the Structural Dialogue, be defined as a "two-way dialogue" (that deals with structural problems in both countries, outside the framework of Section 301). Nonetheless, the reality of the talks was entirely different from this official line. The SII, in effect, involved a very serious set of negotiations primarily aimed at changing structures within Japan. The failure of such negotiations would potentially trigger a damaging blow to the US–Japan relationship and to the Uruguay Round of GATT negotiations. The section below considers whether these were indeed a dialogue or negotiations, two-way or otherwise, and what the risks were in the event of their failure.

5.3.3 A Dialogue or Negotiation?

On paper, the SII was "not a negotiation," yet it differed in nature from the Structural Dialogue, similarly deemed not to be a formal negotiation. US representatives expressed dissatisfaction with the fact that those talks had not gone any further than an exchange of views. One of the joint chairs of the Initiative stated that the approach in the SII was a "clear departure from past practices," and its purpose was designed "to be one not only of identifying problems, but most importantly, of accomplishing change through intensive sessions with the Japanese."[15] What was meant by a "clear departure" is made apparent by the following two points.

The first relates to a change in the US attitude concerning its demands. The USA, in the previous Structural Dialogue, had stated that the talks "were not a negotiation," and, therefore, it would not submit a list of demands, instead making its demands known by its choice of questions and comments. In the SII, however, it produced a long and detailed list of 246 items across six different areas.[16] When the SII became bogged down in the spring of 1990, the US side reduced this list to 18 priority items. This list was handed over to Japanese negotiators and the head of the Liberal Democratic Party.[17] The SII went ahead, with the parties focusing on the items on these lists, while the Japanese side compiled a list of proposed reforms in response. The US team prepared a document that listed the Japanese proposals side by side with amendments suggested by the USA. The list of US demands was, therefore, not merely for show, but played a definite role in defining the exchanges.

The second difference relates to the documentation of agreements. The previous Structural Dialogue was never expected to produce an official report,

---

[15]Statement of Hon. David C. Mulford, Under Secretary for International Affairs, U.S. Department of the Treasury, *United States–Japan Structural Impediments Initiative (SII)*, Hearing before the Subcommittee on International Trade of the Senate Committee on Finance, 101st Congress, 1st session, July 20, 1989, (Part 1 of 3).

[16]The leaked list was published by the *Asahi journal* in four articles appearing between April 20 and May 18, 1990.

[17]Secret Cable, "SII Short List," March 1990, United States Department of State.

but rather the aim was merely to reach agreement on the sort of language used to describe the dialogue in the US congressional briefing and press conferences.[18] In contrast, it had been decided that the SII would ultimately produce a report outlining any agreements.

The report would be more than a mere gesture, largely due to the unofficial threat of invoking Super 301. While the SII was meant to take place outside of the Section 301 framework, in reality, the scheduling of Super 301 and the SII process were closely linked. Under Super 301, the second period of priority country designations was set for April 27, 1990.[19] Meanwhile, five sets of official talks were scheduled to take place after the official start of the SII, with a final report to be released in June. In addition, an interim report emerging from the SII was scheduled to be released in April, just under 3 months prior to the end of 1 year's worth of meetings and immediately prior to the second designation period of Super 301.

Thus, the interim report would be of critical importance. Initially, Japanese negotiators had stated that "as the final report will come out in the summer of next year, issues discussed at the SII, such as Japan's distribution systems, will not be subject to the use of Section 301 of the U.S. Omnibus Foreign Trade and Competitiveness Act in the spring of the following year."[20] Meanwhile, hardliners within the US Congress viewed the SII simply as an alternative to Section 301 and refused to exclude the application of Section 301 to the structural problems. Immediately following the statement from Japan, Max Baucus, chairman of the Senate Finance Committee's International Trade Subcommittee, requested of US negotiators in a July 20 hearing that the interim report be submitted prior to Super 301 priority country designations of the following year, "so that we can take appropriate action."[21] Furthermore, Baucus revealed plans to submit a proposal forcing the application of Section 301 in the event that the SII ended in failure, increasing the pressure to link the SII to Section 301.[22] These actions subsequently continued, and similar statements were made in a November hearing.[23]

---

[18]Scope paper, "U.S.–Japan Structural Dialogue," July 1986, Department of State, NSA, Japan and the U.S., 1977–1992.

[19]March 31, 1990, was a Saturday. Hence reporting occurred on the 30th, and the 30th day after this date, April 29, 1990, also fell on a weekend, so that designations occurred on Friday, April 27, 1990.

[20]*Asahi Shimbun*, July 19, 1989 (Evening edition).

[21]*United States–Japan Structural Impediments Initiative (SII)*, Hearing before the Subcommittee on International Trade of the Senate Committee on Finance, 101st Congress, 1st session, July 20, 1989, (Part 1 of 3).

[22]Statement of Senator Max Baucus, "The Launching of the Structural Impediments Initiative," Working Group on Structural Impediments Initiative (SII), [OA/ID 03684], George Bush Presidential Library. This statement was widely reported on in Japan. *Asahi Shimbun*, August 31, 1989 (Evening edition); *Nihon Keizai Shimbun*, August 31, 1989 (Evening edition).

[23]*United States–Japan Structural Impediments Initiative (SII)*, Hearing before the Subcommittee on International Trade of the Senate Committee on Finance, 101st Congress, 1st session, November 6 and 7, 1989, (Part 2 of 3).

Not only the US Congress but also the government and the negotiation team strongly emphasized the importance of achieving results through the SII prior to the second designation of priority countries.[24] A US–Japan Summit Meeting on September 1, 1989, similarly stressed that tangible progress prior to the interim report in the spring would be critical,[25] while Trade Representative Carla Hills also made strong requests that Japan submit a blueprint as to how structural impediments would be addressed.[26] In the fourth meeting, held just prior to the second designations under Super 301, the US negotiating team was instructed to take advantage of the knowledge that the Japanese side had to finish the interim report. On April 4, 1990, Prime Minister Kaifu sent the Deputy Vice Minister for Foreign Affairs, Hisashi Owada, and the former Japanese Ambassador, Nobuo Matsunaga, to the USA as special envoys to meet with President Bush. At this point, President Bush had received advice against making any definite decisions with regard to Section 301 (no agreement on the interim report had been reached at this stage). Due to the emphasis both the US government and Congress placed on the interim report, by the fall of 1989 the interim evaluations had taken on a special significance as the "interim report."[27]

While the SII was meant to occur outside of the framework of Section 301 of the US Trade Act, the clarity and urgency of US demands, as well as the close scheduling of the Super 301 process with the drafting of SII agreement documentation, shows a clear distinction from the earlier Structural Dialogue. In reality, the SII did not consist of "talks" or "dialogues" aimed at the simple exchange of views, but was in fact a "negotiation" ("a formal discussion between people who are trying to reach an agreement," according to the *Merriam-Webster Dictionary*), aimed at achieving consensus based on argument and compromise.

5.3.4 A Two-Way or One-Way Dialogue?

The US–Japan Structural Impediments Initiative was officially billed as a two-way dialogue. The record of the demands made by each side, however, shows a clear asymmetry between the two. In short, the USA demanded that Japan open its markets, while Japan did not demand the same of the USA. Of course, strictly speaking, there were a number of issues that, if resolved, would have produced

[24]Memorandum, "Issues Paper: Your Discussions with the Japanese," from Desaix Anderson to Lawrence S. Eagleburger, Department of State. Acting Assistant Secretary for East Asian and Pacific Affairs, December 7, 1989, NSA, Japan and the U.S., 1977–1992.

[25]*Asahi Shimbun*, September 2, 1989 (Evening edition).

[26]*Asahi Shimbun*, October 14, 1989 (Morning edition).

[27]In addition, the US suggested that a follow-up on the progress of reforms be carried out for 3 years after the end of the SII. This coincides with the requirement under the US Trade Act for the USTR to monitor progress and report on designated priority practices by 1993 at the earliest (Dougauchi 1991).

immediate gains for Japan. These included the scrapping of the Buy American Act and the Ship American Policy, the removal of short supply provisions that allowed for export restrictions on certain goods in low supply, the adoption of the metric system, the scrapping of the voluntary restraint agreements (VRAs), and the lifting of the ban on exports of Alaskan oil.[28] However, these issues were raised under the pretext of strengthening the competitiveness of US industry and exports.[29] Most of the Japanese demands on the US economy, such as export promotion policies, improvements in labor training and education, promotion of research and development, encouragement of middle- and long-term management perspectives among corporate leaders, and enhanced investment in production facilities, as well as policies aimed at improving the US savings rate, would only serve to increase American competitiveness (Hatakeyama 1996: 33–34). This was well understood by US officials. Glen Fukushima of the USTR stated that the Japanese team pointed out almost exclusively ways to improve the competitiveness of American industry (Fukushima 1992: 206–207).

Needless to say, Japanese representatives had highlighted a number of structural impediments on the US side ever since the earlier Dialogue. Of these, the US fiscal deficit was considered particularly problematic and was the subject of serious discussions in SII talks concerning structural problems on the US side. Nonetheless, without the initiation of the SII, there was never any intention to make such far-reaching demands of the USA. The Deputy Vice-Minister for Foreign Affairs, Koji Watanabe, was somewhat at a loss in making special requests with regard to the US economy, stating after the interim report that he wanted to "conduct further investigations prior to the final report to make systematic requests of the U.S."[30]

The main concern for both the USA and Japan was in reducing the conflict between the two countries by reforming economic structures *in Japan*. While the Japanese representatives urged that the SII should remain "bidirectional in nature," in reality, any claims to having a "two-way" dialogue were largely made for appearances only, which was true from the time of the Structural Dialogue, even from the planning stages prior to the Structural Dialogue, and remained largely unchanged. Accordingly, the difference between the Structural Dialogue and the SII is the difference between a talk and a negotiation; in other words, the difference lay in whether or not problems would occur (mainly via the Super 301) if an agreement was not reached.

[28]Exportation of North Slope oil could have instantly eliminated a large portion of the bilateral trade imbalance, but one US official replied that it was not politically feasible because of the strong opposition from the west coast port workers.

[29]It was argued that protection afforded to US businesses under the Buy American Act and VRAs made it difficult to improve their competitiveness, while short supply provisions made it dangerous to rely on American imports. In 1973, the export of soy beans was banned, an event mentioned in the SII.

[30]*Gaikou forum*, May 1990, p. 28.

5.3.5 The Magnitude of the Risk

If agreements had not been reached through the SII, the consequences could have been disastrous. This was due to the fact that, for US members of Congress who had pushed a hardline stance against Japan, the SII was simply a substitute for action under the Super 301 process. This group had, in fact, sent letters to President Bush and Trade Representative Hills requesting that Super 301 be applied against Japan.[31] Super 301 had, of course, in some of its aspects, been intended to target Japan from its very beginning. Congressman John C. Danforth, who played a significant role in the addition of the provision, stated that while Congress was not thinking only of Japan when Super 301 was created, Japan was certainly within its intended scope.[32]

For this reason, a reaction from Congress would have been unavoidable if Japan were not designated as a priority country. In a 1989 US report on foreign trade barriers, the Japanese automotive and timber industries were highlighted alongside problems related to their distribution systems and the *keiretsu* conglomerates and collusion (USTR 1989). Congress expected that these issues would be targeted for action under the Super 301. If the administration ignored this expectation, Congress could have potentially sought to force the administration to apply Section 301 against Japanese structural impediments or to take legislative measures to obstruct the Uruguay Round of trade talks (Price 1990; Dryden 1995: Chap. 17).

Obviously, the problems were something more than the US internal conflict. The Bush administration thought that dealing with Japanese structural problems, previously been seen as domestic issues, under Super 301 and in the context of potential sanctions, was something that Japan was unlikely to accept.[33] There were also concerns that harming the US–Japan relationship through a wide-ranging application of Super 301 would hinder negotiations in the Uruguay Round. The US ambassador in Japan had warned a number of US government departments that designating Japan as a priority country would provoke an emotional reaction and end up damaging the bilateral relationship.[34]

---

[31]A letter signed by 72 members of the lower house of Congress was sent to Trade Representative Hills (*Asahi Shimbun*, May 20, 1989) (Evening edition). Senator Baucus also sent a similar letter to the President with 13 signatures. In addition, some members of Congress sent individual letters (Letter, from Max Baucus to George Bush, May, 19, 1989, TA003[037033]; Letter, from Carl Levin to George Bush, May, 23, 1989, TA[039063]; Letter, from Rudy Boschwitz to George Bush, May, 19, 1989, TA[039304], George Bush Presidential Library).

[32]Statement, John C. Danforth, "Statement by Senator John C. Danforth," April 27, 1990, Super 301 Decision, [OA/ID 03890], Bush Presidential Records, Office of Legislative Affairs, George Bush Presidential Library.

[33]Furthermore, the structural issues themselves were wide-ranging and required thorough investigation, research, and negotiations. Accordingly, Super 301 processes were considered inappropriate due to the requirement for determinations on results to be made within 1 year. "U.S.-Japan Bilateral Initiative on Structural Impediments to Balance of Payments Adjustment," TPRG: Super 301 and Special 301, [OA/ID CF00506], George Bush Presidential Library.

[34]*The New York Times*, May 16, 1989, Tuesday, Late City Final Edition.

If the approach chosen was either too hardline or too conciliatory, the relationship between the USA and Japan and the multilateral negotiations in the Uruguay Round were likely to be seriously damaged.

5.3.6 Heterogeneity, Interdependence, and Political Focus

What was the role played by interdependence between the two countries, in turning heterogeneity into a political crisis? The US–Japan relationship represents a highly active dyad of international interactions. The emergence of latent structural differences was, consequently, inevitable. This is particularly evident in terms of microeconomic differences and can be seen in the main areas of conflict during the SII. The Large-Scale Retail Act became the most significant issue in the area of the distribution system, when Toys "R" Us, a very well-known retailer in the USA, faced difficulties when opening its first store in Japan. Mutual shareholding among Japanese *keiretsu* conglomerates was also seen as an issue by the USA, as American companies felt obstructed in their efforts to enter the Japanese market due to long-term trading practices among these conglomerates, while demands to strengthen Japanese antitrust laws with regard to exclusive trading practices were also motivated by the efforts of US companies to tender bids in Japan. With regard to the Act against Unjustifiable Premiums and Misleading Representations, the USA singled out regulations on the discount price of confectionary due to the relative importance of "discounts" for US companies seeking new entry to the Japanese market. Interest in the deregulation of takeover bids, shareholders' rights, and the Securities and Exchange Act drew attention when Thomas Boone Pickens, known for greenmailing in the USA, tried a hostile takeover of Koito Manufacturing. In each case, attempts by US companies to conduct and expand operations or direct investments in Japan highlighted problems relating to the difference in Japanese structures and practices. These would then be added to the list of US demands.

Practical demands by the business interests were frequently reinforced by the idea of Japanese "uniqueness." Leading up to the late 1980s, pressure against Japan had already been gaining momentum within the US Congress (Kusano 1991), and, at the same time, a form of revisionism appeared to have gained a foothold across the country (Prestowitz 1988; Fallows 1989; Walferen 1989). Revisionists argued that the Japanese economic system was essentially different from the open-market economies such as the USA and that this difference was the cause of the trade imbalance.

Such arguments were frequently incorporated into attempts to politicize heterogeneity between the two countries. The Pickens case is a good example of this. Having come up against the defensive policies of Koito Manufacturing's management, Pickens sensationally denounced these practices as unfair, and, as a result, by the fall of 1989, Japanese investment practices and regulations, as well as shareholder rights, had all become significant issues. Behind this, allegedly, was the expectation of Mr. Pickens that Koito would try to purchase his shares at a higher price, owing to the desire of Koito's shareholders and customers to avoid further trade frictions (Gotou 1997). Koito's primary customers were Japanese automakers involved in trade frictions with the USA, and its main shareholders included names such as Toyota, Nissan, and Matsushita Electric Industrial Co. (now Panasonic). In a hearing of the Senate Finance Committee's International Trade Subcommittee on November 6, 1989, Pickens named these three companies and emphasized the fact that they accounted for 18% of Japanese exports to the USA. His criticism of them as being the primary cause of the US trade deficit with Japan only served to strengthen the revisionist view.[35]

It was during this period that Toys "R" Us moved to open its stores in Japan. This move was also connected with the SII. Toys "R" Us had begun its operations in Asia from around 1988 while continuing to assess its options with regard to Japan.[36] Eventually, Toys "R" Us announced plans to enter the Japanese market under a joint venture with McDonald's Japan on September 26, 1989, after the specific details of the SII agenda had become clear in the first round of meetings earlier that month. Later, on October 4, representative Hills promptly raised the case of Toys "R" Us in a press conference in order to make the case for deregulation. Den Fujita, the head of McDonald's Japan, gave voice to his own hopes with the following comment: "If procedures relating to the Large-Scale Retail Store Act become tied up and hamper the opening of stores, the U.S. headquarters will likely put pressure on the Japanese government via Washington."[37] Toys "R" Us founder Charles Lazarus may have had just such a plan, having been born in Washington D.C. and as an acquaintance of Hills who was based there also. Each of these cases involved an economic entity consciously seeking to take advantage of the emerging political problems between the USA and Japan.

Thus, the effects of interdependence and heterogeneity should not be underestimated. Without a deep interdependence between the USA and Japan, such political problems would likely never have developed to the level of crisis that they did. The increase in economic exchanges bridging the divide between the two countries and the various interests that emerged as a result of these exchanges turned these very differences into political problems within the political context surrounding them (characterized by an economic downturn, twin deficits, partisan conflict within the USA, and political maneuvering of economic agents).

Nonetheless, it is important to recall that socio-politico-economic structural differences between the USA and Japan have always existed and that they were doubtlessly decreasing rather than increasing throughout the postwar period. Additionally, bilateral interdependence had been growing well before the start of the

---

[35]Statement of T. Boone Pickens, Jr., Chairman, Boone Co., and General Partner, Mesa Limited Partnership, Dallas, TX. *United States–Japan Structural Impediments Initiative (SII),* Hearing before the Subcommittee on International Trade of the Senate Committee on Finance, 101st Congress, 1st session, November 6 and 7, 1989, (Part 2 of 3).

[36]*Nikkei Ryutsu Shimbun*, November 22, 1988; January 1, 1989.

[37]*Nikkei Ryutsu Shimbun*, September 28, 1989.

Structural Dialogue. Despite the potential risks, however, these did not emerge to threaten the diplomatic relationship until the late 1980s. Thus, neither heterogeneity nor interdependence can be considered sufficient to have triggered the crisis.

The same can be said of other instances involving differences between the USA and other nations. In fact, the 1981 report also mentions similar problems faced by US companies in France. Similar to those in Japan, these related to distribution systems and commercial practices, in addition to the language difference. However, these problems did not reach the same level of political significance as the issues that occurred between the USA and Japan around 1990. The USA also experienced numerous instances of trade friction with Canada, though none of these resulted in diplomatic crisis, perhaps due to the linguistic, cultural, and ethnic closeness of the two nations. Compared to such other countries, the differences between the USA and Japan are easily identified. Furthermore, the fact that these were discussed in terms of ideas of fairness and that the trade deficit with Japan accounted for the largest portion of the overall US trade deficit probably enabled these differences to become political targets. As the USA entered the 1990s and began to record an even higher trade deficit with China, a country even more dissimilar to it than Japan, the problems associated with US–Japanese heterogeneity began to dissipate, at least on the surface. The facts suggest that, provided they do not receive significant political attention, problems emerging from heterogeneity may be handled pragmatically.

5.4 Conclusion

This chapter has considered the connection between interdependence and heterogeneity using structural conflict between Japan and the USA as an example. The US–Japan case suggests that interdependence raises the risks associated with heterogeneity. However, deepening interdependence by itself did not necessarily create a political standoff between the two countries. While interdependence increases specific risks, these can emerge as political foci only with the help of some sort of trigger. Economic entities seeking to take advantage of this situation can lead to further moves toward the politicization of the issues.

Further economic growth in China over the medium term may mean a rather gloomy prognosis for future trade friction between the USA and China. Even in the event that China were to democratize itself, abandon its military ambitions, and successfully conclude RTAs with Japan and the USA, it would continue to be the focus of political attention as long as it continued to increase in importance as a US trading partner. At present, there are continuing efforts aimed at applying pressure on Chinese foreign exchange policy by setting deadlines and laying out retaliatory measures, such as the Schumer–Graham bill (s.295) and the Grassley–Baucus bill (s.2467). These may be used in the same way as Section 301 provisions during the US–Japan Structural Impediments Initiative.

Furthermore, the example of Japan indicates that direct US investment in China, generally considered to be a factor relieving friction, may only serve to increase the interests of the relevant US companies in addressing Chinese structural problems. Such companies operating in China are already making significant demands for domestic structural reforms in China via the USCBC. Objections by these companies are more likely to appear when the intention is to sell into the Chinese market itself, as opposed to building production facilities in China and exporting their manufactured products elsewhere. Accordingly, as the Chinese economy continues to grow, lifting wages and increasing the shift toward a domestic demand-driven economy, such grievances may become more apparent. Of course, companies wielding any such objections will not desire any form of trade war between the USA and China, yet the risk of an emotional reaction among other groups within the USA remains. For instance, gaps in reciprocity (whereby Chinese nationals may own land and corporations in the USA, while US nationals may not do the same in China) and security-related concerns (spying against high-tech and military industries, Chinese weapons development) are also involved. If interest groups or political leaders seek to politicize these issues, there is a substantial likelihood that heterogeneity-related risks may bring about a crisis. Further still, these sorts of risks are not limited to US–China and China–Japan relations. Future efforts to produce more detailed assessments of the risks associated with heterogeneity and interdependence between countries would be worthwhile.

References

Bergsten CF, Noland M (1993) Reconcilable differences? United States-Japan economic conflict. Institute for International Economics, Washington, DC

Buzan B, Lawson G (2015) The global transformation: history, modernity and the making of international relations. Cambridge University Press, Cambridge

Destler IM (1979) U.S.-Japanese relations and the American trade initiative of 1977: was this "Trip" necessary? In: William JB (ed) Japan and The United States: challenges and opportunities. New York University Press, New York, pp 190–230

Dougauchi M (1991) Nichibei kouzou mondai kyougi no houteki ichiduke (The legal context of the U.S.-Japan structural impediments initiative). Shoujihoumu 1258:25–31

Dryden S (1995) Trade warriors. Oxford University Press, New York

Fallows J (1989) Nihon fuujikome (Containing Japan). Translated by Omae M. TBS Britanica, Tokyo

Fukushima GS (1992) Nichibei keizai masatu no seijigaku (The politics of U.S.-Japan economic conflict). Asahi Shinbunsya, Tokyo

Gotou M (1997) Koito-Boone Pickens jiken: kokkyouwo koeta kigyoubouei (Koito-Boone Pickens case: defense from transnational takeover). Sannou University Press, Tokyo

Hatakeyama N (1996) Tsusyou kousyou: kokueki wo meguru dorama (Trade negotiation: the drama over national interests). Nihon Keizai Shinbunsya, Tokyo

Kusano A (1991) Amerika gikai no tainichi aturyoku (The pressure from the American Congress). Chuuou Kouron, Tokyo. Chap. 2

Oyane S (2011) Kokusai rejimu to nichibei no gaikou kousou: WTO, APEC, FTA no tenkankyokumen (Constructing international regimes: Japanese and American policy toward the WTO, APEC, and FTAs). Yuhikaku, Tokyo

Prestowitz CV (1988) Trading places. Basic Books, New York

Price JH (1990) Su-pa-301jyouto nichibei kouzou kyougi (Super 301 and the U.S.-Japan structural impediments initiative). Kokusai syouji houmu 18(5):453–461
Suzuki K (2013) Nichibei kouzou kyougi no seiji katei (The political process of the U.S.-Japan structural impediments initiative). Minerva Shobo, Kyoto
U.S.-China Business Council (2013) China and the U.S. Economy: advancing a winning trade agenda. Available via USCBC website. https://www.uschina.org/. Accessed 7 May 2016
U.S.-China Business Council (2014, 2015) China Economic Reform Scorecard. Available via USCBC website. https://www.uschina.org/. Accessed 7 Apr 2016
United States Trade Representative (1989) National Trade Estimate report on Foreign Trade Barriers. U.S. Government Printing Office, Washington, DC
Walferen KV (1989) The enigma of Japanese power. Palgrave Macmillan, London
Yamakage S (1982) Modeling interdependence and analyzing conflict: mathematical representation. Int Pol Sci Rev 3(4):479–503
Yamamoto Y (1989) Kokusaiteki sougoizon (International interdependence). University of Tokyo Press, Tokyo
Yasui A (2005) Beikoku Gikai ha Cyuugokuni naniwo motomete irunoka (What does United States Congress want from China?). Available via Mizuho Research Institute. http://www.mizuho-ri.co.jp/publication/research/pdf/us-insight/USI015.pdf. Accessed at Accessed 5 May 2016
Zeng K (2004) Trade threats, trade wars. The University of Michigan Press, Ann Arbor

Part III
Inside a State

Chapter 6
Role of Third-Party Guarantors in Uncertainty of Preventive Civil War: Can Thucydides Trap Be Resolved?

Kaoru Ishiguro and Kazuya Yamamoto

Abstract The "Thucydides trap" refers to situations where a war is impending between countries in power transition. Formal models of commitment problems in international relations studies demonstrate the ineffectualness of peace promises in such situations. Fearon's temporal power shift model associated with resource division problems is a typical one. His model has been expanded to include third-party guarantors while retaining complete information. This study incorporates uncertainty in the model and addresses the question of why some conflicts are resolved by guarantors while others are not. It argues that uncertainties about intervention and costs that accompany conflicts cause the difference. The main findings suggest that suspicions about third-party intervention on the part of domestic actors lead to fighting. Additionally, maintaining peace is more likely to be difficult if the declining actor's cost of fighting is uncertain, while power shifts of large magnitude prolong conflicts.

Keywords Civil conflict · Third-party intervention · Thucydides' trap · Commitment problems · Uncertainty

6.1 Introduction

Among many implications for contemporary international relations suggested in Thucydides' *History of the Peloponnesian War*, the "Thucydides trap" is the most famous one. It asserts that a rising power causes a declining power's anxiety and the latter's suspicion leads to war eventually. Thucydides observed this trap in the

K. Ishiguro
Graduate School of Economics, Kobe University, Kobe, Japan
e-mail: ishiguro@econ.kobe-u.ac.jp

K. Yamamoto (✉)
Center for Global Public Goods Studies, Kyoto Sangyo University, Kyoto, Japan
e-mail: uhi09142@nifty.ne.jp

M. Tadokoro et al. (eds.), *Emerging Risks in a World of Heterogeneity*, Evolutionary Economics and Social Complexity Science 10,
https://doi.org/10.1007/978-981-10-7968-9_6

rivalry between emerging Athens and established Sparta that sought to defend the status quo. The power transition theory in international relations studies developed this argument and explained war in modern history from perspectives of the rise and fall of great powers (e.g., Organski 1968; Gilpin 1981; Modelski 1987; Kennedy 1987). Recently, China's relations with the USA have been discussed from the same perspective (Allison 2017).

Meanwhile, this argument has been applied to cases of civil conflict since the end of the Cold War. In the former Yugoslavia and Africa in the 1990s, civil conflicts were characterized by competition between ethnic groups in changing balance of power. Once a dominant group in the Cold War period lost its legitimacy in a country, other groups began to dissent and their competition escalated into armed conflict. Formal analysis of international relations studies connects this type of civil conflict with commitment problems, instead of describing it as Thucydides' trap. In their terminology, commitment problems refer to the inability to keep promises despite them benefitting all parties, thus resulting in war.

Fearon (1995) divided wars into three types: preemptive wars, preventive wars, and wars over strategically critical objects. Among these, Fearon's preventive war thesis formalized the relationship between the occurrence of war and power shifts from one actor to another over time, despite their agreement for peaceful resolution. Specifically, in bargaining problems in which competing parties are required to negotiate a set of issues, or resource division problems such as territorial disputes, Fearon demonstrated that when power shifts from one actor to another over time, underlying commitment problems inevitably give rise to a preventive war launched by the declining side. Even if the rising actor promises to abide by an agreement or accepts a certain division of resources, the declining actor cannot trust the rising actor's words because there exists no guarantee that the rising actor will continue to follow through on its promise once it has become sufficiently strong enough to defeat the declining side. Thus, without means of ensuring that the promise is maintained, the declining actor is skeptical about the rising actor's future intentions. Consequently, this type of commitment problems induces the declining actor to initiate an attack before its rival has consolidated its power. Since the application of this model to the Yugoslav wars by Fearon (1998), his temporal power shift model associated with resource division problems has become renowned for offering a persuasive explanation for civil conflicts as well as for the traditional interstate ones.

Following Fearon's argument, Ishiguro (2007, Chap. 10; 2010, Chap. 4) sought to find mechanisms that prevent the occurrence of these types of preventive wars. His finding was that outside third parties could play a significant role. He expanded Fearon's (1998) model and demonstrated that, if information is complete between actors, preventive wars are avoidable by the intervention of third parties who guarantee the implementation of promises agreed upon by rival actors. Certainly, Ishiguro's complete information model can explain the peaceful resolutions of civil conflicts in some cases. For example, in Macedonia, clear manifestations of an intention to intervene by the UN Preventative Deployment Force (UNPREDEP) in the 1990s and the USA and the EU in the early 2000s (i.e., complete information about third parties' involvement) played a pivotal role in preventing the conflict from descending into further violence (Ramsbotham et al. 2005, 127–129). However, a question remains: why do third parties succeed in maintaining (or restoring) peace in some cases while they fail to do so in others? For example, in contrast to the Macedonian case, in Sierra Leone immediately after the conclusion of the Lomé Peace Accord in 1999, the Revolutionary United Front (RUF) continued to violate the ceasefire despite the deployment of the UN Mission in Sierra Leone (UNAMSIL) (Ramsbotham et al. 2005, 151–153; Ero 2003; Richards and Vincent 2008).

We address this puzzle. We argue that in order to explain different outcomes of civil conflicts in which outside third parties play similar roles as guarantors, uncertainties should be taken into account. Specifically, our model demonstrates that unlike Ishiguro's (2007, 2010) findings obtained by assuming complete information, peace led by outside third-party guarantors becomes more difficult to achieve if uncertainties exist between actors in conflict.

The next section describes the relevant literature in greater detail. Section 6.3 formally describes Fearon's and Ishiguro's arguments. Section 6.4 develops a generalized version of Ishiguro's third-party intervention model, through which the above puzzle is addressed. Sections 6.5 and 6.6 investigate the effects of uncertainties in two distinct ways. Section 6.5 investigates uncertainty over intervention. Meanwhile, Sect. 6.6 addresses the uncertainty about the costs of war borne by domestic disputants – or rather, the strength of their resolves. Section 6.7 investigates situations in which fights have occurred because of these kinds of uncertainties. Section 6.8 presents conclusions.

6.2 Related Literature

Three types of research are related to our topic: studies that expand Fearon's (1995, 1998) models and deepen his arguments, those that investigate the role of third parties in civil conflicts, and those that connect the above two.

The work of Robert Powell notably develops Fearon's temporal power shift model. Powell (2004, 2006) generalized Fearon's argument and presented conditions in which socially inefficient outcomes brought by commitment problems arise in broader social situations, such as political transitions between an elite and a poor majority in a more institutionalized state. Also, Powell (1999, Chap. 4) developed a model in which the declining country (or hegemon), rather than the emerging one, makes an offer for a new distribution of territory and revealed that the traditional power transition school's argument that a shift in the distribution of power ends in war is not persuasive. Tingley (2011) offered another important development, particularly in terms of methodology. He tested the implications derived from Fearon's model by using laboratory experiments. These experiments confirmed that the increasing influence of the future (i.e., players' longer time horizons) leads to more socially inefficient outcomes.

Second, models that attempt to investigate the role of third parties in civil conflict have proliferated following the intensification of ethnic conflicts in the post-Cold War period.[1] Using a game of perfect and complete information, Carment and Rowlands (1998) investigated the optimal level of involvement and studied how this level changes depending on factors such as the salience of a given dispute to a third party and the relative capacity of combatants. Walter (2002, Chap. 2) developed a model in which a third party attempts to intervene in an ongoing militarized conflict between rebels on the one hand and the incumbent government on the other and argued that the more the combatants are convinced that the third party will enforce demobilization, the more likely that the combatants will begin negotiations, and a peace settlement will be realized. Meanwhile, Fortna and Martin's (2009) comparative statics reveal that the type of government, the benefits of peace, the costs of accepting peacekeepers, and the costs of enduring exploitation for the rebels affect the implementation of peacekeeping in militarized disputes.[2]

Finally, Cetinyan (2002) and Grigoryan (2010) combined resource division problems with third-party involvement. Assuming that an ethnic group makes a demand on the government for the reallocation of resources and that a foreign third party may intervene to help that group, Cetinyan (2002, 650–657) argued that when information is complete, the ethnic group's demands are reduced to a set of concessions deemed acceptable by the government, and thereby the intervention will be avoided. Meanwhile, in contrast to the conventional interventionist's assertion that violence against minorities monotonically decreases with intervention, Grigoryan

[1]International relations studies have distinguished between intervention and mediation, based on the intensity of third parties' involvement. Intervention may include coercive means by which third parties attempt to force conflicting parties to accept a certain distribution of power, abide by the terms of a peace agreement, and so forth. Military operations such as peacekeeping activities and air strikes are sometimes employed. Meanwhile, mediation usually indicates diplomatic measures in which third parties serve as messengers to convey one party's intentions to another or arbitrators to convene conferences between competing groups. As described later, this chapter addresses the intervention type of involvement. In particular, our model focuses on the kind of intervention in which third parties play a role in ensuring agreements between rival parties, rather than the ones that attempt to intervene in ongoing fighting such as air strikes. A variety of formal models that address third-party mediation have also been developed. For these models, see Kydd (2003, 2006), Rauchhaus (2006), and Smith and Stam (2003).

[2]Although the recent literature on intervention focuses more on domestic conflict scenarios, international relations studies have traditionally investigated the functions and effects of intervention in interstate conflicts. The theories of extended deterrence and military alliance have studied how allies will react, or intervene, if their friends are attacked by adversaries. For recent formal and statistical models, see Werner (2000) and Smith (1996).

(2010) indicated that when incomplete information about the state and the third party exists, intervention might escalate, rather than resolve, state-minority conflicts.

Both Cetinyan (2002) and Grigoryan (2010) have advanced Fearon's model in that they considered the role of third-party intervention in connection with resource division problems. However, their models fail to incorporate the type of power shifts that evolve as time passes, which is the core concept of Fearon's preventive war argument. In fact, although Grigoryan (2010) did address changes in the power balance between the minority and the state, these changes do not depend on time, but on the actions taken by the intervener and the state. As a result, his model does not capture the kind of power shifts envisaged by Fearon. Undoubtedly, the types of power shifts investigated by Grigoryan are also an important aspect of civil conflicts. However, temporal power shifts have characterized as many conflicts as the ones addressed by Grigoryan. Situations characterized by temporal power shifts have driven competing actors to be belligerent (e.g., the ethnic Serbs in Croatia in 1991, the Khmer Rouge in Cambodia in the 1990s, and the Sunni minority in Iraq at the present time). Thus, considering this fact, a model that addresses power shifts as Fearon did is as much needed as Grigoryan's approach.

In this respect, as mentioned in the first section, Ishiguro (2007, 2010) first linked temporal power shifts with both intrastate resource division problems and third-party intervention. However, as argued, his model is confined to complete information situations. As a result, that model is unable to address situations in which uncertainties encompass civil conflicts. Given the trend in the literature up to the present, addressing uncertainties is our purpose.[3]

6.3 The Baseline Argument

This section describes the arguments advanced by Fearon, Ishiguro, and Powell formally. We call this model the base model (see Fig. 6.1). In the next section, we develop a generalized version of this model so that we can address the puzzle described above.

Consider three players: a rising actor, a declining actor, and a potential third-party guarantor. The rising and declining actors live together in the same state and are

[3]Uncertainty, or asymmetric information, in bargaining and war has been studied in the previous literature. For example, Powell (1999) studied how asymmetric information about actors' willingness to use force influences the course of conflicts. Walter (2002) investigates the effects of uncertainty about third parties' involvement on achieving peace in civil conflicts. However, the effects of uncertainty under the situations addressed by this chapter (i.e., the situations in which commitment problems are caused by temporal power shifts and third parties are attempting to resolve these problems) have not been studied. We will investigate these situations here.

competing for resources in that state.[4] The rising actor is becoming dominant in the country whereas the declining actor's power is waning. To illustrate, as Fearon (1998) described, the Croats in independent Croatia in 1991 may be seen as the rising actor, while the ethnic Serbs in the new country are considered the declining actor. Similarly, in Cambodia in the 1990s, the new government was consolidating its power while the Khmer Rouge was losing ground.[5]

We now consider that the rising actor is unofficially presenting a pre-negotiation resource division proposal α. α represents the rising actor's share of resources and lies in the interval [0, 1]. A larger value of α indicates a larger share of resources for the rising actor. It is assumed that the declining actor prefers negotiations to a fight if the payoffs for participating in negotiations are equal to those for fighting. In order to prevent the declining actor from launching a fight in D_1, the rising actor is now presenting a pre-negotiation resource division proposal that satisfies $1–\alpha = 1–p_1–c_d$. Rewriting,

$$\alpha^{**} = \begin{cases} p_1 + c_d, & \text{if } 1 - p_1 - c_d \geq 0 \\ 1, & \text{if } 1 - p_1 - c_d < 0. \end{cases}$$

The game starts with this arrangement. All of these actors are assumed to be risk-neutral.

The game has four moves. The first move is that the declining actor decides whether or not to start negotiations with its rising counterpart in D_1. If it decides to do so, then the game proceeds to the next move, R_1. Otherwise, the declining actor begins fighting and the game ends (CQ_3). Assume that the rising actor wins the combat before entering into negotiations with probability p_1. In R_1, the rising actor officially proposes the resource division plan. This plan might be either a plan that is the same one as the pre-negotiation proposal or a plan that is more favorable to the rising actor than the original version. Then, in D_2, the declining actor decides whether or not to accept this plan. If the declining actor decides to accept it, then the game proceeds to the next move, I. Otherwise, the declining actor launches a fight, and the game ends (CQ_2). Assume that the rising actor wins the combat following negotiations with probability p_2. Since we consider situations in which power is shifting from the declining actor to the rising one over time, it is assumed that $p_2 > p_1$.

The third-party guarantor's objective is to resolve commitment problems between the domestic rivals and to prevent fighting between them by ensuring that the terms

[4]The previous literature refers to this type of competition between two domestic actors in various ways: negotiation on a set of issues (Fearon 1995), division of "benefits" (Fearon 1998), bargaining over territory (Powell 2006), and resource division (Tingley 2011). Although any and all of these representations are applicable in our argument, this chapter uses the term resource division following the latest study by Tingley.

[5]Rising and declining actors in this model refer to any actors who are competing for resources in a single state and are in situations in which power is shifting from the latter actor to the former one over time. Therefore, domestic competing actors in this model may be ethnic groups, rebels, central governments, and so forth.

of the pre-negotiation proposal are respected. In I, the third party who observed the rising actor's behavior in R_1 decides whether or not intervention is necessary. If the third party finds that the rising actor abides by its initial promise that was presented before entering the negotiations, the third party does not enforce sanctions, s, where $s = 0$. On the other hand, if it finds that the rising actor in R_1, which has now become stronger (i.e., $p_2 > p_1$), reneges on its pre-negotiation promise and demands greater concessions from the declining actor, then the third party will punish the rising actor by imposing s, where $s > 0$. After the third party's move, the game ends in CQ_1.[6]

The players' payoffs are as follows. Assuming that any side winning a war takes all the resources, the expected payoffs for the rising actor are $p_1 \times 1 + (1–p_1) \times 0–c_r = p_1–c_r$ in CQ_3 and $p_2–c_r$ in CQ_2, where c_r is the rising actor's costs of war ($c_r > 0$). Meanwhile, the rising actor receives $\alpha–s$ in CQ_1, where s is sanctions imposed by the third-party guarantor. If the third party imposes no sanctions, the rising actor's payoffs are α in CQ_1. The rising actor prefers peaceful settlement to resorting to battle and suffering the costs of war, $\alpha–s > p_2–c_r$. Likewise, the expected payoffs for the declining actor are $p_1 \times 0 + (1–p_1) \times 1–c_d = 1–p_1–c_d$ in CQ_3 and $1–p_2–c_d$ in CQ_2, where c_d is the declining actor's costs of war ($c_d > 0$).[7] Meanwhile, by avoiding a fight, the declining actor receives its own share of resources in the state, $1–\alpha$, in CQ_1. Finally, the payoffs received by the third party are Π_f when fights occur, whereas it receives Π_a when fights are avoided. It is assumed that the third-party guarantor prefers peace to war and has sufficient will and ability to intervene, $\Pi_a > \Pi_f$.[8]

Fearon (1995, 1998) and Powell (2006) demonstrated that when information is complete and third parties are absent, commitment problems arise between domestic actors and preventive wars occur. By cutting off the third party's move from the base model, we can trace their argument. Working backward, the expected payoffs for the

[6]The third-party guarantor in this model is distinguishable from other types of third parties in two respects. First, the role of the third party in the model is to preserve and ensure agreements between conflicting parties. Therefore, the forms of intervention in this model are different from the ones that are employed after the breakdown of bargaining and are conducted to end ongoing fighting (see Cetinyan 2002; Grigoryan 2010 for a discussion of these types of intervention). Second, the third party in this model plays a balanced role in that it demands that both domestic parties keep their original resource division promise, rather than siding with one actor in the conflict. Thus, this third party is distinguishable from, for example, NATO in the Libyan civil war in 2011, which was biased toward the rebels. In sum, the type of intervention addressed by this model has most typically been undertaken by the UN and/or groups of countries that attempt to operate on the basis of the UN initiative. For instance, the Cambodian peace process in the late 1980s and 1990s is a fitting example: countries encouraged four Cambodian factions to enter into negotiations and guaranteed the Paris Peace agreements by establishing the UN Transitional Authority in Cambodia (UNTAC).

[7]It may be reasonable to assume that, along with power shifts from the declining actor to the rising one (i.e., $p_2 > p_1$), the former's costs of war increase (i.e., $c_{d1} < c_{d2}$) while those of the latter decrease (i.e., $c_{r1} > c_{r2}$). However, assuming the different costs of war between D_1 and D_2 leads to the same findings as the ones derived from assuming unchanged costs. Therefore, this chapter employs the fixed values of costs and simplifies the analysis.

[8]The later sections modify the base model and consider situations in which the third party may choose not to intervene.

declining actor in D_2 are 1–α when it accepts plan α, whereas its payoffs are 1–p_2–c_d when it chooses to fight. Assume that the declining actor accepts the plan if the resulting payoffs are equal to those for fighting. Then, it chooses

$$\rho = \begin{cases} a, & \text{if } 1 - \alpha \geq 1 - p_2 - c_d \\ f, & \text{if } 1 - \alpha < 1 - p_2 - c_d. \end{cases}$$

Anticipating this behavior on the part of the declining actor, the rising actor decides the amount of α in R_1. If the rising actor prefers peace to fighting (i.e., $\alpha > p_2 – c_r$), it will propose the greatest amount of α that it can while still persuading the declining actor not to fight in D_2. That is, plan α^* proposed by the rising actor that prefers peace to fighting is

$$\alpha^* = \begin{cases} p_2 + c_d, & \text{if } 1 - p_2 - c_d \geq 0 \\ 1, & \text{if } 1 - p_2 - c_d < 0. \end{cases}$$

Meanwhile, since $c_d > 0$ and $c_r > 0$, $\alpha^* > p_2 – c_r$ is always satisfied. Thus, the rising actor always prefers peace to fighting and proposes α^* in R_1 when no third parties exist. Anticipating this move by the rising actor, the declining actor decides in D_1. While the declining actor receives 1–p_1–c_d by choosing a fight, it receives 1–α^* = 1–p_2–c_d by choosing negotiations. Since the balance of power shifts over a lapse of time ($p_2 > p_1$), 1–p_1–c_d is greater than 1–p_2–c_d. Knowing this, the declining actor decides to fight preventively in D_1. Thus, the type of preventive war as described by Fearon (1995) occurs.

As argued by Ishiguro (2007, 2010), third-party involvement is a solution to the above commitment problems. Rejoin move *I* into the base model. The third-party guarantor will impose sanctions *s* on the rising actor when the latter reneges on its pre-negotiation promise. Thus, the third party imposes sanctions:

$$s = \alpha^* - \alpha^{**} \tag{6.1}$$

Anticipating the third party's move in *I*, the rising actor abandons the idea of exploiting the declining actor and proposes α^{**} in R_1. Anticipating the rising actor's behavior, the declining actor decides to enter into negotiations in D_1. Thus, peace is maintained in this case.

Base Proposition In situations where information is complete, competing domestic actors are unable to avoid fighting by themselves due to underlying commitment problems. Meanwhile, settlements can be realized if third parties definitively intervene in the negotiation process.

6.4 The General Model

The base proposition is what Fearon, Powell, and Ishiguro demonstrated. Although the proposition is persuasive in some civil conflicts, this argument is unable to capture those that are plagued by uncertainty. In reality, this type of civil conflict is rather common. Civil conflicts involving third parties usually entail uncertainty concerning whether third parties intervene. As a result, rival actors in a given conflict may underestimate third parties' resolve and ignore their mandates. Meanwhile, the intentions of competing actors in civil conflicts are often unclear. By overestimating the declining actor's costs of war, the rising actor may underestimate the degree to which the declining actor is resolved to fight. As a result, the rising actor may mistakenly demand larger concessions from the declining actor than the latter is actually willing to concede. The following sections consider how these uncertainties change the argument of the base proposition. We demonstrate that the uncertainties regarding intervention and the costs of war solve the puzzle described in the first section and explain why some third-party guarantors achieve peace while others fail.

Before addressing these uncertainties, however, we modify the base model. Regarding the third party's choice, by making the costs of intervention implicit, the base model assumes that the third party does not have the option of not intervening. As a result, the third-party actor in Fig. 6.1 always intervenes if the rising actor reneges on its promise. In fact, situations in which third parties' defection is inconceivable are not as unusual as they seem to be. For example, it was

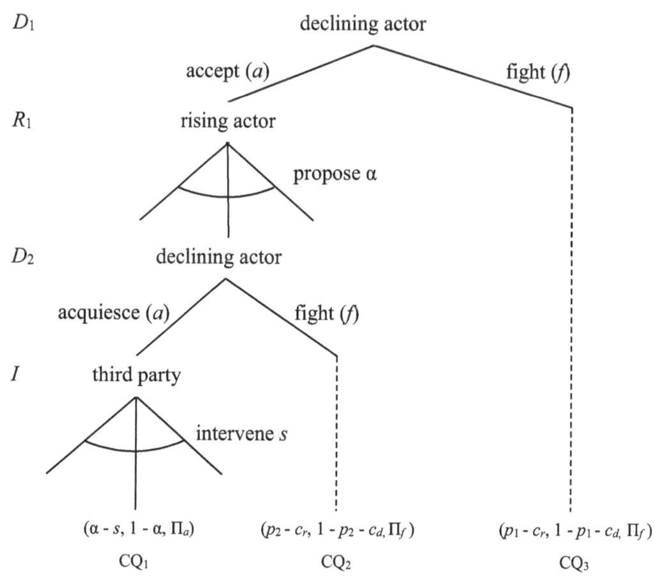

Fig. 6.1 The base model. Note: The payoffs are those of the rising actor, the declining actor, and the third party, in that order

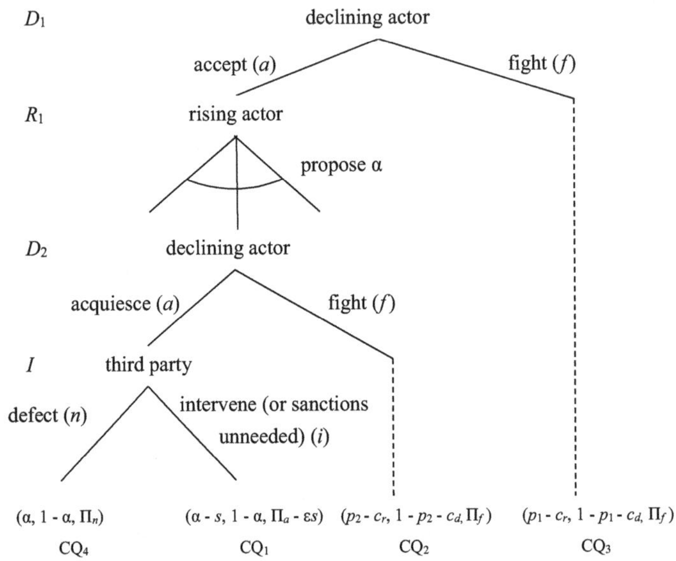

Fig. 6.2 The general model. Note: The payoffs are those of the rising actor, the declining actor, and the third party, in that order. When the rising actor abides by its initial promise, no sanctions are required and the third party actor's payoffs are Π_a in I

unimaginable that the UN and countries involved in the Cambodian peace process would decide to leave the process after the Paris Peace agreements were concluded and that Cambodian state rebuilding plans such as UNTAC would eventually be aborted. The base model properly illustrates this type of third-party intervention. However, there are also cases in which third parties are forced to defect at the final moment of their decision because of costs such as declining domestic support in their own countries and increasing expected expenditures. In order to include the latter situations, we generalize the base model by making the costs of intervention explicit and by incorporating the third party's choice of nonintervention into the model.

In Fig. 6.2, when the rising actor in R_1 presents α that is greater than α^{**} and sanctions become necessary, the third-party actor may also choose defection as well as intervention on move I. The third party's payoffs when it chooses to intervene are $\Pi_a - \varepsilon s$, where $\varepsilon \geq 0$. ε represents the third party's sensitivity to the costs of intervention (i.e., the third-party actor that is more sensitive to costs has a greater ε). By contrast, the third party's choice of defection leads to Π_n. Although the choice of defection allows the third party to save the costs of intervention, the choice to defect at the final stage also entails another type of cost such as the loss of reputation in the international community and the decline of influence in global politics. Meanwhile, if the rising actor proposes α^{**}, then no sanctions are needed and the third party can receive Π_a. Maintaining the base model's assumption that the third party prefers peace to fighting, the third party's preferences are $\Pi_a > \Pi_a - \varepsilon s > \Pi_f$ and $\Pi_a > \Pi_n > \Pi_f$.[9]

In this setting, the situation investigated by the base model is replicated if $\Pi_a - \varepsilon s \geq \Pi_n$ and $\varepsilon = 0$ are assumed. Thus, this modified model includes not only situations in which intervention costs are implicit but also those in which the third party's actions are influenced by intervention costs and the third party can choose defection. We call this modified version the general model. In the following sections, we use this model to investigate our puzzle.

6.5 Third-Party Intervention

This section addresses uncertainty regarding third-party intervention. Outside actors may hesitate to become fully involved in conflicts. Meanwhile, domestic actors may be unsure of the third parties' true intentions. This Section investigates how this type of uncertainty changes the results that are derived from a game of complete information. Instead of assuming that $\Pi_a - \varepsilon s \geq \Pi_n$ and setting ε to 0, we now consider that the third party's preference is either $\Pi_a > \Pi_a - \varepsilon s \geq \Pi_n > \Pi_f$ or $\Pi_a > \Pi_n > \Pi_a - \varepsilon s > \Pi_f$.[10] Domestic actors are not convinced of the third party's commitment to intervention, possibly because of weak support from citizens in a third-party country or a large amount of expected spending borne by the third party. Let $\gamma \in [0, 1]$ be the domestic actors' subjective probability of third-party intervention on I. Assume that both domestic actors have a common probability. These actors believe that the third-party guarantor in I intervenes in the conflict and imposes sanctions s on the rising actor with probability γ, whereas the guarantor eventually defects with probability $1-\gamma$. In other words, the domestic actors believe that the third party's payoffs are $\Pi_a > \Pi_a - \varepsilon s \geq \Pi_n > \Pi_f$ with probability γ and $\Pi_a > \Pi_n > \Pi_a - \varepsilon s > \Pi_f$ with probability $1-\gamma$.

The rising actor thus proposes α^{**} in R_1 if the payoffs gained by proposing α^{**} exceed the expected payoffs from proposing α^*:

---

[9]The following sections assume that the third party actor chooses to intervene if intervention and nonintervention are indifferent, i.e., $\Pi_a - \varepsilon s = \Pi_n$.

[10]We might consider situations in which the third party prefers war to bearing any costs pertaining to intervention, such as $\Pi_f > \Pi_a - \varepsilon s$ and $\Pi_f > \Pi_n$. Moreover, we might consider situations where war is the most preferable outcome for the third party among the possible outcomes, such as $\Pi_f > \Pi_a$. However, these situations imply that the third party is unwilling to be involved with the conflict from the outset and that move I does not exist in the model. Obviously, in these situations, the game returns to the earlier one played by the two domestic actors and results in a fight in D_1. Since this chapter's purpose is to investigate the third party's role, we assume situations in which, although the third party prefers peace without costs, Π_a, to any possible outcomes and has incentives to be involved with the conflict at the outset, $\Pi_a - \varepsilon s > \Pi_f$ and $\Pi_n > \Pi_f$, the costs of intervention may eventually force it to defect from the peace process in I.

$$(1-\gamma)\alpha^{*}+\gamma(\alpha^{*}-s)\leq\alpha^{**}.$$

Rewriting the inequality yields

$$s\geq\frac{\alpha^{*}-\alpha^{**}}{\gamma} \tag{6.2}$$

If the third party imposes sanctions $\bar{s}$ that satisfy inequality (6.2), the rising actor in R_1 proposes α^{**}. Anticipating this action by the rising actor, the declining actor in D_1 chooses to enter the official negotiations when inequality (6.2) is satisfied. Otherwise, the latter launches an attack in D_1. Thus, the equilibria are

$$[\alpha^{**};a,(a,\ldots,f);(i,\ldots,n)] \quad \text{if } \bar{s}\geq(\alpha^{*}-\alpha^{**})/\gamma, \tag{6.3}$$

$$[\alpha^{*};f,(a,\ldots,f);(i,\ldots,n)] \quad \text{if } \bar{s}<(\alpha^{*}-\alpha^{**})/\gamma, \tag{6.4}$$

where semicolons are used to separate actors and commas are used to separate the moves of an individual actor. That is, in order, the moves in the square brackets represent the rising actor's proposal in R_1, the declining actor's actions in D_1 and D_2, and the third party's decision in I.[11] The parentheses of D_2 and I denote the declining and the third party actors' decisions in the infinite possible paths that might follow R_1. In R_1, the rising actor can present infinite possible proposals between 0 and 1. Specifically, the declining actor in D_2 chooses to acquiesce (a) when it reaches paths that follow the rising actor's α that is equal to or less than α^{*} (i.e., $\alpha\leq\alpha^{*}$). Meanwhile, the declining actor chooses to fight (f) when $\alpha>\alpha^{*}$ in R_1. Similarly, the third party in I chooses to intervene (i) when $\Pi_a-\varepsilon s\geq\Pi_n$ while choosing to defect (n) when $\Pi_n>\Pi_a-\varepsilon s$. Of the two equilibria, peace is only realized in equilibrium (6.3), where the sequence of the players' actions on the equilibrium path is $a\rightarrow\alpha^{**}\rightarrow a\rightarrow i(s=0)$.[12]

In earlier sections, we considered situations in which the third party always intervenes ($\Pi_a-\varepsilon s\geq\Pi_n$) and the domestic actors know it ($\gamma=1$). Moreover, the third party only attempts to impose sanctions that return the rising actor's benefits to its initial promise $\left(\bar{s}=\alpha^{*}-\alpha^{**}\right)$ in the earlier arguments. This situation is represented by a special case of equilibrium (6.3), in which $\varepsilon=0$ and $\bar{s}=(\alpha^{*}-\alpha^{**})/1$. However, inequality (6.2) indicates that the amount $\bar{s}=\alpha^{*}-\alpha^{**}$ is insufficient for peace if the domestic actors are skeptical of the third party's true intentions (i.e., $\gamma<1$). Thus, when uncertainty exists, the third party's action to impose $\bar{s}=\alpha^{*}-\alpha^{**}$ results in equilibrium (6.4), and a fight occurs.

---

[11]In this version of the model, because the third party moves last, the domestic actors do not update their beliefs regarding intervention.

[12]When the third party reaches paths that follow the rising actor's α that is equal to or less than α^{**} (i.e., $\alpha^{*}\leq\alpha^{**}$), sanctions are not required. In these cases, the third party can dispense with its intervention and receive Π_a. In our model, this type of nonintervention is formally equivalent to the third party's choice of intervention (i) with no sanctions (i.e., $\Pi_a-\varepsilon s=\Pi_a>\Pi_n$, where $s=0$).

Proposition 1 If a third-party guarantor attempts to impose sanctions that only reduce the rising parties' benefits to the initial promise between domestic actors, even slight suspicions on the part of domestic parties regarding the credibility of a third party's intervention cause fighting, and the third party fails to prevent war.

Meanwhile, inequality (6.2) indicates that a level of sanctions that is greater than $\bar{s} = \alpha^{*} - \alpha^{**}$ can prevent war even under uncertainty. When sanctions that satisfies this inequality are presented by the third party, the rising actor expects that the guarantor intervenes and chooses to propose α^{**} in R_1 even if the rising actor is unsure of the intervention ($\gamma < 1$).

Proposition 2 If a third-party guarantor attempts to punish rising parties by imposing sanctions more severe than those that only diminish the rising parties' benefits to the pre-negotiation arrangement, the rising parties follow through on their promise and peace is realized.

In addition, when uncertainty about intervention exists, the domestic actors do not know the third party's true payoffs and are unable to know how much of the costs of the sanctions compel the guarantor to leave the peace process. The third party is able to capitalize on these situations. Specifically, in cases in which the third party indicates an amount $\bar{s}$ that makes its payoffs $\Pi_n > \Pi_a - \varepsilon\bar{s}$, it does not really prefer sanctions to defection. Thus, the third party's bluffing successfully induces the rising actor to propose α^{**} in these cases, despite that if the rising actor proposed α^{*} in R_1, the third party would not impose such $\bar{s}$.

Proposition 3 If domestic parties are uncertain about third-party intervention, a third-party guarantor can take advantage of this uncertainty and is able to realize peace by pretending to be a firmly resolved intervener who is willing to impose severe sanctions that would not be implemented should it really has to do so.

6.6 Costs of War

Next, we add uncertainty about the costs of fighting to our model. Consider that although the declining actor knows its own costs of war, both the rising actor and the third-party guarantor do not know the declining actor's true costs. For the sake of simplicity, we assume that the declining actor's costs of fighting take a value that is uniformly distributed over the interval $[c_{dL}, c_{dH}]$ and that the third party and the rising actor only know that the declining actor's costs lie within this interval.[13] Thus, the third party and the rising actor do not know the declining actor's true payoffs but can only consider that the declining actor's payoffs range from $1-p_1-c_{dL}$ to $1-p_1-c_{dH}$ in CQ_3 (and from $1-p_2-c_{dL}$ to $1-p_2-$

[13]Although we assume a uniform distribution for the declining actor's costs of fighting, the same argument holds for any standard probability distributions that are employed.

Table 6.1 Equilibria under uncertainty about intervention and costs of war

Equilibrium	c_d	p_2–p_1	s	Moves on the equilibrium path
$\gamma = 0$				
I. $[\alpha_u^*; a, (a, \ldots, f); (i, \ldots, n)]$	$c_d \geq p_2 - p_1 + (\gamma s + c_{dH} - c_r)/2$	$\forall(p_2 - p_1)$	$\forall s$	$a \to \alpha_u^* \to a \to i$ or $n^{(+)}$
II. $[\alpha_u^*; f, (a, \ldots, f); (i, \ldots, n)]$	$(\gamma s + c_{dH} - c_r)/2 \leq c_d < p_2 - p_1 + (\gamma s + c_{dH} - c_r)/2$	$\forall(p_2 - p_1)$	$\forall s$	$f \to \alpha_u^* \to a \to i$ or n
III. $[\alpha_u^*; f, (a, \ldots, f); (i, \ldots, n)]$	$c_d < \gamma s + c_{dH} - c_r)/2$	$\forall(p_2 - p_1)$	$\forall s$	$f \to \alpha_u^* \to f \to i$ or n
$\gamma \neq 0$				
IV. $[\alpha_u^*; a, (a, \ldots, f); (i, \ldots, n)]$	$c_d \geq p_2 - p_1 + (\gamma s + c_{dH} - c_r)/2$	$p_2 - p_1 \geq (c_{dH} + c_{dL})/2 + c_r$	$\forall s$	$a \to \alpha_u^* \to a \to i$ or $n^{(+)}$
V. $[\alpha_u^*; f, (a, \ldots, f); (i, \ldots, n)]$	$(\gamma s + c_{dH} - c_r)/2 \leq c_d < p_2 - p_1 + (\gamma s + c_{dH} - c_r)/2$	$p_2 - p_1 \geq (c_{dH} + c_{dL})/2 + c_r$	$\forall s$	$f \to \alpha_u^* \to a \to i$ or n
VI. $[\alpha_u^*; f, (a, \ldots, f); (i, \ldots, n)]$	$c_d < (\gamma s + c_{dH} - c_r)/2$	$p_2 - p_1 \geq (c_{dH} + c_{dL})/2 + c_r$	$\forall s$	$f \to \alpha_u^* \to a \to i$ or n
VII. $[\alpha_u^*; a, (a, \ldots, f); (i, \ldots, n)]$	$c_d \geq p_2 - p_1 + (\gamma s + c_{dH} - c_r)/2$	p_2–$p_1 < (c_{dH} + c_{dL})/2 + c_r$	$s \leq \underline{s}$, $s \geq \bar{s}$	$a \to \alpha_u^* \to a \to i$ or $n^{(+)}$
VIII. $[\alpha_u^*; f, (a, \ldots, f); (i, \ldots, n)]$	$(\gamma s + c_{dH} - c_r)/2 \leq c_d < p_2 - p_1 + (\gamma s + c_{dH} - c_r)/2$	p_2–$p_1 < (c_{dH} + c_{dL})/2 + c_r$	$s \leq \underline{s}$, $s \geq \bar{s}$	$f \to \alpha_u^* \to a \to i$ or n
IX. $[\alpha_u^*; f, (a, \ldots, f); (i, \ldots, n)]$	$c_d < (\gamma s + c_{dH} - c_r)/2$	p_2–$p_1 < (c_{dH} + c_{dL})/2 + c_r$	$s \leq \underline{s}, s \geq \bar{s}$	$f \to \alpha_u^* \to f \to i$ or n
X. $[\alpha_u^{**}; a, (a, \ldots, f); (i, \ldots, n)]$	$c_d \geq (c_{dH} + c_{dL})/2$	p_2–$p_1 < (c_{dH} + c_{dL})/2 + c_r$	$\underline{s} < s < \bar{s}$	$a \to \alpha_u^{**} \to a \to i(s = 0)^{(+)}$
XI. $[\alpha_u^{**}; f, (a, \ldots, f); (i, \ldots, n)]$	p_1–$p_2 + (c_{dH} + c_{dL})/2 \leq c_d < (c_{dH} + c_{dL})/2$	p_2–$p_1 < (c_{dH} + c_{dL})/2 + c_r$	$\underline{s} < s < \bar{s}$	$f \to \alpha_u^{**} \to a \to i(s = 0)$
XII. $[\alpha_u^{**}; f, (a, \ldots, f); (i, \ldots, n)]$	$c_d < p_1$–$p_2 + (c_{dH} + c_{dL})/2$	p_2–$p_1 < (c_{dH} + c_{dL})/2 + c_r$	$\underline{s} < s < \bar{s}$	$f \to \alpha_u^{**} \to f \to i(s = 0)$

Note: $\underline{s} = (c_{dH} + c_r - [(c_{dH} - c_{dL})\{c_{dH} + c_{dL} + 2c_r - 2(p_2 - p_1)\}]^{(1/2)})/\gamma$, $\bar{s} = (c_{dH} + c_r + [(c_{dH} - c_{dL})\{c_{dH} + c_{dL} + 2c_r - 2(p_2 - p_1)\}]^{(1/2)})/\gamma$. (+), which is added at the end of the equilibrium paths in the last column, indicates the equilibrium paths that reach peace. For the players' beliefs, see the Appendix

c_{dH} in CQ_2) before the game starts. The cost burden of fighting indicates the degree to which the declining actor is resolved to fight. That is, smaller costs of fighting imply that the declining actor has a firmer resolve to fight.

The equilibria in this version of our model are described in Table 6.1 (see the Appendix for the full description of equilibrium analysis).

In terms of the effects of uncertainty about costs of war, three suggestions can be obtained from the analysis in Table 6.1. First, the base proposition argues that when no third-party intervener exists, fighting between competing domestic actors is unavoidable. However, when uncertainty about costs of war exists, peace is possible even if the domestic actors consider that no third party joins (i.e., $\gamma = 0$). Equilibrium I indicates that when the declining actor's resolve is weak (i.e., $c_d \geq p_2 - p_1 + (\gamma s + c_{dH} - c_r)/2$), the uncertainty about its resolve to fight allows peace to be maintained.

Proposition 4 In situations in which declining parties are weak-willed and uncertainty about their costs of fighting exists, fights between competing domestic parties are avoidable even if domestic actors do not believe that a third party will intervene.

Second, the base proposition argues that if the third party always intervenes, fighting between domestic actors is avoidable. However, when uncertainty about costs of war exists, there are cases in which peace is difficult to achieve even if the domestic actors are sure of the guarantor's intervention (i.e., $\gamma = 1$, which is included in the case of $\gamma \neq 0$ in Table 6.1). If the declining actor is firmly resolved (i.e., $c_d < p_2 - p_1 + (\gamma s + c_{dH} - c_r)/2$ in equilibria V, VI, VIII, and IX or $c_d < (c_{dH} + c_{dL})/2$ in equilibria in XI and XII), convincing the domestic actors of third-party intervention does not lead to peace.

Proposition 5 In situations in which uncertainty exists about the costs of fighting, a third-party guarantor fails to prevent fights initiated by firmly resolved declining parties even if third-party intervention is certain and the competing domestic parties are sure of it.

Finally, the earlier arguments indicate that when the rising actor induced by commitment problems reneges on its initial promise, no peace is attainable. However, when uncertainty about costs of war exists, the declining actor whose resolve is weak may accept the rising actor's revised terms in R_1, α_u^*, and no fight occurs in some cases (i.e., $c_d \geq p_2 - p_1 + (\gamma s + c_{dH} - c_r)/2$ in equilibria I, IV, and VII).

Proposition 6 In situations in which uncertainty exists about the costs of fighting, even if commitment problems occur and rising parties renege on their promises, fights can be avoided when declining parties are weak-willed.

6.7 Protracted Conflicts

Thus far, we find that third-party guarantors are successful in preventing wars in complete information settings, while third parties who face uncertainties might fail to do so. The remaining question is how long the realization of peace will be prolonged once wars have occurred due to uncertainties. This section addresses this question. In order to capture the cycles of fighting and renegotiations in civil conflicts, consider that after domestic actors fight with each other following D_1 or D_2, the game returns to the first move; D_1 and renegotiation processes begin. This expanded model, which is solved numerically, comprises the following moves[14]:

Premove The rising actor's subjective probability for the declining actor's costs of war is set to c_d^r. For simplicity, c_d^r is uniformly distributed over the interval [0, 1]. The rising actor presents pre-negotiation proposal α_w^{**}, where $\alpha_w^{**} = p_1 + c_d^r$ if $p_1 + c_d^r \leq 1$ or $\alpha_w^{**} = 1$ if $p_1 + c_d^r > 1$.

D

$\boldsymbol{D_1}$: *The declining actor's response to the rising actor's pre-negotiation proposal.*

Case $\boldsymbol{D_{11}}$ If α_w^{**} exceeds the acceptance threshold of the declining actor (i.e., $\alpha_w^{**} > p_1 + c_d$, where c_d is the declining actor's true costs), then the declining actor rejects the proposal and begins fighting. The result of fighting is determined using probability p_1. That is, the declining actor prevails in fights with probability $1–p_1$. If the declining actor prevails, p_1 is favorably updated by setting it to a uniformly distributed number from $[0, p_1]$. On the other hand, if the rising actor prevails, p_1 is set to a uniformly distributed number from $[p_1, 1]$. Then, the cycle returns to the Premove.

Case $\boldsymbol{D_{12}}$ If α_w^{**} does not exceed the threshold of the declining actor's acceptance (i.e., $\alpha_w^{**} \leq p_1 + c_d$), then the declining actor considers whether or not the third-party guarantor will truly intervene. The declining actor's decision depends on the amount of sanctions required by the guarantor $s_w \in [0, 1]$, where $s_w = \alpha_w^* - \alpha_w^{**}$, $\alpha_w^{**} = p_1 + c_d^r$ if $p_1 + c_d^r \leq 1$ or $\alpha_w^{**} = 1$ if$p_1 + c_d^r > 1$, $\alpha_w^* = p_2 + c_d^r$ if $p_2 + c_d^r \leq 1$ or $\alpha_w^* = 1$ if $p_2 + c_d^r > 1$, $s_w \neq s = \alpha^* - \alpha^{**}$, and $s_w \neq s_u = \alpha_u^* - \alpha_u^{**}$. The

[14]Although models that incorporate discount factors are usually employed when games are repeated, we do not use this approach in this section. Instead of using standard game theoretic models, this section adopts an agent-based model. Typically, discount factors are employed in order to investigate whether or not actors' long-term time horizons affect results. For example, the iterated prisoner's dilemma indicates that longsighted actors are more likely to cooperate than shortsighted ones. Players' time horizons may certainly be important. However, this chapter's purpose is to investigate the effects of third parties' presence, not those of long-term time horizons, on peace and war. Therefore, although time horizons may also influence peace and war, this chapter focuses on the third party's effects by not incorporating discount factors; it thus avoids confusing the effects of the two variables (i.e., third parties and time horizons) in the analysis. This approach is similar to the one adopted by Axelrod's (1984) repeated prisoner's dilemma competition, which does not use discount factors and focuses on the effects of different strategies on payoffs. See Yamamoto (2009) for another dynamic agent-based model for analyzing commitment problems by using a computer simulation.

amount of s_w indicates the size of the burden borne by the guarantor. That is, larger values of s_w imply heavier burdens for the guarantor. Therefore, larger s_w values imply that the implementation of sanctions by the guarantor is less credible. The declining actor begins a fight with probability s_w. If a fight occurs, the result of the fighting is determined by the same procedure as used in D_{11}, and the process returns to the Premove. Otherwise, the process proceeds to R_1.

$\boldsymbol{R_1}$: *The rising actor's decision at the formal negotiations.* If the rising actor believes that the third-party guarantor will actually impose sanctions s_w, it proposes α_w^{**}. Otherwise, it proposes α_w^{*}. The rising actor's decision also depends on the credibility of the potential intervention and is determined by the probability s_w. After the rising actor proposes either α_w^{**} or α_w^{*}, the process proceeds to D_2.

$\boldsymbol{D_2}$: *The final decision by the declining actor.* If the rising actor proposes α_w^{**}, peace is reached because both domestic actors have accepted this plan. As a result, no sanctions are imposed by the third-party guarantor, and the game ends. On the other hand, if the rising actor proposes α_w^{*}, the process proceeds to I.[15]

$\boldsymbol{I}$: *The decision made by the third-party guarantor.* The third party intervenes with probability $1–s_w$. That is, the lower the burden for intervention, the more likely the third party is to intervene. If it intervenes, peace is realized, and the game ends. If not, the value of p_1 is set to p_2, and the cycle returns to the Premove.

The game repeats until it finally ends in either D_2 or I. The model has three parameters: c_d, p_s, and λ. c_d controls the declining actor's true costs of war. p_s is the initial value of p_2. λ controls the magnitude of power shifts from the declining actor to the rising one. Specifically, p_1 is given by $p_1 = \lambda p_2$, where $\lambda \in (0,\ 1)$. Therefore, smaller values of λ imply larger shifts of power from the declining actor to the rising one. A total of 100 runs were collected for each combination of the parameters.[16]

Figure 6.3 indicates the number of times the game repeats in each run. *MR* in the z-axis is the mean of repetitions of 100 runs.

Two characteristics of the results are observed in the figure. The first is that smaller values of λ cause larger values of *MR*. In other words, larger shifts in power prolong conflicts. This is caused by two mechanisms. First, since, given a p_2 value, smaller values of λ provide smaller values of p_1, smaller values of λ imply greater burdens borne by the guarantor. Therefore, smaller values of λ enhance the probability of the declining actor's rejection of the negotiations in D_1, the rising actor's proposal of α_w^{*} in R_1, and the third party's unwillingness to impose sanctions in I. Due to these factors, protracted conflicts are more likely to accompany decreasing values of λ. Second, since smaller values of λ decrease the values of p_1, smaller values of λ enhance the likelihood of the declining actor's victory in D_1. Once the declining actor prevails, it is more likely that the declining actor will win again in later rounds, because its victory further decreases the values of p_1 and thereby

[15]Since the declining actor concluded at D_1 that the third-party guarantor's promise to intervene would be fulfilled, it again chooses not to fight at this move.

[16]The source code of the model is written in Java.

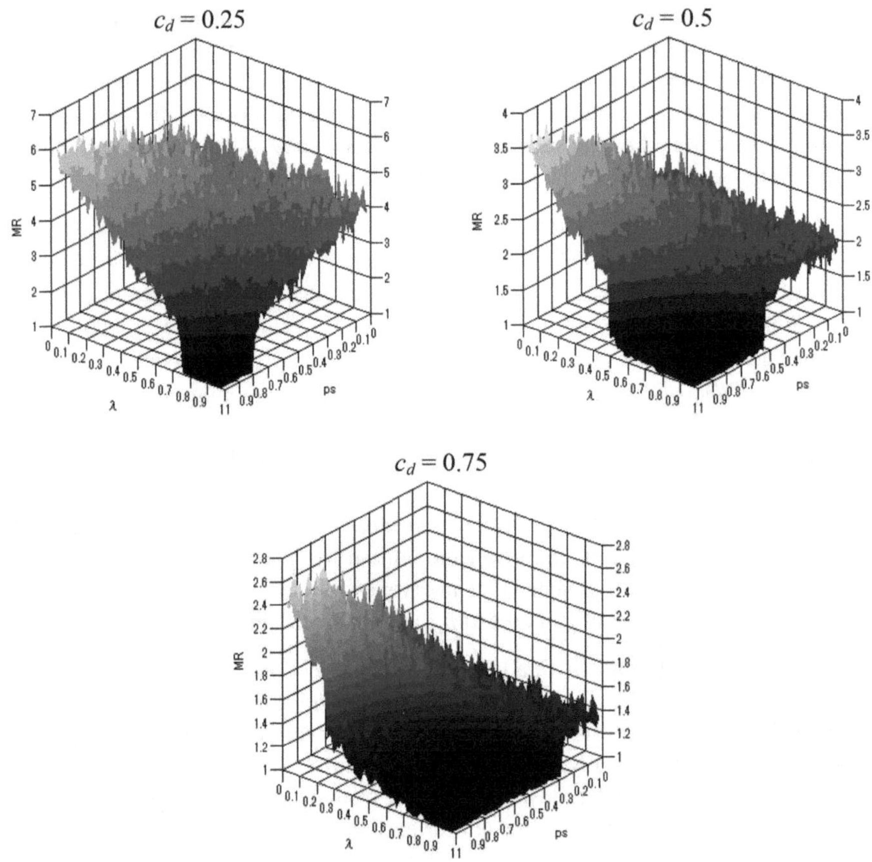

Fig. 6.3 The effect of power shifts on the duration of conflict

continues to enhance the probability of future wins. Due to this cycle, the declining actor increasingly becomes belligerent, and warfare is repeatedly chosen in D_1. On the other hand, larger values of λ increase the values of p_1 and thereby enhance the probability of the declining actor's defeat in D_1. Once the declining actor is defeated, it is more likely that it loses in later rounds due to the opposite logic that applies to cases in which values of λ are smaller. A series of defeats eventually forces the declining actor to concede and accept any demands made by the rising actor (i.e., $p_1 + c_d^r > 1$). As a result, the game ends in an agreement that is reached with the declining actor's complete concession.

Implication 1: The larger the power shift involved, the longer a civil conflict continues.

The second characteristic is that smaller values of c_d produce larger values of *MR*. Smaller values of c_d imply firmer resolve of the declining actor to fight. Meanwhile, smaller values of c_d enhance the probability that c_d^r exceeds c_d. Therefore, when the

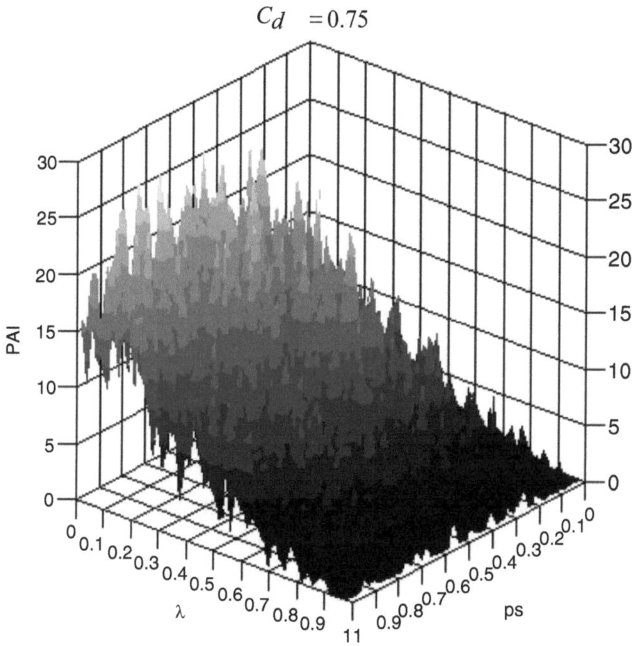

Fig. 6.4 The effect of power shifts on intervention

declining actor's resolve is firm, the rising actor tends to underestimate the declining actor's true resolve $\left(c_d^r > c_d\right)$. As a result, with smaller values of c_d, the rising actor is more likely to propose an excessive demand; thereby, the declining actor is likely to reject the proposal, and thus fighting continues.

Implication 2: The firmer the declining actor's resolve, the longer a civil conflict continues.

Next, we analyze how the dynamics in the model influence the role of the third-party guarantor. Figure 6.4 indicates the relation between λ, p_s, and the number of agreements realized through intervention (*PAI*). More specifically, *PAI* indicates the number of runs in which a settlement is reached through the third-party guarantor's intervention in *I*.[17] As Fig. 6.4 indicates, smaller values of λ increase the overall value of *PAI* if c_d is sufficiently large.

Large values of c_d imply that the declining actor's true resolve is weak, and, in contrast to the cases in which values of c_d are smaller, there is greater probability that c_d exceeds c_d^r. Therefore, in these cases, the rising actor tends to overestimate the declining actor's resolve and propose a more modest demand than it actually can. Meanwhile, larger values of λ reduce the burden borne by the guarantor, and the

[17]Since the total number of runs for each combination of parameters is 100, the maximum value of *PAI* is 100.

credibility of intervention increases. Therefore, when both c_d and λ are large, a negotiated settlement without intervention in D_2 is more likely to occur through the combination of modest demands made by the rising actor and domestic actors' confidence in intervention. On the other hand, if values of λ are smaller, intervention becomes more burdensome. As a result, even if the declining actor accepts a modest division proposal by the rising actor in D_1, the latter is more likely to renege on the earlier promise and advance α_w^* in R_1. Consequently, the game is more likely to proceed to *I*, where the third party will be forced to implement sanctions.

Implication 3: In situations in which the declining actor has weak resolve, the larger the power shift, the more important a third-party intervention becomes.

6.8 Conclusion

Although the assumption of complete information illuminates important aspects of civil conflicts, a number of conflicts are plagued by uncertainties. Formal models that address domestic resource division problems need to consider such uncertainties. In contrast to Ishiguro's (2010) argument, even if third parties are involved in civil conflicts, these conflicts are more likely to lead to war when uncertainties exist. This study demonstrates that uncertainties about third-party intervention and those about the costs of war induce declining actors to begin preventive wars. In addition, it reveals that large shifts of power and firm resolve of declining actors in conditions of uncertainty allow protracted conflicts to emerge.

These results suggest several policy implications for achieving successful intervention by third-party guarantors. First, foreign actors who have already decided to be involved in disputes should avoid ambiguity and express the clearest possible commitment. Second, third parties should also present themselves as firmly resolved interveners, even if that is not the case. Third, establishing close communication with domestic actors is also important so that uncertainty about domestic actors' resolve is reduced and the true intentions of declining players who have a firm resolve are shared among the relevant parties. Fourth, measures that can promote the declining actors' choice to pursue cooperative and peaceful approaches would be useful for preventing conflicts from becoming bogged down and protracted. Finally, the role of foreign actors is even more important when conflicts evolve with weak-willed declining actors. Thus, combining models of complete information with those incorporating uncertainty allows us to more comprehensively investigate the role of third-party guarantors in resource division problems in civil conflicts.[18]

[18] Although some of the above policy implications suggest that third parties are required to keep enforcing agreements that reflect the balance of power before the shift in power, as Werner and Yuen (2005) and Beardsley (2008) argued, intervention may be difficult to continue in the long term. Addressing this potential problem should be the next step for research along this study's lines.

Acknowledgments Kazuya Yamamoto, Masayuki Tadokoro and Yoshihiro Shima for their helpful comments.

Appendix: Equilibrium Analysis in Section 6.6

Before the game starts, the rising actor believes that the declining actor's costs of fighting are uniformly distributed between c_{dL} and c_{dH}. The probability density function of the costs is $1/(c_{dH}–c_{dL})$. Therefore, the rising actor's expected value for the declining actor's payoffs in CQ_3 is

$$\int_{c_{dL}}^{c_{dH}} (1 - p_1 - x) \cdot \frac{1}{c_{dH} - c_{dL}} \mathrm{dx} = 1 - p_1 - \frac{c_{dL} + c_{dH}}{2} \tag{6.A1}$$

Thus, consider that the game starts with the rising actor's pre-negotiation offer that is equal to (6.A1)= $1 - \alpha_u^{**}$, where

$$\alpha_u^{**} = p_1 + \frac{c_{dL} + c_{dH}}{2}$$

(i) The Rising Actor's Move

If R_1 is reached, the rising actor that observed the declining actor's decision in D_1 to participate in the negotiations updates its belief about the declining actor's costs of war to the interval $[(c_{dL} + c_{dH})/2, c_{dH}]$. Based on the updated belief, the rising actor in R_1 maximizes its expected utility, $EU^r(\alpha)$, where $\alpha \in [0, 1]$.

(i-a) The case where $\alpha \in [0, \alpha_u^{**}]$. Because $1–\alpha$ is greater than $1–p_2–c_d$, the rising actor expects that the declining actor in D_2 always chooses to acquiesce. In addition, when the rising actor presents $\alpha \in [0, p_1 + (c_{dL} + c_{dH})/2 (= \alpha_u^{**})]$, it abides by the initial promise, and no sanctions are imposed by the third party. Thus, the maximized value of $EU^r(\alpha)$ is

$$\mathrm{EU}^r(\alpha_u^{**}) = \alpha_u^{**} = p_1 + \frac{c_{dL} + c_{dH}}{2} \tag{6.A2}$$

(i-b) The case where $\alpha \in [\alpha_u^{**}, p_2 + (c_{dL} + c_{dH})/2]$. In this case, although the declining actor chooses to acquiesce in D_2, α presented by the rising actor exceeds the amount of α_u^{**}. As a result, the third party in I may impose sanctions against the rising actor. Therefore, $EU^r(\alpha)$ is $(1–\gamma)\alpha + \gamma(\alpha–s) = \alpha–\gamma s$. Thus, the maximized value of this function is

$$\mathrm{EU}^r(\alpha_u^{*}) = p_2 + \frac{c_{dL} + c_{dH}}{2} - \gamma s \tag{6.A3}$$

where $\alpha_u^{*} = p_2 + (c_{dL} + c_{dH})/2$.

(i-c) The case where $\alpha \in [p_2 + (c_{dL} + c_{dH})/2, p_2 + c_{dH}]$. Because the rising actor's belief about the declining actor's costs is uniformly distributed between $(c_{dL} + c_{dH})/2$ and c_{dH}, the cumulative distribution function of the declining actor's costs that are believed by the rising actor is $F(x) = \{x-(c_{dL} + c_{dH})/2\}/\{c_{dH}-(c_{dL} + c_{dH})/2\}$. Therefore, $EU^r(\alpha)$ is written as

$$\mathrm{EU}^r(\alpha) = \left(1 - \frac{\alpha - p_2 - \frac{c_{dL}+c_{dH}}{2}}{c_{dH} - \frac{c_{dL}+c_{dH}}{2}}\right)[(1-\gamma)\alpha + \gamma(\alpha - s)]$$
$$+ \frac{\alpha - p_2 - \frac{c_{dL}+c_{dH}}{2}}{c_{dH} - \frac{c_{dL}+c_{dH}}{2}}(p_2 - c_r)$$

The first-order condition for this quadratic function is $d(\mathrm{EU}^r(\alpha))/d\alpha = (-4\alpha + 2\gamma s + 4p_2 + 2c_{dH} - 2c_r)/(c_{dH}-c_{dL}) = 0$. Rewritten, this is

$$\alpha_u^* = p_2 + \frac{\gamma s + c_{dH} - c_r}{2}.$$

The second-order condition is $d^2(\mathrm{EU}^r(\alpha))/d\alpha^2 = 4/(c_{dL}-c_{dH})$, which is always less than zero. Hence, substituting α_u^*, the maximized value of $\mathrm{EU}^r(\alpha)$ is

$$\mathrm{EU}^r\left(\alpha_u^*\right) = p_2 + \frac{\gamma^2 s^2 - 2c_{dH}\gamma s - 2c_r\gamma s + c_{dH}^2 + c_r^2 + 2c_{dL}c_r}{2(c_{dH} - c_{dL})} \tag{6.A4}$$

(i-d) The case where $\alpha \in [p_2 + c_{dH}, 1]$.The rising actor expects that the declining actor in D_2 always chooses to fight. Therefore, the maximized valuse of $\mathrm{EU}^r(\alpha)$ is

$$\mathrm{EU}^r\left(\alpha_u^*\right) = p_2 - c_r \tag{6.A5}$$

where $\forall\alpha_u^* \in [p_2 + c_{dH}, 1]$.

Comparing (6.A3) and (6.A4),

$$\left(p_2 + \frac{\gamma^2 s^2 - 2c_{dH}\gamma s - 2c_r\gamma s + c_{dH}^2 + c_r^2 + 2c_{dL}c_r}{2(c_{dH} - c_{dL})}\right) - \left(p_2 + \frac{c_{dL} + c_{dH}}{2} - \gamma s\right)$$
$$= (\gamma s - c_r - c_{dL})^2 \geq 0.$$

Thus, (6.A4)≥(6.A3) is always satisfied. Similarly, comparing (6.A4) and (6.A5),

$$\left(p_2 + \frac{\gamma^2 s^2 - 2c_{dH}\gamma s - 2c_r\gamma s + c_{dH}^2 + c_r^2 + 2c_{dL}c_r}{2(c_{dH} - c_{dL})}\right) - (p_2 - c_r)$$
$$= (\gamma s - c_r - c_{dH})^2 \geq 0.$$

Therefore, (6.A4) ≥(6.A5) is also always satisfied. Hence, the rising actor in R_1 always prefers (6.A4) to (6.A3) and (6.A5). (Assume that (6.A4) is preferred when the equalities are satisfied.) Meanwhile, setting Eqs. (6.A4)– (6.A2) = 0 generates

$$\left(p_2 + \frac{\gamma^2 s^2 - 2c_{dH}\gamma s - 2c_r\gamma s + c_{dH}^2 + c_r^2 + 2c_{dL}c_r}{2(c_{dH} - c_{dL})}\right) - \left(p_1 + \frac{c_{dL} + c_{dH}}{2}\right)$$
$$= \gamma^2 s^2 - 2(c_{dH} + c_r)\gamma s + c_r^2 + 2c_{dL}c_r + 2(p_2 - p_1)(c_{dH} - c_{dL}) + c_{dL}^2 = 0.$$

When $\gamma = 0$, the left side of the above equation is always positive. Therefore, (6. A4) > (6.A2) always holds in this case. Meanwhile, when $\gamma \neq 0$, if the discriminant of the quadratic polynomial with respect to s (i.e., $\gamma^2(c_{dH}-c_{dL})[c_{dH} + c_{dL} + 2c_r-2(p_2-p_1)]$) is equal or negative, (6.A4) ≥ (6.A2) is always satisfied (assume that (6.A4) is preferred when the equality is satisfied). Therefore, if $c_{dH} + c_{dL} + 2c_r-2(p_2-p_1) \leq 0$, which is rewritten as

$$p_2 - p_1 \geq \frac{(c_{dH} + c_{dL})}{2} + c_r \tag{6.A6}$$

(6.A4) ≥ (6.A2) always holds. In contrast, if (6.A6) is not satisfied, (6.A4) ≥ (6.A2) holds only when $s \leq \underline{s}$ or $s \geq \bar{s}$, where

$$\underline{s} = c_{dH} + c_r - \frac{\left[(c_{dH} - c_{dL})\left\{c_{dH} + c_{dL} + 2c_r - 2(p_2 - p_1)\right\}\right]^{\frac{1}{2}}}{\gamma},$$
$$\bar{s} = c_{dH} + c_r + \frac{\left[(c_{dH} - c_{dL})\left\{c_{dH} + c_{dL} + 2c_r - 2(p_2 - p_1)\right\}\right]^{\frac{1}{2}}}{\gamma}.$$

$(c_{dH} + c_r)^2-(c_{dH}-c_{dL})\{c_{dH} + c_{dL} + 2c_r-2(p_2-p_1)\}$ yields $c_r^2 + c_{dL}^2 + 2(p_2-p_1)(c_{dH}-c_{dL})$, which is always greater than zero. Because $\left[(c_{dH} - c_{dL})\left\{c_{dH} + c_{dL} + 2c_r - 2(p_2 - p_1)\right\}\right]^{\frac{1}{2}} > 0$ and $c_{dH} + c_r > 0, c_{dH} + c_r > \left[(c_{dH} - c_{dL})\left\{c_{dH} + c_{dL} + 2c_r - 2(p_2 - p_1)\right\}\right]^{\frac{1}{2}}$ also holds. Hence, $\underline{s} > 0$.

Overall, the rising actor in R_1 chooses

$$\alpha_u^* = p_2 + \frac{\gamma s + c_{dH} - c_r}{2} \tag{6.A7}$$

if (I) $\gamma = 0$, (II) $\gamma \neq 0$ and $p_2 - p_1 \geq \frac{(c_{dH}+c_{dL})}{2} + c_r$, (III) $\gamma \neq 0$, $p_2 - p_1 < \frac{(c_{dH}+c_{dL})}{2} + c_r$, and $s \leq \underline{s}$, or if (IV) $\gamma \neq 0$, $p_2 - p_1 < \frac{(c_{dH}+c_{dL})}{2} + c_r$, and $s \geq \bar{s}$. Meanwhile, it chooses

$$\alpha_u^{**} = p_1 + \frac{c_{dL} + c_{dH}}{2} \tag{6.A8}$$

if $\gamma \neq 0$, $p_2 - p_1 < \frac{(c_{dH}+c_{dL})}{2} + c_r$, and $\underline{s} < s < \bar{s}$.

(ii) The Declining Actor's Moves

When the rising actor's proposal in R_1 is (6.A7), the declining actor in D_2 chooses to acquiesce if $1 - p_2 - (\gamma s + c_{dH} - c_r)/2 \geq 1 - p_2 - c_d$, which is rewritten as

$$c_d \geq \frac{\gamma s + c_{dH} - c_r}{2} \tag{6.A9}$$

Otherwise, it chooses to fight in D_2. By contrast, when the proposal is (6.A8), the declining actor chooses to acquiesce in D_2 if $1 - p_1 - (c_{dH} + c_{dL})/2 \geq 1 - p_2 - c_d$, which is rewritten as

$$c_d \geq p_1 - p_2 + \frac{c_{dH} + c_{dL}}{2} \tag{6.A10}$$

Otherwise, it chooses to fight.

Meanwhile, the declining actor that anticipates (6.A7) and whose costs satisfy (6.A9) chooses to accept in D_1 if $1 - p_2 - (\gamma s + c_{dH} - c_r)/2 \geq 1 - p_1 - c_d$, which is rewritten as

$$c_d \geq p_2 - p_1 + \frac{\gamma s + c_{dH} - c_r}{2}.$$

Otherwise, it chooses to fight. By contrast, the declining actor that anticipates (6.A7) but whose costs do not satisfy (6.A9) chooses to fight in D_1, because $1{-}p_2{-}c_d < 1{-}p_1{-}c_d$ is always satisfied. Meanwhile, the declining actor that anticipates (6.A8) and whose costs satisfy (6.A10) chooses to accept in D_1 if $1 - p_1 - (c_{dH} + c_{dL})/2 \geq 1 - p_1 - c_d$, which is rewritten as

$$c_d \geq \frac{c_{dH} + c_{dL}}{2}.$$

Otherwise, it chooses to fight. Alternatively, the declining actor that anticipates (6.A8) but whose costs do not satisfy (6.A10) chooses to fight in D_1 because $1{-}p_2{-}c_d < 1{-}p_1{-}c_d$ is always satisfied.

In sum, in the case of (6.A7), the declining actor chooses (f, f) if $c_d < (\gamma s + c_{dH} - c_r)/2$, (f, a) if $(\gamma s + c_{dH} - c_r)/2 \leq c_d < p_2 - p_1 + (\gamma s + c_{dH} - c_r)/2$, and (a, a) if $c_d \geq p_2 - p_1 + (\gamma s + c_{dH} - c_r)/2$. Meantime, in the case of (6.A8), it chooses (f, f) if $c_d < p_1{-}p_2 + (c_{dH} + c_{dL})/2$, (f, a) if $p_1 - p_2 + (c_{dH} + c_{dL})/2 \leq c_d < (c_{dH} + c_{dL})/2$, and (a, a) if $c_d \geq (c_{dH} + c_{dL})/2$. Actions in the parentheses are those in D_1 and D_2, respectively.

(iii) The Third-Party Actor's Move

The third-party actor in I who observed the declining actor's acceptance in D_1 and D_2 updates its belief about the declining actor's costs of war. When the rising actor's proposal in R_1 is (6.A7), the third party who observed that the declining actor prefers $1 - \alpha_u^*$ to both $1{-}p_2{-}c_d$ and $1{-}p_1{-}c_d$ updates its belief to the interval $[(\gamma s + c_{dH}{-}c_r)/2 + p_2{-}p_1, c_{dH}]$. Similarly, when the proposal is (6.A8), the third party who observed that the declining actor prefers $1 - \alpha_u^{**}$ to both $1–p_2–c_d$ and $1–p_1–c_d$ updates its belief to $[(c_{dH} + c_{dL})/2, c_{dH}]$.

If the proposal is α_u^*, the third party whose preference is $\Pi_a - \varepsilon s \geq \Pi_n$ decides to impose sanctions (i), whereas those who prefer Π_n to $\Pi_a–\varepsilon s$ choose to defect (n). Meanwhile, if the official proposal is α_u^{**}, the third party is not required to impose sanctions, and $s = 0$.

Taken all together, the equilibria described in Table 6.1 are obtained

References

Allison G (2017) Destined for war: can America and China escape Thucydides's trap? Houghton Mifflin Harcourt, Boston

Axelrod R (1984) The evolution of cooperation. Basic Books, New York

Beardsley K (2008) Agreement without peace? International mediation and time inconsistency problems. Am J Polit Sci 52(4):723–740

Carment D, Dane R (1998) Three's company: evaluating third-party intervention in intrastate conflict. J Confl Resolut 42(5):572–599

Cetinyan R (2002) Ethnic bargaining in the shadow of third-party intervention. Int Organ 56 (3):645–677

Ero C (2003) Sierra Leone: the legacies of authoritarianism and political violence. In: Cawthra G, Luckham R (eds) Governing insecurity: democratic control of military and security establishments in transitional democracies. Zed Books, London, pp 232–253

Fearon JD (1995) Rationalist explanations for war. Int Organ 49(3):379–414

Fearon JD (1998) Commitment problems and the spread of ethnic conflict. In: Lake DA, Rothchild DS (eds) The international spread of ethnic conflict: fear, diffusion, and escalation. Princeton University Press, Princeton, pp 107–126

Fortna VP, Martin LL (2009) Peacekeepers as signals: the demand for international peacekeeping in civil war. In: Milner HV, Moravcsik A (eds) Power, interdependence, and nonstate actors in world politics. Princeton University Press, Princeton, pp 87–107

Gilpin R (1981) War and change in world politics. Cambridge University Press, Cambridge

Grigoryan A (2010) Third-party intervention and the escalation of state-minority conflicts. Int Stud Q 54(4):1143–1174

Ishiguro K (2007) *Nyumon kokusaiseijikeizai no bunseki* [introduction to the study of international political economy]. Keiso Shobo, Tokyo

Ishiguro K (2010) *Insenchibu na kokusaiseijigaku* [incentive analysis of international politics]. Nihon Hyoron Sha, Tokyo

Kennedy P (1987) The rise and fall of the great powers. Random House, New York

Kydd A (2003) Which side are you on? Bias, credibility and mediation. Am J Polit Sci 47 (4):597–611

Kydd A (2006) When can mediators build trust. Am Polit Sci Rev 100(3):449–462

Modelski G (1987) Long cycle in world politics. Macmillan, London

Organski AFK (1968) World politics, 2nd edn. Knopf, New York

Powell R (1999) In the shadow of the power: states and strategies in international politics. Princeton University Press, Princeton

Powell R (2004) The inefficient use of power: costly conflict with complete information. Am Polit Sci Rev 98(2):231–241

Powell R (2006) War as a commitment problem. Int Organ 60(1):169–203

Ramsbotham O, Woodhouse T, Miall H (2005) Contemporary conflict resolution: the prevention, management and transformation of deadly conflicts, 2nd edn. Polity, Cambridge

Rauchhaus RW (2006) Asymmetric information, mediation, and conflict management. World Polit 58:207–241

Richards P, Vincent J (2008) Sierra Leone: marginalization of the RUF. In: De Zeeuw J (ed) From soldiers to politicians: transforming rebel movements after civil war. Lynne Rienner, Boulder, pp 81–102

Smith A (1996) To intervene or not to intervene: a biased decision. J Confl Resolut 40(1):16–40

Smith A, Stam A (2003) Mediation and peacekeeping in a random walk model of civil and interstate war. Int Stud Rev 5(4):115–135

Tingley DH (2011) The dark side of the future: an experimental test of commitment problems in bargaining. Int Stud Q 55(2):521–544

Walter BF (2002) Committing to peace: the successful settlement of civil wars. Princeton University Press, Princeton

Werner S (2000) Deterring intervention: the stakes of war and third-party involvement. Am J Polit Sci 44(4):720–732

Werner S, Yuen A (2005) Making and keeping peace. Int Organ 59(2):261–292

Yamamoto K (2009) Kokunai Funso to Kokusai Kainyu no Doteki Bunseki [The dynamics of intrastate conflict and international intervention]. In: Yoshida K, Ihori I, Sejima M (eds) *Chikyu Chitsujo no Shimyureishon Bunseki* [The numerical analysis of global order]. Nihon Hyoron Sha, Tokyo, pp 189–205

Chapter 7
Public Opinion and Foreign Policy: The Effect of Information Stimulus on Levels of Support for Foreign Aid and Coalition Withdrawal

Yoshitaka Komiya, Mari Miyagawa, and Atsushi Tago

Abstract The chapter uses two survey experiments to see how information stimulus can change public perception on two key foreign policy instruments: *foreign aid* and *military coalition*. Foreign aid is financed by tax revenue and must be supported by a wide range of general public to continue. In a similar vein, use of force abroad needs public support, and this is especially true in democracies. To conduct comparative survey experiments on these two foreign policy instruments, Japan was selected as a field of experiment. This is because the country is an interesting case due to its constitutional prohibition of using force abroad and heavy reliance on foreign aid as a means to exercise its influence abroad. We take advantage of this unique setting and reveal how political information can change the level of public support for key foreign policy agendas.

Keywords Public opinion · Survey experiment · Foreign aid · Use of force · Coalition of the willing

7.1 Introduction

A state leader needs domestic backing in order to achieve key foreign policies. This is particularly true among democracies and when the policy in question needs the engagement of significant resources. A notable literature on audience costs has emerged (see, e.g., Schultz 1999, 2001a, b) exploring the connection between public backing and foreign policy. Additionally, following Michael Tomz's seminal work on audience costs (Tomz 2007), recent scholarly efforts have emphasized the importance of using *survey experiments* to study how public backing can be secured.

Y. Komiya · A. Tago (✉)
Graduate School of Law, Kobe University, Kobe, Hyogo, Japan
e-mail: tago@dragon.kobe-u.ac.jp

M. Miyagawa
Graduate School of Arts and Sciences, University of Tokyo, Komaba, Tokyo, Japan

M. Tadokoro et al. (eds.), *Emerging Risks in a World of Heterogeneity*, Evolutionary Economics and Social Complexity Science 10,
https://doi.org/10.1007/978-981-10-7968-9_7

Indeed, there are many articles examining how public support for a particular foreign engagement policy can be secured by providing information stimuli.

In this study, we join such a rising research trend of using survey experiments and conduct two different experimental studies to see how information stimulus can change public perception on two key foreign policy instruments: *foreign aid* and *military coalition*.

Foreign aid is financed by tax revenue and must be supported by a wide range of general public to continue. Accordingly, when people believe that industrial nations are facing economic difficulties, the provision of foreign aid to less developed countries is subject to more criticism. Given such attacks on aid, public perception of foreign aid is one of the key research areas of studies on public opinion and foreign policy (see, e.g., Milner and Tingley 2013). In a similar vein, public perception toward military coalition participation is also an important issue, due to casualty sensitiveness of the general public (e.g., Gelpi et al. 2009). The two foreign policy instruments share a similarity in terms of the necessity of generating public support for securing a successful implementation.

To conduct comparative survey experiments on these two foreign policy instruments, Japan was selected as a field of experiment. This is because the country is a unique case due to its constitutional prohibition of using force abroad. The post-WWII constitution of Japan prohibits threats and the use of force as means of settling international disputes. This has meant that economic aid has been the only major instrument which Japan can use to engage with foreign countries for a long time. Accordingly, domestic audiences should have a high shared consensus on the aid policy, and thus it may be difficult to change perceptions by a single stimulus in a survey experiment.

By contrast, the use of force, which used to be strictly prohibited before the end of Cold War, is now becoming a realistic option as a foreign engagement instrument. Prime Minister Shinzo Abe has engaged in a major national security policy reform in the summer of 2015. With a new law, it is becoming an actual policy choice for Japan to send its military troops abroad, especially as a part of US-led military coalitions. It is possible that information stimuli may easily affect the perception of people on the newly emerged foreign engagement instrument since it is yet a hypothetical stage and people cannot yet fully form their opinions. Expectation of people would vary widely for a new policy choice.

Our experiments in Japan thus enable us to do an interesting comparison of a traditional instrument (foreign aid) and a new instrument (the use of force). We are going to proceed this chapter first by focusing on foreign aid and public opinion. After that, we will focus on the relationship between military coalition and public perception. For both cases, an original survey experiment is used to reveal how we can change the perception of people toward key foreign policy agendas.

7.2 Foreign Aid and Public Opinion

7.2.1 *Literature Review*

Before the Vietnam War, scholars believed that public opinion was unstable and unstructured, meaning that it did not provide sufficient foundations for effective foreign policy; therefore, it was not taken seriously as a key factor to influence foreign policy (Lippmann 1925; Almond 1956; Holsti 1992). However, seeing the power of the antiwar movement in the late 1960s, scholars started to change their mind and admitted that the US government unavoidably decided to withdraw from Vietnam due to the public antiwar opinion. For instance, some studies argued that public opinion is likely formed rationally (Hurwitz and Peffley 1987; Shapiro and Page 1988) and has a clear impact on foreign policy (Holsti 1992; Kuklinski and Quirk 2000).

Recent studies repeatedly confirm these post-Vietnam War "findings" and further explore the close relationship between public opinion and foreign policy. Aldrich et al. (2006) find that public forms their coherent attitudes toward foreign policy by using information from media and rhetoric of political and administrative elites. The authors reinforce their argument by showing some cases in the USA such as missions in Lebanon, Somalia, and the Iraq War (2003). The cases of Lebanon and Somalia illustrate that an elite perception of public opinion can be a material determinant in foreign policy-making. In the case of the Iraq War, American foreign policy of coalition-based occupation became an issue in the 2004 presidential election. The American public made their choices in part by evaluating whether President Bush was right in conducting his Iraq policy or not.

Moreover, Baum and Potter (2008) find that the influence of public opinion on foreign policy becomes more effective as the information gap between the public and leaders becomes smaller. They suggest that the public, in foreign policy area, always faces informational disadvantage vis-à-vis leaders and thus is susceptible to information framed by elites. The public can be independent on the framing attached by elites if this information gap narrows. In Baum and Potter's view, the information gap narrowing is mainly undertaken by media since it controls the main flow of information between public and leaders. They explain this relationship between public, leaders, and media by using the idea of market equilibrium. They regard foreign policy as the equilibrium outcome of a foreign policy marketplace where three strategic actors – public, leaders, and media – act over information, a key market commodity.

Likewise, Milner and Tingley (2013) emphasize that public opinion has the ability to affect foreign aid policy. In particular, they make an important argument suggesting that there are two-way interactions between public and policy-makers. First, public opinion ties the hands of policy-makers. The government faces an accountability challenge from the public because the government has been delegated the authority for using tax money by the public (Milner 2006). Second, policy-makers would take advantage of their knowledge and information to change public perception in their favor. Milner and Tingley (2013) are not alone in finding this "elite effect" (e.g., Aldrich et al. 2006; Baum and Potter 2008).

While there are numerous studies confirming some public opinion impact on foreign policies, it has been difficult to determine the precise nature of this impact, especially in terms of cross-national comparison. Otter (2003) analyzed five case studies and found the following three groups. First, the USA and Denmark have positive correlations between public attitudes and foreign aid policy; the amount of aid decreases with the decline of public support for aid in the USA, and the amount of aid increases with the rise of public support in Denmark. Second, by contrast, Japan and Australia have negative correlations; the amount of aid does not change despite the increase in public support for aid in Japan, and the amount of aid decreases despite the increase in public support in Australia. Finally, Canada is an unclear case since public support for aid fluctuates too much, and thus it was not possible to determine the trend of support for aid. Otter's study suggests a possible cross-national variation, and while this is an interesting finding, we must note that his analysis is just based on these five countries, and public opinion may be influenced by where and by how the aid is delivered but not by how much.

In addition to the research connecting public opinion and foreign aid policy, there are emerging empirical studies on factors affecting public support for foreign aid. According to Milner and Tingley (2013), there are at least three kinds of factors that influence public support for foreign aid: *ideological*, *material/economic*, and *cultural* factors.

First, liberals are likely to give more support for foreign aid than conservatives (Paxton and Knack 2012; Milner and Tingley 2010, 2013; Prather 2014). A root of this ideological divide in preferences for foreign aid policy can be found in preferences for national domestic redistribution policy. Liberals are often more supportive for domestic redistribution policy and therefore favor providing aid assistance to developing countries more, compared to conservatives.

Second, as a material/economical explanation, Milner and Tingley (2013) find that the level of public support for foreign aid in rich donor countries with higher level of endowments of capital is higher than in those with less endowments of capital. They suggest that those with better education are more likely to be exposed to information on international affairs and the global distribution problem, and thus they tend to generate positive attitudes toward foreign aid. In a similar vein, Paxton and Knack's (2012) study finds that skilled workers and high-income households favor more foreign aid.

Finally, Paxton and Knack (2012) emphasize the importance of cultural factors as determinants of public support for foreign aid. They suggest that trust in people and institutions, beliefs about the causes of poverty, awareness of international affairs, and religiosity have positive impact on the level of public support for foreign aid. Furthermore, they find that people in countries whose level of existing aid are high are likely to express less support for increasing foreign aid and that people from countries whose history has experience of colonization are likely to give more support for foreign aid. Besides these factors, recent studies find some evidence that racial paternalism also drives public support for foreign aid (Baker and

Fitzgerald 2012; Baker 2015); for instance, white Americans are more supportive for providing aid to black Africans than white Eastern Europeans.

These factors underpin levels of public support for foreign aid. However, their relations are not clearly understood. For instance, material factors and cultural factors cannot easily be distinguished since the same variable (such as "education level") may be positively related to both material and cultural source for public support of foreign aid (Milner and Tingley 2013). To avoid such an identification issue, we control for these factors by the use of a survey experiment. Experiment-based research through *randomization* enables us to focus on how aid effectiveness information (treatment) would change public perceptions on foreign aid by comparing with the control group, to which we provide no effectiveness information.

7.2.2 Aid Effectiveness and Hypotheses

An emerging topic among scholars who study the factors which influence public support for foreign aid is aid effectiveness. "Skepticism about aid effectiveness" reduces the level of public support for foreign aid policy (Hudson and vanHeerde-Hudson 2012). The aid effectiveness can be interpreted in two ways: *whether* the aid works effectively to develop the national interest of the donor country or not and *whether* the aid works effectively to help people in recipient countries or not.

Donor country aid effectiveness is evaluated by considering whether the aid is functioning as a part of the national security and diplomatic strategy to promote national interests. One of the well-known mechanisms as to how foreign aid is connected to promotion of the national interest is the economic one. By providing aid, the supplier country will receive a critical natural resource (such as minerals) from an aid recipient. Or, it is also possible to buy policy position by aid. For instance, it is often mentioned that the votes of less developed members of the United Nations General Assembly are often bought through foreign aid from developed nations.

By contrast, skepticism about aid effectiveness for recipient countries is often generated by perceptions of poor governmental quality of the aid recipient countries and their corruption (Bauhr et al. 2013). When people feel that foreign aid is not effective, they feel that the foreign aid budget is waste of money. People assuming poor government quality and corruption in the aid recipient states would thus express less support for foreign aid policy (Atkinson and Eastwood 2007).

Given this existing literature, we consider that *proper professional information input* on foreign aid effectiveness diminishes aid skepticism and thus increases the level of public support for foreign aid. Aid effectiveness can be divided into two as noted above: one is the aid effectiveness for donor countries and the other is the aid effectiveness for recipient countries.

Public support is essential for the donor governments when they carry out their foreign aid policies because a huge amount of national budget which comes from taxpayers' money is allocated not for domestic problems but for foreign countries.

Considering the importance of public opinion, the donor governments emphasize that foreign aid policy serves their national interests such as economic benefit, positive effects related to soft power, and good political relationships. For example, the US Japanese governments both regard foreign aid policy as one of their most effective diplomatic strategies. Foreign aid policy, therefore, seems to be intimately related with national interests.

In order to increase public support for foreign aid, many governments have attempted to persuade the public by explaining the benefits which foreign aid policy brings to the aid providers. For instance, the Japanese government in February 2015 changed its official "ODA principle" to emphasize national interests by continuing the ODA program more strongly than in the previous version. According to a poll conducted by the cabinet office of the Japanese government (2013), the most common reason for supporting ODA is the *economic benefit* to Japan, and the second is the *soft-power effect* on Japan. It is therefore clear that the Japanese believe their foreign aid policy should contribute to the national interests of Japan.

Hypothesis 7.1 Economic benefit and soft-power benefit information increases levels of public support for a state's foreign aid policy.

By contrast, what we propose here as an alternative hypothesis is a theory to emphasize "bottom-up *direct* effectiveness." We consider that the public is tired of listening about national-level, macro aid effectiveness in terms of their value to the national interest.[1] The general public would believe their aid is more useful if it is actually helping people in need. Also, they need to believe that the aid is being used to make positive, long-term changes to the society of the recipient nation. Owen Barder (2011) argues that "the more we defend aid mainly on the basis that it is in our national interest, the more likely it is to be bent to our short-term commercial and strategic interests, the more ineffectively it will be used, the harder it will be to demonstrate its benefits, and the greater the justification for public skepticism." According to foreign aid advocates, direct, intuitive effectiveness information like "your penny enables us to increase school enrollment in Ethiopia by 50%" would appeal to sense of justice and empathy for "our fellow human beings" (Barder 2011). We therefore hypothesize that education aid effectiveness is a key factor to change the perception of people to support foreign aid.

Hypothesis 7.2 Educational aid effective information, especially at the microlevel (i.e., a direct, example-based proof of aid effectiveness), increases public support for a state's foreign aid policy.

[1]For the ideas that we need to emphasize, the marginal aid effectiveness appears in blog posts by foreign aid advocates as Kenny (2011) and Barder (2011).

7.2.3 Research Design

We use survey experiment as a research strategy to test the hypotheses. In our study, respondents read a scenario about the Japanese foreign aid policy and were asked if they supported the provision of foreign aid in the developing countries.[2] The scenario is divided into two parts. In the first part, in order to prime respondents equally, we provided them with both positive and negative information about the Japanese foreign aid policy. The positive information was that Japan provides foreign aid continuously because foreign aid benefits the national interest, and developed countries have a responsibility to support developing countries. For the negative case, the respondents were informed that there was some opposition to the Japanese foreign aid policy because Japan had a national debt which was more than 10 million yen per person.

In the second part, respondents were asked to read a hypothetical "expert's" assessment on the effectiveness of the Japanese foreign aid. There were six different manipulations in the expert's assessment – (i) uncertain effect on recipient countries, (ii) definitive effect on recipient countries, (iii) economic effect on Japan, (iv) soft-power effect on Japan, (v) macrolevel educational effect on recipient countries, and (vi) microlevel educational effect on recipient countries. These six patterns were randomly assigned to respondents.

Immediately after this, respondents were asked if they support Japanese foreign aid policy – this is our dependent variable. Possible choices were as follows: *we should* (1) stop foreign aid, (2) reduce foreign aid, (3) maintain the status quo, and (4) increase foreign aid. Respondents could select either "I do not know" or "I do not want to answer"; we recoded those answers as a missing variable.

Our survey was conducted from February 6–12, 2015, through Nikkei Research Inc. (http://www.nikkei-r.co.jp/english/). The survey covered 976 individuals between the ages of 20 and 69. Table 7.1 shows the sample size, mean age, gender balance, income level, educational level, and the mean scores for a question regarding level of support for developed countries' foreign aid policy, for the six manipulations. The table clearly shows that the random assignment of the six manipulations was implemented successfully and that there is therefore no systematic difference among the six sample groups in terms of basic attribution and key political positions and attitudes.

Nikkei Research Inc. has a nationwide pool of respondents; however, our study inevitably suffers from a sampling bias since it is based on an internet survey. Individuals in our sample had to have internet access and voluntarily preregistered with the survey company. We should not and do not claim that the results of this experiment can be extended to the whole Japanese population. However, by

[2]Somewhat surprisingly, levels of support for foreign aid in Japan are relatively low when compared with other developed countries. Indeed, a cross-national survey of 17 countries (Paxton and Knack 2012: 27) reveals that Japan had the lowest level of support (about 45%) for an increase to level of foreign aid. It was about 20 points lower score compared with the overall mean of 67%.

Table 7.1 Mean value of key variables and sample size (foreign aid)

Manipulations	Uncertain effect on recipient countries	Definitive effect on recipient on countries	Economic effect on Japan	Soft-power effect on Japan	Macrolevel educational effect on recipient countries	Microlevel educational effect on recipient countries
Pre-experimental support for developed countries' foreign aid policy[a] (*N*)	3.02 (147)	2.96 (137)	2.96 (130)	2.83 (170)	2.84 (129)	2.99 (136)
Age (*N*)	45 (167)	44 (161)	45 (148)	43 (187)	44 (153)	45 (160)
Gender (1 = male, 2 = female; *N*)	1.50 (167)	1.54 (161)	1.45 (148)	1.45 (187)	1.47 (153)	1.51 (160)
Education level (*N*)	5.77 (167)	5.72 (161)	5.83 (148)	5.99 (187)	5.84 (153)	5.85 (160)
Income level (*N*)	3.00 (166)	2.93 (161)	2.82 (148)	2.81 (187)	2.83 (152)	3.03 (158)

[a]Respondents answered *before* receiving stimulus (effect information). Although we prepared choices "I do not know" and "I do not want to answer", we manipulated these answers as missing variables

Table 7.2 Estimated treatment effects (foreign aid)

Support for Japanese foreign aid	Coefficient	Standard error	t	95% confident interval	
Pre-experimental support for developed countries' foreign aid policy[a]	0.43***	0.03	15.29	0.38	0.49
Uncertain effect on recipient countries	Baseline				
Definitive effect on recipient countries	0.10	0.07	1.37	−0.04	0.24
Economic effect on Japan	0.11	0.07	1.51	−0.03	0.25
Soft-power effect on Japan	0.11	0.07	1.60	−0.02	0.25
Macro-level educational effect	0.17**	0.07	2.26	0.02	0.31
Microlevel educational effect	0.15**	0.07	2.06	0.01	0.29
R^2	0.24				
N	775				

*$p < 0.10$; **$p < 0.05$; ***$p < 0.01$
[a]Respondents answered before receiving stimulus (effect information)

carefully observing the differences among people with randomly assigned stimuli, we are able to claim that the test provides valuable information about how different stimuli on foreign aid effect can affect support for foreign aid policy.

7.2.4 *Result*

We use OLS regression analysis to summarize our data. This is simply because we would like to insert the variable reflecting the "pre-experiment level of support for foreign aid." By inserting the variable, we can show how respondents' attitudes toward foreign aid policy changed *after* the stimuli. Table 7.2 and Fig. 7.1 show a result of the regression analysis. The dependent variable is support for Japanese foreign aid. A baseline of the regression analysis is the uncertain effect on recipient country. The most powerful predictor for the level of support for foreign aid after the experiment is indeed the pre-experiment attitude toward aid (one level increase in the pre-experimental aid support increases the level of support by 0.43 after the experiment).

As to information stimuli, economic effects and soft-power effects on Japan failed to cause a statistically significant increase in support for foreign aid. Hypothesis 7.1 (*economic benefit* and *soft-power benefit* information increase public support for foreign aid policy) is rejected. However, the expected directions of coefficients of both are positive, indicating that economic effect information and soft-power effect information may raise the level of support for foreign assistance among respondents. This result might be statistically significant if the survey sample size was larger.

By contrast, as expected, both macro and micro educational effects increase the level of foreign aid support by 0.17 and 0.15, respectively, which is statistically significant ($p < 0.05$). This result offers support for Hypothesis 7.2 (*educational aid*

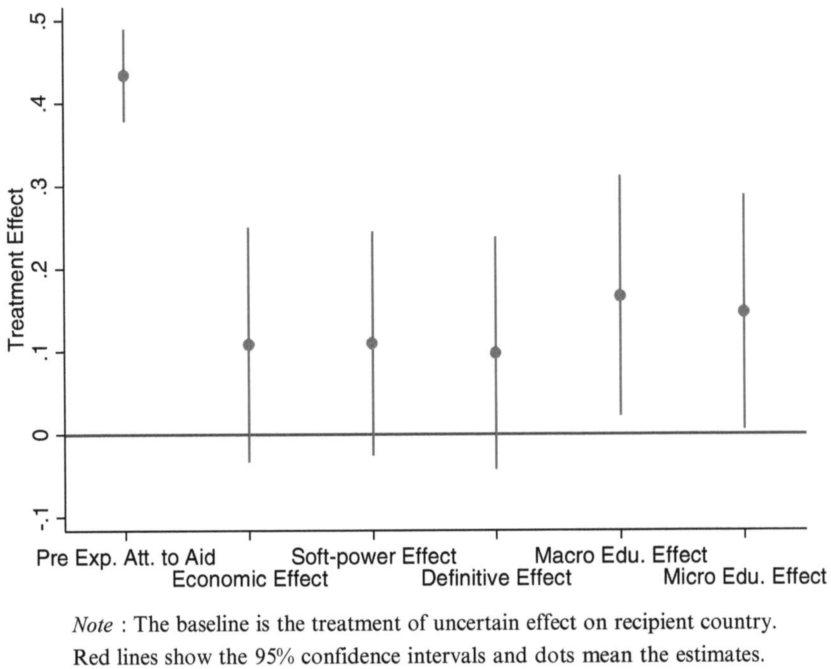

Fig. 7.1 Estimated treatment effects (foreign aid)
Note: The baseline is the treatment of uncertain effect on recipient country. Red lines show the 95% confidence intervals and dots mean the estimates

effective information, especially at microlevel, increases public support for foreign aid policy). As Fig. 7.1 illustrates, we can see a difference between the educational effect stimuli and the others. The result also indicates that there are few differences between the macrolevel educational effect and the microlevel educational effect. This outcome suggests that regardless of whether the educational effect information about aid is at macrolevel (abstract) or at microlevel (concrete/episodic), those who have received the information become more favorable to foreign aid.

In short, our experiment shows that the Japanese respondents react to the aid effect information if it is seen to be used effectively for the development of local education. It is rather surprising that a perceived boost in Japan's national interest would not really increase the level of support for foreign aid. While recent Japanese Foreign Ministry and aid agencies emphasize the ODA's *economic benefit* to Japan and its *soft-power effect* on Japan, the PR of foreign aid by emphasizing only those factors may not be as productive as the government wishes to mobilize the general public support for foreign assistance.

7.3 Military Coalition and Public Opinion

7.3.1 Literature Review

Public attitudes toward warfare are also a central theme among international relations scholars studying public opinion and foreign policy. Military action needs public support, and again, this is especially true in democracies.

In studying public support for military operations, scholars tend to focus on *casualties* as a crucially important factor. Casualties are believed to undermine the public's willingness to support military missions. Mueller (2005) argues that the support of the general public decreases as casualties mount. However, it is also true that casualties alone cannot be the only determinant of support for military deployments. For instance, demographic factors such as race and gender have an impact on public support for military operations. Eichenberg (2003) provides us with survey-based evidence that women are less supportive to war than men. Gartner and Segura (2000) find the racial factor to be a key determinant of war support. Significant difference exists between African-Americans and white Americans.

Besides these demographic factors, previous studies on casualties and public opinion focus on *when* casualty information would undermine levels of public support for a war. According to Gelpi et al. (2009), public tolerance for the human cost of war is mainly shaped by whether people believe the war is likely to succeed. If they believe in success of the war, they continue to support it even if they had initial doubts about the use of military force in the first place. On the other hand, if they think a military operation will be unsuccessful, they will be less supportive for the military mission even if they believed that the resort to military force was the right thing. In the success case, they regard casualties as a necessary evil to get the greater goods that come from victory in a war. In a similar vein, Kriner and Shen (2013) observe a statistically significant difference in reactions to casualty levels between rich and poor. The poor, who would be more likely to suffer in a war compared with the rich, are less supportive for a war. In US data, people in poor regions are more sensitive to casualties than people in the high-income regions.

Aside from the issue of casualties, international backing should generate favorable perceptions in the general public. Gelpi et al. (2011) assert that international backing from NATO and the UN increases levels of American public support for military operations. They claim this is because respondents generally favor multilateral operations. In particular, their finding is interesting since the effect of international backing is more salient among those who are not confident in the US President. In a similar vein, Johns and Davies (2014) analyze public opinion in the UK by using a survey experiment. They conclude that international backing translates into greater public support. However, they argue that support from the US government does not have positive effect on the general public in the UK; rather it has a negative effect because they have doubts about the US intervention in Iraq. Moreover, Ikeda and Tago (2014) find that the Japanese general public tends to support sending its Self-Defense Forces abroad as a part of a coalition led by the USA if there are more states to support the use of force in the coalition.

Given these studies, we consider that our study should pay attention to the issue of casualties as well as international backing. Information about the number of casualties and the level of international backing is crucial in helping people decide whether they support the use of force. When the use of force concerns a major existential issue, such as a state's independence or over disputed territories considered to be important, the general public would approve the military measures without international backing and with a high expectation of likelihood of troop casualties. The issues at stake are considered to be worth paying the cost of the military operation. By contrast, if the use of force is over something perceived to be a less vital interest, or is for the sake of an alliance obligation (i.e., to assist other countries in danger), domestic support for the military action may not be robust.

Therefore, troop contributions to military coalitions are always controversial to the public in a country sending the military forces as a *follower* state. Follower governments that decide to make a troop contribution will face a tough time to convince their domestic audience why such a military move is necessary and how long it must be maintained. In many cases, governments cannot successfully persuade their domestic audience; this is due to the fact that coalition participation would not be necessarily seen as serving the *core* national interest (Tago 2009, 2014). To make matters worse, those operations would be very costly since there are casualties to the deployed soldiers. In fact, in Iraq, 178 UK soldiers were killed for the US-led coalition occupation forces (Ministry of Defense of the U.K. 2013) which was close to the level of British casualties in the Falklands War, which was purely for self-defense of the territory – an obvious core national interest. The casualties in Iraq – battle deaths in operation for a non-core interest – affect the probability of the early departure of troops, i.e., a "defection" from a coalition (Tago 2009).

What is somehow puzzling about public opinion and coalition participation is that, in some countries, domestic opposition can be contained by the political elites. While in other countries, strong opposition to coalition participation is formed, and thus a government is forced to announce its premature troop withdrawal. What determines this difference, and how can we understand the attitudes of the general public toward a military action performed for a not necessarily core national interest? We examine how the general public can be tolerant to the cost of coalition participation and sustain support for sending troops to the coalition when there are a *risk* of casualties and *actual* casualties in a multinational operation.

7.3.2 Theory on Coalition Defection and Hypothesis

The general public cares about the costs and benefits of wars. As was discussed earlier, casualties represent a large cost. To maintain a level of public support, casualties must be avoided. Looking at the Korean War and the Iraq War, Mueller

(2005) finds that large numbers of casualties will lead to a decrease in the level of public support. In their more refined empirical research, Gelpi et al. (2009) argue that the general public would not be "casualty-shy" or "casualty phobic," which sets any type of casualty as the definitive reason to withdraw troops from the front zone. The American general public, according to their analyses, can tolerate casualties under the condition where they can expect that the use of force will be successful. That is, the American public would care a lot about casualties when the military operation is expected be a failure and lacks any justification. This type of casualty sensitiveness in the public matters to government decision-making, and, for instance, Tago (2009) finds that the higher the number of casualties, the greater the likelihood of premature troop withdrawal from the coalition forces in Iraq.

Hypothesis 7.3 Troop casualties in a coalition military operation lead to more support for the premature troop withdrawal from a coalition since the general public sees military casualties as a direct cost of the operation.

However, no matter how many soldiers are killed and how much domestic opposition appears, a defection (i.e., premature troop withdrawal) from a coalition will damage ties within an alliance (Tago 2009). For instance, the Spanish government faced strong opposition from its general public to its continued membership of the Iraqi occupational coalition in 2004. It finally decided to withdraw troops from Iraq in April 2004, and this caused disappointment in the US government. For a while after the decision, US-Spain bilateral ties were soured.

Moreover, the logic of fear of abandonment is quite powerful to citizens in a country facing tough enemy and rival states like Japan. For instance, according to a public opinion poll conducted by the Ministry of Foreign Affairs of Japan (2006), 70.9% of respondents believe that one of the key determinants to guarantee peace and security in Japan is its alliance with the USA.[3] Indeed, this is a significantly greater percentage of people who believe that Japan's pacifist constitution is a key determinant of its peace and security (55.5%).

Japanese people see the American alliance commitment is somehow sensitive and may not be there if Japan fails to meet American requests for basing rights and host-nation support budget. Moreover, in recent national security law reform, many people have started to take the perspective that the Japanese Self-Defense Forces must contribute to US military operations. The same people also know that American nuclear umbrella deters an enemy's hostile actions toward Japan – or it is often so argued in the media. Therefore, the Japanese general public under the fear of abandonment must care how the US government reacts to its possibly disloyal action in a coalition operation. That is, if Japan decides to withdraw its troops from a coalition, there must be approval from the US government. If not, people would think there will be a backlash from the USA, and in the worst case, it will trigger the abandonment of Japan by the USA. As long as the White House somehow shows its

[3]This survey was conducted with multiple choice methods, which are perhaps not the most appropriate to determine public opinion on peace and security.

understanding regarding Japan's premature withdrawal, then Japanese people would think that they do not need to be worried about the fear of abandonment. Our second hypothesis is:

Hypothesis 7.4 US opposition to the premature withdrawal of troops leads to less support for leaving a coalition due to the fear of abandonment.

7.3.3 Research Design

We conducted a survey experiment in February 6–12, 2015. The scenario was based on Japanese withdrawal from a US-led military operation in a fictional "State A." We employed six scenarios by combining the following three conditions – (i) an attack condition, (ii) a damage condition, and (iii) a US reaction condition. The attack condition involves a terrorist attack on one either the military coalition forces or the citizens of State A. The damage condition looks at the human cost caused by the terrorist attack. There are three types of damage: possible casualties of the Self-Defense Forces, actual casualties of the Self-Defense Forces, and actual casualties of another military coalition force member and the announcement to withdraw by that state.[4] The US reaction condition is the reaction by the USA after the Japanese government decides to withdraw from the military coalition operation. This condition has two reactions: the USA opposes the decision and the USA understands the decision (Table 7.3).

This study was carried out by the Nikkei Research Inc. The survey covered 1021 individuals between the age of 20 and 69. As it can be seen in Table 7.4, random assignment was carried out successfully.

To measure the level of support for withdrawal, the respondents were asked how much they support the Japanese government's decision to withdraw troops from the military coalition. *Oppose* is coded 1, *Somehow oppose* is coded 2, *Somehow support* is coded 3, *Support* is coded 4, *I do not know* is coded 5, and *I do not want to answer* is coded 6. However, this research treats 5 and 6 as missing value.

7.3.4 Results

Tables 7.5 (t-test) and 7.6 (regression analysis) as well as Figs. 7.2 (t-test) and 7.3 (regression analysis) show how strongly stimuli conditions affect the public support for premature troops withdrawal. The "SDF casualty" factor does not increase the support for premature withdrawal when the USA opposes the decision to exit prematurely (Hypothesis 7.3 is rejected). However, under the condition that the

[4]In the Japanese survey, we consistently asked respondents to consider the impact of injuries/deaths.

Table 7.3 Six scenarios (military coalition)

	Attack condition	Damage condition	US reaction condition
Scenario 1	Military coalition	Possible of SDF death/injuries	Oppose
Scenario 2	Citizen in State A	Possible of SDF death/injuries	Oppose
Scenario 3	Military coalition	Actual SDF death/injuries	Oppose
Scenario 4	Military coalition	Actual another state force death/injuries	Oppose
Scenario 5	Military coalition	Actual SDF death/injuries	Understand
Scenario 6	Military coalition	Actual another state force death/injuries	Understand

Table 7.4 Mean value of key variables and sample size (military coalition)

Manipulations	Scenario 1	Scenario 2	Scenario 3	Scenario 4	Scenario 5	Scenario 6
Cannot accept use of force as a mean of conflict resolution (*N*)	2.9 (167)	3 (172)	3 (155)	3.1 (161)	3.1 (168)	3 (198)
Age (*N*)	47 (167)	45 (172)	49 (155)	46 (161)	47 (168)	46 (198)
Gender (1 = male, 2 = female; *N*)	1.4 (167)	1.5 (172)	1.3 (155)	1.5 (161)	1.5 (168)	1.5 (198)
Education level (*N*)	5.7 (167)	5.7 (172)	5.5 (155)	5.9 (161)	5.6 (168)	5.9 (198)
Income level (*N*)	2.9 (166)	2.9 (172)	2.7 (153)	3 (160)	2.9 (163)	2.8 (196)

Table 7.5 Mean treatment effects: t-test (military coalition)

Manipulation	*N*	Mean	Standard error	95% confident interval	
Potential casualty	149	3.040	0.767	2.888	3.191
Citizen casualty	151	2.993	0.730	2.848	3.137
SDF casualty	129	3.038	0.084	2.870	3.206
Coal. casualty	137	3.087	0.075	2.937	3.237
SDF casualty and US approval	149	3.335	0.066	3.204	3.466
Coal. casualty and US approval	174	3.356	0.061	3.234	3.477

Table 7.6 Estimated treatment effects: results of regression analysis (military coalition)

Support for troops withdrawal	Coefficient	Standard error	*t*	95% confident interval	
US approval	0.310***	0.063	4.89	0.185	0.434
SDF casualty	−0.009	0.066	−0.14	−0.138	0.119
R^2	0.027				
N	889				

$^*p < 0.10$; $^{**}p < 0.05$; $^{***}p < 0.01$

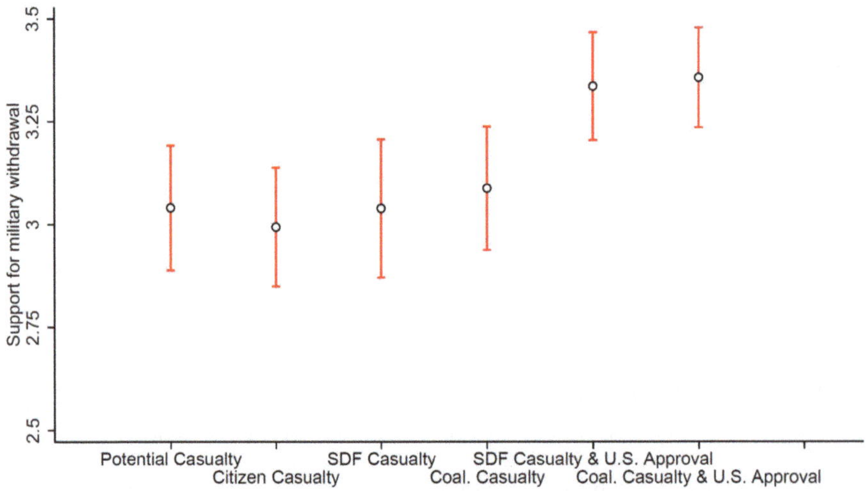

Note: Red lines show the 95% confidence intervals and dots mean the estimates.

Fig. 7.2 Estimated treatment effects: t-test (military coalition)
Note: Red lines show the 95% confidence intervals and dots mean the estimates

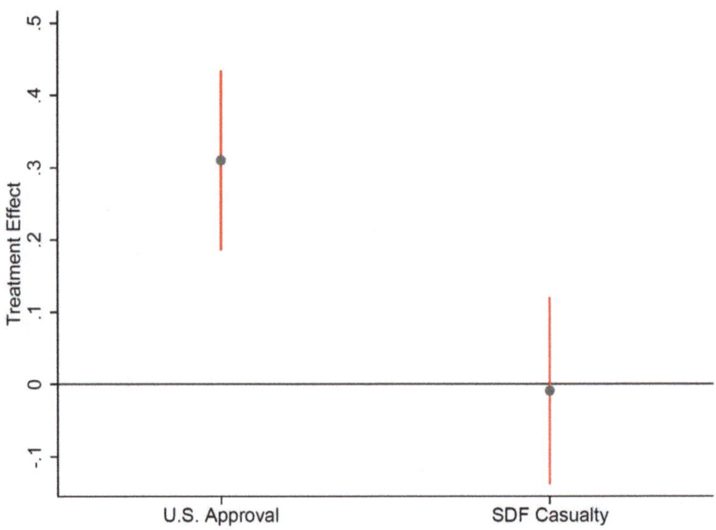

Note: Red lines show the 95% confidence intervals and dots mean the estimates.

Fig. 7.3 Estimated treatment effects: regression analysis (military coalition)
Note: Red lines show the 95% confidence intervals and dots mean the estimates

USA understands the Japan decision to withdraw prematurely, the general public in Japan are likely to support the premature withdrawal of troops withdrawal compared with the case that Japan cannot get the understanding of the USA (Hypothesis 7.4 is supported).

If the US government makes a statement that it would understand the early Japanese withdrawal from a coalition, the Japanese general public support leaving a coalition prematurely. If the US government opposes the early withdrawal from a coalition, the respondents feel that Japan may be abandoned by the USA when there is a crisis facing Japan and thus consider it important to stay in a coalition even if there are actual casualties to the Self-Defense Forces in a coalition.

Fear of abandonment drives Japanese respondents to care more about how the USA considers its premature withdrawal of troops. As Gelpi et al. (2009) argue, the public is not casualty-shy and casualty phobic. They think of a state's national security as part of a larger picture.

7.4 Conclusion

Our experiments in Japan enabled us to do an interesting comparison of a traditional foreign engagement instrument (foreign aid) and an emerging one (use of force). Interestingly, in the former experiment, rather than the national interest, people care about how human beings could be helped by Japanese aid. Effectiveness of aid at the individual level matters. By contrast, in a coalition defection experiment, casualties in an operation did not matter. That is, individual costs were not seen as important. Rather, the general fear of alliance abandonment, seen as affecting the national interest, affects how people think of the right policy choice.

This is indeed a highly contrasting result. It could be possible that the particular scenarios and setting of the experiments generated such a puzzling outcome; however, it is also quite plausible that there are some systematic reasons why this contrast emerges. We think that further experimental studies should enable us to have an answer for this question.

Appendix for Aid Experiment

Part 1 Scenario provided to all respondents

> Japan has been providing foreign aid to developing countries because foreign aid contributes to the national interests of Japan and providing it is a responsibility of advanced countries. However, considering the fact that Japan has a national deficit of more than 10 million yen per person, there has been some criticism of the foreign aid policy.

Recently, in an article contributed by a specialist, the following opinion was presented as a part of government public relations.

Part 2 There are six scenario patterns in our experiment and the sentences in non-italic are the key stimuli.

Scenario 1. (Uncertain effect on recipient countries)

Japanese foreign aid attempts to improve infrastructure in recipient countries but in fact, its effect is not certain.

Scenario 2. (Definitive effect on recipient countries)

Japanese foreign aid improves infrastructure in recipient countries and promotes economic growth.

Scenario 3. (Economic effect on Japan)

Providing foreign aid benefits Japan, as it helps us to secure our energy resources.

Scenario 4. (Soft-power effect on Japan)

The provision of foreign aid creates a positive image of Japan in the world, engendering feelings of trust.

Scenario 5. (Macro-level educational effect on recipient countries)

Japanese foreign aid enables children in many countries to receive education and therefore has a positive effect for the training of future generations.

Scenario 6. (Micro-level educational effect on recipient countries)

Japanese foreign aid enabled a girl named Sally (6 years old) in a developing country to receive compulsory education 30 years ago. Now she is working to spread education in poor areas.

Appendix for Coalition Experiment

There are six scenario patterns in our experiment and the sentences in non-italic are key stimuli.

Scenario 1
The Japanese government has dispatched its Self-Defense Forces to State A in the Middle East as a member of the U.S.-led coalition forces to provide back-up logistical support. A large-scale terrorist attack targets the military coalition. There is the possibility of Self-Defense Force casualties. *As a result, the Japanese government decides to withdraw 2000 troops from State A.* The U.S. opposes this decision.

Scenario 2
The Japanese government has dispatched its Self-Defense Forces to State A in the Middle East as a member of the U.S.-led coalition forces to provide back-up logistical support. A large-scale terrorist attack targets the citizens in State A in a

specific area. *There is the possibility of Self-Defense Force casualties. As a result, the Japanese government decides to withdraw 2000 troops from State A.* The U.S. opposes this decision.

Scenario 3
The Japanese government has dispatched its Self-Defense Forces to State A in the Middle East as a member of the U.S.-led coalition forces to provide back-up logistical support. A large-scale terrorist attack targets the military coalition. The Self-Defense Forces suffer a number of casualties. *As a result, the Japanese government decides to withdraw 2000 troops from State A.* The U.S. opposes this decision.

Scenario 4
The Japanese government dispatches its Self-Defense Forces to State A in the Middle East as a member of the U.S.-led coalition forces to provide back-up logistical support. A large-scale terrorist attack targets the military coalition. The Self-Defense Forces have not suffered any casualties, but another member state of the military coalition force has, leading to its withdrawal. *As a result, the Japanese government decides to withdraw 2000 troops from State A.* The U.S. opposes this decision.

Scenario 5
The Japanese government has dispatched its Self-Defense Forces to State A in the Middle East as a member of the U.S.-led coalition forces to provide back-up logistical support. A large-scale terrorist attack targets the military coalition. The Self-Defense Forces suffer a number of casualties. *As a result, the Japanese government decides to withdraw 2000 troops from State A.* The U.S. understands this decision.

Scenario 6
The Japanese government has dispatched its Self-Defense Forces to State A in the Middle East as a member of the U.S.-led coalition forces to provide back-up logistical support. A large-scale terrorist attack targets the military coalition. The Self-Defense Forces have not suffered any casualties, but another member state of the military coalition force has, leading to its withdrawal. *As a result, the Japanese government decides to withdraw 2000 troops from State A.* The U.S. understands this decision.

References

Almond GA (1956) Public opinion and national security. Public Opin Q 20:371–378
Aldrich JH, Gelpi C, Feaver P, Reifler J, Sharp KT (2006) Foreign policy and the electoral connection. Ann Rev Polit Sci 9(1):477–502
Atkinson R, Eastwood A (2007) Public attitudes to overseas giving: does government make a difference? S3RI Applications & Policy Working Papers, A07/05. Southampton Statistical Sciences Research Institute, Southampton

Baker A (2015) Race, paternalism, and foreign aid: evidence from U.S. public opinion. Am Polit Sci Rev 109(1):93–109

Baker A, Fitzgerald J (2012) Racial paternalism and mass support for foreign aid. University of Colorado at Boulder, Institute of Behavior Sciences, Boulder

Barder O (2011) Does the public care about development? Owen abroad. http://www.owen.org/blog/4363. Last Accessed 1 May 2015

Bauhr M, Charron N, Nasiritousi N (2013) Does corruption cause aid fatigue? Public opinion and the aid corruption paradox. Int Stud Q 57(3):568–579

Baum MA, Potter PBK (2008) The relationships between mass media, public opinion, and foreign policy: toward a theoretical synthesis. Annu Rev Polit Sci 11(1):39–65

Eichenberg RC (2003) Gender differences in public attitudes toward the use of force by the United States, 1990–2003. Int Secur 28(1):110–141

Gartner SS, Segura GM (2000) Race, casualties, and opinion in the Vietnam War. J Polit 62 (1):115–146

Gelpi C, Feaver PD, Reifler J (2009) Paying the human costs of war. Princeton University Press, Princeton

Grieco J, Gelpi C, Reifler J, Feaver PD (2011) Let's get a second opinion: international institutions and American public support for war. Int Stud Q 55:563–583

Holsti OR (1992) Public opinion and foreign policy: challenges to the almond-Lippmann consensus. Int Stud Q 36:439–466

Hudson D, VanHeerde-Hudson J (2012) 'A mile wide and an inch deep': surveys of public attitudes towards development aid. Int J Dev Educ Global Learn 4(1):5–23

Hurwitz J, Peffley M (1987) How are foreign policy attitudes structured? A hierarchical model. Am Polit Sci Rev 81:1099–1120

Ikeda M, Tago A (2014) Winning over foreign domestic support for use of force: power of diplomatic and operational multilateralism. Int Relat Asia-Pacific 14(2):303–324

Johns R, Davies GAM (2014) Coalitions of the willing? International backing and British public support for military action. J Peace Res 51(6):767–781

Kenney C (2011) Lies, damn lies and surveys about foreign aid. Center for Global Development Blogpost. http://www.cgdev.org/blog/lies-damn-lies-and-survey-about-foreign-aid. Last Accessed 1 May 2015

Kriner DL, Shen FX (2013) Reassessing American casualty sensitivity: the mediating influence of inequality. J Confl Resolut 58(7):1174–1201

Kuklinski JH, Quirk PJ (2000) Reconsidering the rational public: cognition, heuristics, and mass opinion. Elements of Reason: Cognition, Choice, and the Bounds of Rationality, 153–182

Lippmann W (1925) The phantom public. Harcourt, Brace, New York

Milner H (2006) Why multilateralism? Foreign aid and domestic principal-agent problems. In: Hawkins DG, Lake DA, Nielson DL, Tierney MJ (eds) Delegation and Agency in International Organizations, Cambridge University Press, New York, pp 107–139

Milner H, Tingley D (2010) The domestic politics of foreign aid: American legislators and the politics of donor countries. Econ Polit 22(2):200–232

Milner H, Tingley D (2013) Public opinion and foreign aid: a review essay. Int Interact 39 (3):389–401

Ministry of Foreign Affairs of Japan (2006) Research about Japan-U.S. Security Arrangement http://www.mofa.go.jp/mofaj/area/usa/hosho/chosa05/. Last accessed 1 May 2015

Ministry of Defense of the UK (2013) UK armed forces commissioned officers casualty figures for operation veritas and telic. http://www.gov.uk/government/publications/uk-armed-forces-commisioned-officers-casualty-figures-operations-veritas-and-telic. Last Accessed 1 May 2015

Mueller J (2005) The Iraq syndrome. Foreign Aff 84(6):44–54

Otter M (2003) Domestic public support for foreign aid: does it matter? Third World Q 24 (1):115–125

Paxton P, Knack S (2012) Individual and country-level factors affecting support for foreign aid. Int Polit Sci Rev 33(2):171–192

Prather L (2014) Values at the water's edge: social welfare values and foreign aid. Stanford University Working Paper

Program on International Policy Attitudes (PIPA) (2001) Americans on foreign aid and world hunger: a study of U.S. public attitudes. http://www.pipa.org/OnlineReports/ForeignAid/ForeignAid_Feb01/ForeignAid_Feb01_rpt.pdf. Accessed 6 July 2015

Schultz KA (1999) Do democratic institutions constrain or inform? Contrasting two institutional perspectives on democracy and war. Int Organ 53(2):233–266

Schultz KA (2001a) Democracy and coercive diplomacy. Cambridge University Press, New York

Schultz KA (2001b) Looking for audience costs. J Confl Resolut 45(1):32–60

Shapiro RY, Page BI (1988) Foreign policy and the rational public. J Confl Resolut 32:211–247

Tago A (2009) When are democratic friends unreliable? The unilateral withdrawal of troops from the 'coalition of the willing'. J Peace Res 46(2):219–234

Tago A (2014) Too many problems at home to help you: domestic disincentives for military coalition participation. Int Area Stud Rev 14(3):262–278

Tomz M (2007) Domestic audience costs in international relations: an experimental approach. Int Organ 61(4):821–840

Part IV
Interactions Between the International System, Domestic Society, and Individuals

Chapter 8
Agent-Based Simulation as a Method for International Political Science: A Way of Expressing Diversity

Susumu Egashira

Abstract This chapter tried to demonstrate utility of agent-based simulation (ABS) for the studies of international relations (IR). Traditionally, IR studies have been heavily dependent on historical approaches emphasizing detailed empirical analyses. Although more "scientific" approaches such as mathematical methods and game theories were introduced, empirical approaches are still much more dominant than economics.

However, it is impossibility of verification through experiments in this field, because IR studies have an inherent difficulty. That is, elements of the events discussed in this field are usually diverse and complicated which forces researcher to shed lights on a variety of elements of specific events. To discuss specific events in the detailed way within the framework of a general theory, one would need to make more presumptions, or they have to be replaced with more concrete alternatives. But how can one select appropriate presumption?

ABS model, we are proposing in this chapter, has advantages in overcoming the difficulties we discussed above. We create agents in computer and let them interact with each other within the virtual world setup in a computer. By "cultivating" nations this way, we can reduce, if not completely eliminate, risks of introducing arbitrary presumptions by the model builder. It also allows us to observe dynamic process of interactions of nations or to conduct an experiment of virtual history by obtaining path-dependent properties of agents.

Keywords Agent-based modeling · Methodology · Complex system · International relationship · Cultivation of nations

S. Egashira (✉)
Otaru University of Commerce, Hokkaido, Japan
e-mail: egashira@res.otaru-uc.ac.jp

M. Tadokoro et al. (eds.), *Emerging Risks in a World of Heterogeneity*, Evolutionary Economics and Social Complexity Science 10,
https://doi.org/10.1007/978-981-10-7968-9_8

8.1 Introduction

This chapter attempts to demonstrate the utility of agent-based simulation (ABS) for studies on international relations (IR). Traditionally, IR studies have heavily depended on historical approaches emphasizing on detailed empirical analyses. Although more "deductive" approaches, such as mathematical methods and game theories, were introduced, empirical approaches continue to be significantly more dominant in comparison to economics.

If an explanation of the past were the only purpose of IR study, it would not be necessary to discuss the appropriateness of historical approaches. However, if it attempts to gain certain useful knowledge about the current policy choices and even tries to predict the future, a general understanding of the structure of the world is indispensable. Essentially, IR scholars often attempt to draw some lessons for the future based on their studies of the past by implicitly assuming some regularity in history; however strictly, induction from history does not offer any conclusive ideas on general theory.

Any future forecast requires detection of a general law in social phenomenon. Considering economics in the nineteenth century, there were controversies on the methodologies between inductive approaches, such as historical and statistical methods, and deductive approaches that were constructed on mathematical hypothesis from clear-cut "axioms." Although their consequences were not necessarily fruitful, they had influenced the logical positivism and falsificationism of Popper (1972). Popper (1972) concluded that one cannot derive universal "law" in social and natural sciences, but obtain "temporal hypothesis." Moreover, he proved that it is impossible to derive falsifiable hypothesis through deductive methods and that their role is only the verification of hypothesis.

In modern economics, for example, in neoclassical economics, a temporal hypothesis consists of widely accepted "axioms," such as a smooth utility function and production function, and presumptions added by researchers according to their interests. The relationship between variables, particularly explanatory and explained variable, is specified in this hypothesis. A researcher verifies the possibility of its defense by comparing variables and economic data observed in a real society.

Recently, experimental methods have been actively introduced into economics and it makes the relationship between theoretical hypothesis and positive methods stricter. However, all researchers assert that a theoretical hypothesis is required beforehand (Smith 1976; Camerer et al. 2005) as an explanation of causality requires a theory even when positive approaches have been developed. Any hypothesis proposed by an inductive method is not accepted in economics from the viewpoint of generality, even when it is well-sophisticated.

The most serious problem in modern economics is an assumption of independency of economic variables from other variables ignored in a hypothesis. Economic researchers have safely accepted that we can arbitrarily cut variables off their environment and create a condition in a laboratory. This tradition has been maintained implicitly since Marshall (1890), who is the founder of modern economics, set the important assumption "ceteris paribus" in his book in 1890. However, independency of variables from environments is an important problem that has to be verified in social science. Modern economics was born at the end of the nineteenth century under considerable influence of classical physics. Science of dynamic system in that time supposed the closed system that ignores interactions to its outer system, such as a calculation of orbital paths of planets. It is not natural to suppose in social science that the human mind is not affected by an individual's circumstances that they are based on decision-making of humans (Lawson 1997).

Still, however, studies in IR that regards interactions between agents and a historical continuity more important than economics have an inherent challenge that the elements of the events discussed in the field are generally diverse and complicated, which forces researchers to shed light on a variety of elements of specific events (Evera 1997). To discuss specific events in a detailed manner within the framework of a general theory, one requires to make more presumptions. However, how can one select appropriate presumptions? As deductions only make information more intelligible without changing the amount of information, whether one can generate an appropriate theory depends upon the selection of presumptions. Thus, if more presumptions are introduced, there is a larger room for arbitrary selection of the presumptions, which will bias the theory. This problem can occur in economic theories, which deal with less diverse events, and thereby require less presumptions for theory building. However, in IR studies whose objects of research are more diverse, there appears to be stronger emphasis on analyses of unique events, which paradoxically requires more presumption for theories. Even in economics, which has a method of construction with an axiom and additional presumptions, this problem is encountered and it is challenging to create a theory that can predict the future.

The ABS model that we are proposing in this chapter has the advantages in overcoming the challenges we discussed above. We create agents and interactions among each other on computers within the virtual world setup in a computer. It is comparable to a biological experiment. A researcher cultivates cells in a container to observe how they develop, mutate, reproduce, and interact in the environments, with changes to elements, such as temperature, humidity, and PH. Considering our ABS model, we assume that subagents (population) have the basic characteristics of agents (nations), resulting in interactions between different agents that change the population structure of the subagents. Interactions between nations repeat over a thousand years and each nation adaptively develops a national identity through historical mutation. By "cultivating" nations in this manner, we can very much reduce, if not completely eliminate, the risks of introducing arbitrary presumptions by the model builder. It also allows us to observe the dynamic process of interactions of nations or to conduct an experiment of virtual history by obtaining path-dependent properties of agents. Researchers can create ABS models that are detailed and logical, utilizing agents developed in such a manner that arbitrariness is avoided.

8.2 Model for IR

Mathematical models are not as prevalent in political studies as in economics, and they are applied in limited fields. Most of the qualitative researches of politics have adopted a historical approach and an inductive method. The reasons for these are the objectives of politics that make it challenging to identify a general structure that incorporates related events, factors, and environments. Moreover, relationships between the factors studied in politics are not merely correlations but causal connections. This means that theoretical models are required for explanations of causal connections, in addition to quantitative models. If statistical methods are adopted, serious problems are encountered as reversed causal relationships and loop causality are frequently observed. Although in an economic model, there is a possibility of avoiding a problem of multicollinearity by simplifying the model settings, in an IR model it is challenging to suppose the independence of variables, and there are many cases that contain an essence of problems in the interactions between the variables. For example, when we create a model to explain the relationship between nations from viewpoints of productivities, populations, religions, technologies, and natural conditions, it is obvious that there are dependencies between factors, and there is a possibility of obtaining biased results in an analysis using a linear model. If it is supposed that nesting interactions of variables are important and that a present international political situation has emerged as a result of interdependency, a researcher should create a model including multi-dependencies.

As political phenomena are more diverse and complicated in comparison to economic phenomena, mathematical models tend to become very complicated by introducing more parameters to realistically present the objects of research. However, there are serious problems involved in creating such complicated models. First, no matter how many parameters are incorporated into the model, it is impossible for one to cover all the relevant factors. Thus, we may not be able to understand the structure of phenomena even with the complicated model. Second, complicated models tend to produce equally complicated conclusions. The problem here is that it is often impossible to draw relevant political implications out of the complicated conclusions.

In economics, the abovementioned challenges are less intense as it is relatively easier for economists to isolate economic phenomena from the other elements of a society and to assume an isolated and fairly simple system of economic variables. Under this assumption, they can simplify their research agenda and can be successful in reaching clear conclusions through a deductive method. However, although such simplification assists mathematical manageability of the model, it does not necessarily contribute to a better understanding of realities. In other words, even economic models are not descriptions of the reality as such, but are pronouncements of a perspective or thought of an observer. The same limitation applies to a quantitative model. An even quantitative model that is supposed to validate the explanatory power of the model is not free from the cognitive "cage" imposed by the observation based on a preexisting theoretical framework as it filters data according to the observer's cognitive framework in the selection of variables.

Despite the limitations, a cognitive framework is useful in political studies. It is effective in understanding uncertain objects, such as social phenomenon. Objects of social science cannot be generally grasped by simple experiences and require epistemological approaches. Most concepts in social sciences are tools for dealing with unsubstantial items as if they were substantial. For example, concepts such as GDP, unemployment rate, profit, firm, and household in economics are defined by academic agreements. The same word has different meanings in different paradigms (e.g., the term "cost" has different meanings in economics and accounting). Although it is at all times possible that the cognitive framework will fail to recognize aspects of the real, it has also evolved along with the changes in situations and is continuously revised to maintain its evaluation capability.

The same can be stated about international politics. Although "power" is the key concept in the field, its definition is multifaceted and dependent on each researcher's interests (Evera 1999; Nye 2009; Kamiya 2009). Moreover, it is a very dynamic concept that has changed in the context of the real world. The concept of "power" has developed and changed in order to understand the dynamic process of international politics in the real world. In politics, one has to deal with subjects that have strong path dependency and individuality. It is challenging to make high-level abstractions, but researchers are often expected to contribute to the policy-making process. In other words, political scientists face the problem that although they do not possess a method, such as the natural sciences, they are asked to predict the future, similar to other scientists, and provide clear explanations that ordinary people can understand. Thus, there is a fundamental gap in political studies between its methods and expectations.

How can we overcome the challenge of analyzing the complex phenomenon? Hayek (1973) proposed "pattern prediction" as a solution. We live in a society as a complex system. Although we tend to regard the future as decisive and predictable in this system, we rarely come across a situation where we fail to make a decision. Hayek explained the reason why we can continue with our daily lives without serious challenges as there are social patterns as a result of interactions between our behaviors, and we unconsciously use them and decide our behaviors.

In the next section, we propose an agent-based model of computer simulation as a method of pattern prediction. The advantage of this model is that it is possible to demonstrate the powers that consist of multiple factors and relationships between the players in real international politics, as much as the limits allow. However, the problem of simulation models is arbitrarily selecting variables and parameters, similar to other models in the social sciences. Simulation models require the types of functions to be specified. If we attempt to create a model that reflects several aspects of an object, there could be a problem that we would arbitrarily assume functions. In order to avoid the arbitrariness, we set up a system which automatically generates behavior functions of agents without relying upon assumptions of a model builder. In our ABS, agents are nations. We define only the very fundamental characteristics that are common to every primitive social group based on insights of cultural anthropology, history, and archaeology. As each nation develops and interacts with each other, more complicated and multilayered functions are designed to emerge. The features of agents that have been "cultivated" in this manner are diverse and independent from arbitrary assumption of model builders. Researchers select some developed agents and apply the ABS on those agents for their final objective. ABS could be useful to find new aspects of an object while ensuring some degree of generality. Repeated simulation games using "cultivated" agents in a "laboratory" demonstrate new and path-dependent facts that cannot be imagined.

The characteristics of the actual nations are developed through interactions between internal and external conditions. Although we can discuss the individual and micro relationships (e.g., wars involve significant cost and decrease populations, trade creates inflow and outflow of wealth, and types and quantities of resources influence the development of industries), the continuous and holistic entity of micro relationships is not predictable. There is a danger of lapsing into ad hoc settings as those who create models have to generally assume this type of unpredictable factors in the first step of creating a model. However, it creates the possibility to discuss the general characteristics in the political process by making simple assumptions that are also the objectives of the retroductive analysis and utilizing the results of a simulation, while arbitrary settings are removed. In the following section, we will present a conceptual model without theoretical and empirical foundations. However, we can adequately demonstrate that our model requires significantly less arbitrarily presumptions in comparison to the other approaches. It requires further inputs from disciplines such as cultural anthropology, history, and archaeology, to develop a fully satisfactory model. However, it is beyond the scope of this chapter.

8.3 Basic Model

Our model has an internal structure that influences governments' decision-making. There are other well-known models where the governments face audience costs, such as those by Fearon (1994) and Schultz (1999). However, in the model proposed in this paper, the trends and economic situations of nations and diplomacy are decided not only by democracy but also by other factors, such as religions, histories, and unique natural conditions. We cultivate nations with these fundamental elements in a society without the intention to establish a democracy. There is a possibility that the pattern of nations' behaviors that emerges may be democratic at one time and religious at another. The important point is that we cultivate appropriate agents for applied games of international politics.

8.3.1 Definition of the Variables

In this model, there are N ($N \geq 0$) nations that have p ($p \geq 0$) varied citizens. All the citizens have fundamental characteristics and we assume the following five characteristics:

Sociality: θ_{cl} collective: cl – individual: i
Dynamics: θ_{cn} conservative: cn – revolutionary: r
Attitude to change: θ_t tolerant: t – strict: st
Diligence: θ_d lazy: lz – diligent: d
Decision-making method: θ_m top-down: td – bottom-up: bu
Attitude to life: θ_h hedonistic: h – stoic: so

In this model, the fundamental characteristics are provisionally decided without any empirical reasoning and should be defined according to the results of anthropological and historical studies.

Each citizen has a characteristic. For example, if we assume that p_{cl} citizens have a collective character and p_i have individuality in a nation, sociality is expressed as $f_{\mathrm{cl}} = p_{\mathrm{cl}} - p_i$. Further, the population of the nation is:

$$C_{\mathrm{pp}} = p_{\mathrm{cl}} + p_i + p_{\mathrm{cn}} + p_r + p_t + p_{\mathrm{sr}} + p_{\mathrm{lz}} + p_d + p_{\mathrm{td}} + p_{\mathrm{bu}} + p_h + p_{\mathrm{so}} \tag{8.1}$$

The characteristics of a nation, such as the attitude toward policy and economy, religion, and culture, are composed of the basic characteristics of the people.

Further, we define the indexes of national capability as below. They are a fundamental part of a nation's power, which is often discussed in international politics. C_{pp} denotes the population, C_c is the quantity of capital, C_{tq} is the average technology level, C_{tr} is the quantity of trade, C_{pr} is productivity, and C_m is the power of the military. However, these variables are dependent on each other.

$$C_{\mathrm{pp}} = \varphi_{\mathrm{pp}}\left(C_{\mathrm{pr}}, C_{\mathrm{tq}}\right) \tag{8.2}$$
$$C_c = \varphi_c(C_{\mathrm{tr}}, C_{\mathrm{pr}}, C_{\mathrm{tq}}, R) \tag{8.3}$$
$$C_{\mathrm{tq}} = \varphi_{\mathrm{tq}}\left(C_c, C_{\mathrm{pp}}, \theta_{\mathrm{cl}}, \theta_t, \theta_d\right) \tag{8.4}$$
$$C_{\mathrm{tr}} = \varphi_{\mathrm{tr}}(C_{\mathrm{pr}}, C_{\mathrm{tq}}, \theta_d, R) \tag{8.5}$$
$$C_{\mathrm{pr}} = \varphi_{\mathrm{pr}}\left(C_{\mathrm{tq}}, C_c, \theta_d, \theta_h\right) \tag{8.6}$$
$$C_m = \varphi_m(C_{\mathrm{pp}}, C_{\mathrm{tq}}, C_c, \theta_{cl}, \theta_d, R) \tag{8.7}$$

R denotes an initial quantity of a resource. The initial values of each variable are decided randomly. The diversity in the composition of nations' populations is low in the initial stage of a simulation.

8.3.2 *Structure of the Simulation*

In this simulation model, each nation decides its foreign strategy at the beginning of each year. A nation has three options—"war," "trade," or "nothing"—and chooses one of them against all the other nations. Here, we introduce the concept of "distance." Although a nation requires a certain level of technology to interact with others, it is challenging to overcome the problem of distance in earlier periods as technology would not have matured. In this case, the nation has to choose "nothing" as its strategy against others. $D_{x,\ y}$ denotes the distance between nations x and y. If $D_{x,\ y}/C_{\mathrm{tq}} > a$, both the nations interact with each other, and a is positive and a constant.

A nation selects its strategy according to relative proportions between home and the other, other's strategy in the past, and domestic trends. In this simulation, an agent memorizes all the nations' strategies of the last 10 years, and if a foreign nation has adopted a war strategy more than five times, the nation decides that the other is "pugnacious."

Nations calculate benefits and losses when they choose war or trade before making a decision. If the difference in the nations' capabilities is large, they generally exclude war and choose trade. However, if they predict that the damage will be too severe when they choose trade and the other chooses war, they have to choose war. Figure 8.1 shows the expected payoff matrix of this game.

$$
\begin{aligned}
r_1 &= C_{c2} + R_2 + C_{\mathrm{pp2}} - |C_{m1} - C_{m2.}| \\
r_2 &= C_{c1} + R_1 + C_{\mathrm{pp1}} - |C_{m2} - C_{m1}| \\
r_3 &= C_{c2} + R_2 + C_{\mathrm{pp2}} - |C_{m1}/2 - C_{m2}| \\
r_4 &= C_{c1} + R_1 + C_{\mathrm{pp1}} - |C_{m2}/2 - C_{m1}| \\
r_5 &= C_{\mathrm{tr2}} \\
r_6 &= C_{\mathrm{tr1}}
\end{aligned}
$$

An important point to note is that $(r_1, \cdots, r_6)$ is merely an expected vector that each nation forecasts in a subjective manner, and it is different from the result the nation actually receives at the end of the year. The nation has memories of adverse nations' strategies going back 10 years and knows the probability that they will choose "war."

We defined a set of strategies by a nation as $\mathrm{s} = (s^{\mathrm{trade}}, s^{\mathrm{war}}) = (0, 1)$. Thus, the probability of war can be illustrated as:

Fig. 8.1 Payoff matrix

		Nation 2: War	Nation 2: Trade
Nation 1	War	r1, r2	r3, r4
	Trade	r4, r3	r5, r6

$$w = \frac{\sum_{t=1}^{10} s_t^{\mathrm{war}}}{10} \tag{8.8}$$

The nation calculates an expected benefit π^e and selects the best strategy according to those conditions. However, the winner of a war is decided by different factors in this model. It is not only dependent on a simple military power but also on the total ability to continue war.

$$\varphi = C_c + C_{\mathrm{tq}} + C_{\mathrm{tr}} + C_{\mathrm{pr}} + C_m \tag{8.9}$$

If nations 1 and 2 come into contact, the result π is as follows:

$$\pi^r = \begin{cases} \delta(\varphi_1 - \varphi_2), & \textit{if } s_1 + s_2 = 2 \\ \delta(\varphi_1 + \varphi_2), & \textit{if } s_1 + s_2 = 0 \\ \delta(\varphi_1 - \varepsilon\varphi_2), & \textit{if } s_1 = 1, s_2 = 0 \\ \delta(\varepsilon\varphi_1 - \varphi_2), & \textit{if } s_1 = 0, s_2 = 1 \end{cases} \tag{8.10}$$

δ, $(0 \le \delta \le 1)$ and ε, $(-1 \le \varepsilon \le 1)$ are random numbers. In this game, the difference between forecast and reality is more important than winning and losing. The ultimate result has three patterns: (1) the forecast and reality are not very different, (2) the reality is much better than the forecast, and (3) the reality is much worse than the forecast. We set a rule that the composition of the population does not change if the forecast and reality are not very different $(-0.5 \le (\pi^r - \pi^e)/\pi^e \le 0.5)$. If the reality is much better than the forecast, $0.5 < (\pi^r - \pi^e)/\pi^e$, the number of people with major characteristics increases by θ, but those with minor characteristics decrease by θ, which is decided randomly. On the other hand, if the former is much worse than the latter, $(\pi^r - \pi^e)/\pi^e \le -0.5$, the number of people with minor characteristics increases by θ, but those with major characteristics decrease by θ. This means that the majority has power and domestic political initiative when the policy is successful, but the minority obtains power when the policy supported by the majority does not work.

This game comprises of five steps: step 1, calculating national power; step 2, deciding the international policy; step 3, action; step 4, evaluation of the results of the policy; and step 5, changing the composition of the population. A year consists of these five steps, and they are repeated a thousand times in a trial.

One feature of this model is that the historical processes underlying the nations' development not only influence national powers but also cultures, politics, and national characteristics. The basic concept of this model is that national characteristics are path-dependent. In other words, political decisions are not made based on objective rationality, but on the peculiar tradition of the nation.

Although a repeat count in social simulations is generally rationalized as highlighting problems, whether the repeat count in the simulation is sufficient to reflect, the objective can be questioned as the game in this type of computer simulation is a limited repeated game, but daily life in the real society is infinite. There is the possibility that too many iterations make for an unrealistic evolution, but too few make for uncertain results. However, the history of real nations encapsulates thousands of years at most; thus, the problem of a repeat count is not serious for this simulation. This simulation is simple as it is merely a sample of the "cultivation" model. If we create a more complicated and detailed model, this problem will require a discussion again.

8.4 Results of the Simulation

We now present some sample results from the simulation. The results of the simulation themselves do not have any implications for real politics as the objective of this chapter is, as repeatedly mentioned, to propose a new methodological concept in international political studies. It should be noted that these are not the final results, but the processes and characteristics of "cultivated" nations.

First, we will discuss the changes in populations of nations. Seven nations were successfully developed over a thousand years in this trial (Fig. 8.2). Some nations initially experienced an increase in population followed by a decrease. The patterns of development were diverse and dependent on random number sequences, such as δ. In other cases, most nations experienced a decrease in population in the initial period and then maintained a constant population (Fig. 8.3).

Next, let us observe the population compositions of the top two (No. 32 and 82) and seventh (No. 58) nations. Nations that survived for a 1000 years had a one-sided population composition, showing either of the two opposing characteristics. For example, Figure 8.4 shows that the indicator of dynamics C_{cn} (revolutionary conservative) had the smallest share, but "revolutionary" was dominant in the relationship between "revolutionary conservative" in No. 82. Diversity disappeared owing to the rule of the game where population increased only when war and trade were successful, but cultural diffusion through immigration and transfer was not considered. The results suggest that nations that survived did not necessarily have a cultural commonality, and it is possible for them to survive and develop without cultural commonality and standard strategies (Figs. 8.5 and 8.6).

We now discuss the changes in national capability, which are more complicated than the changes in population. Although a number of nations increased their capability in the initial period, most of them failed to maintain it. Moreover, it is important to note that the changes in population and capability were not parallel. In this trial, only No. 58 was successful in increasing and maintaining both its population and capability until the end. Strong national capability was not necessarily an advantage in increasing the population; although it strengthened the hand of the nation both in war and trade in this model, it also had a tendency to increase the length of war (Figure 8.7 shows the times of war). If war time continued for a long period of time, it became prolonged as the nation memorized its opponent's

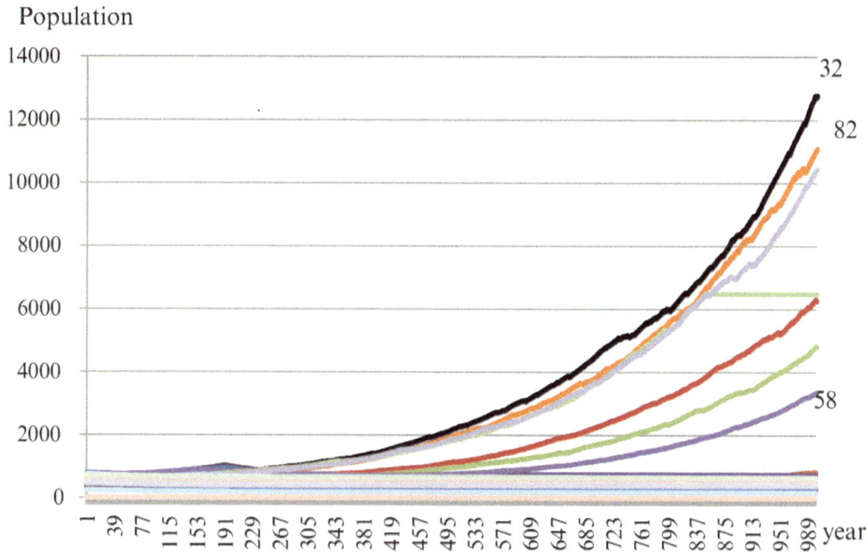

Fig. 8.2 Population

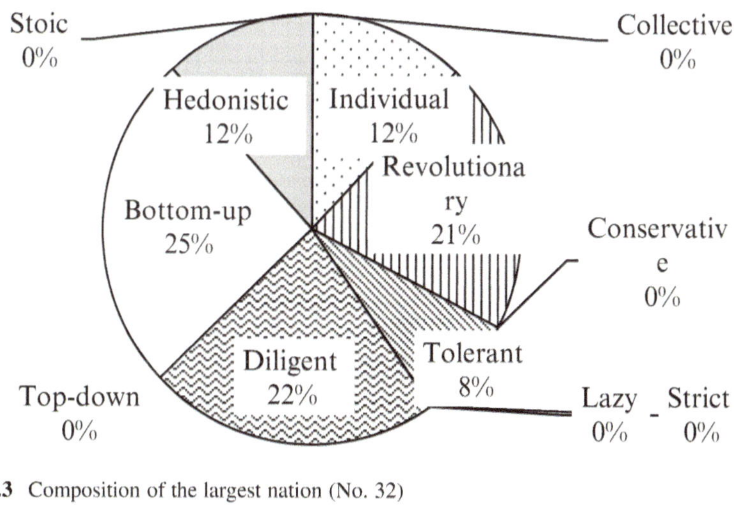

Fig. 8.3 Composition of the largest nation (No. 32)

strategies from the past 10 years. As a result, strong nations failed to increase their populations after a massive nation appeared.

Figures 8.8, 8.9, and 8.10 show the population compositions that maintained national capabilities until the end.

Nation No. 17, which increased its capability in the early period and maintained it till the end, contained opposite characteristics as it entered a stationary state before

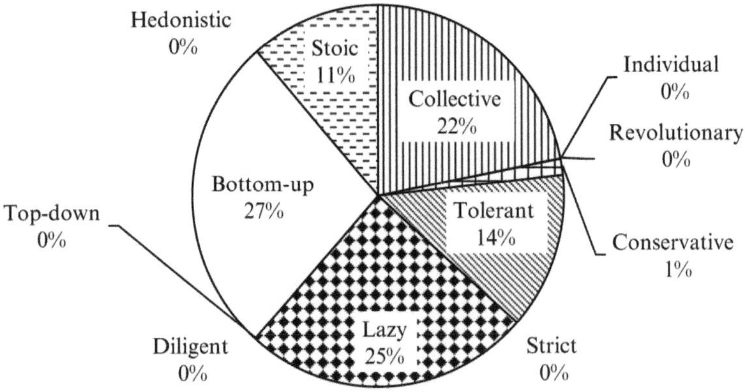

Fig. 8.4 Composition of the second largest nation (No. 82)

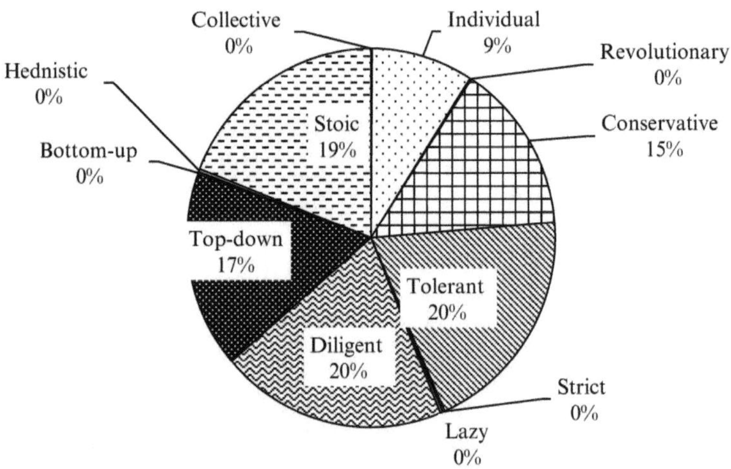

Fig. 8.5 Composition of the small nation (No. 58)

the pressure of selection substantially worked. A nation that stops changing in the earlier period has more diversity in this model.

In this manner, although the nations that developed in this model had a strong tendency toward path dependency, their processes and final situations could be clearly explained through the first few assumptions. Therefore, we were able to appreciate the validity of a certain "cultivated" model by examining the validity of the assumptions. The results of the simulation verify the validity of the assumptions as the results of computer simulations do not contain more information than the ones

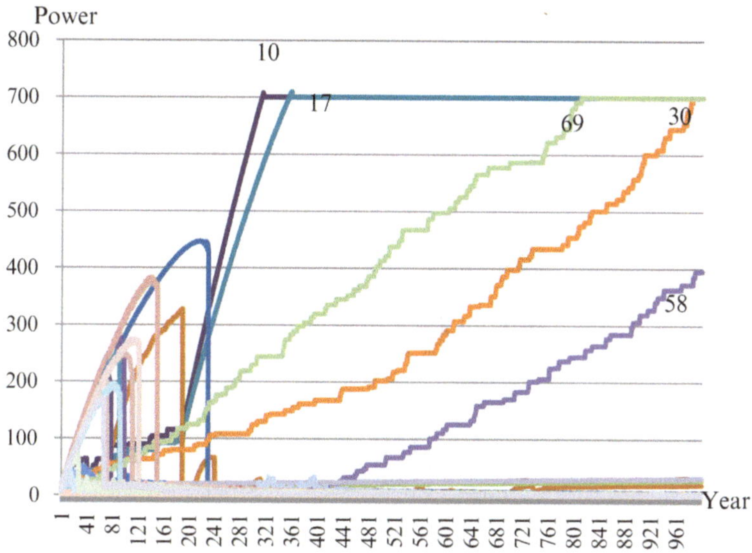

Fig. 8.6 Changes in national capability

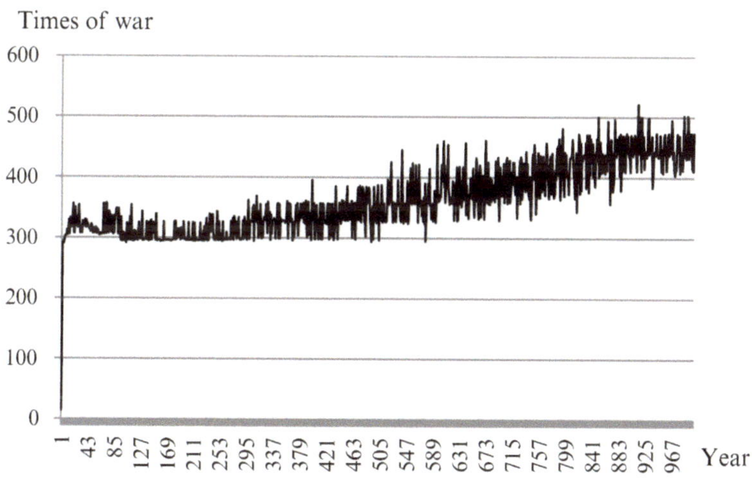

Fig. 8.7 Times of war

contained in the assumptions or mathematical deductive models. On the other hand, it is possible to "cultivate" appropriate agents for problems in international politics if we are successful in obtaining theoretical foundations and empirical evidence in the background, such as cultural anthropology and history.

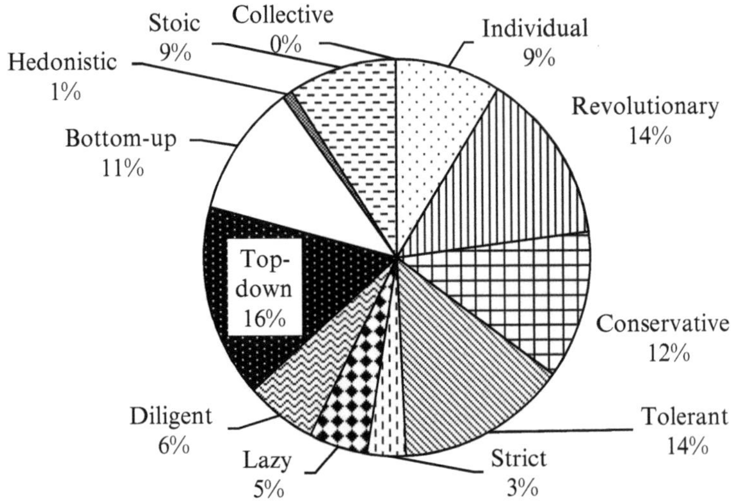

Fig. 8.8 Composition of the strongest nation (No. 17)

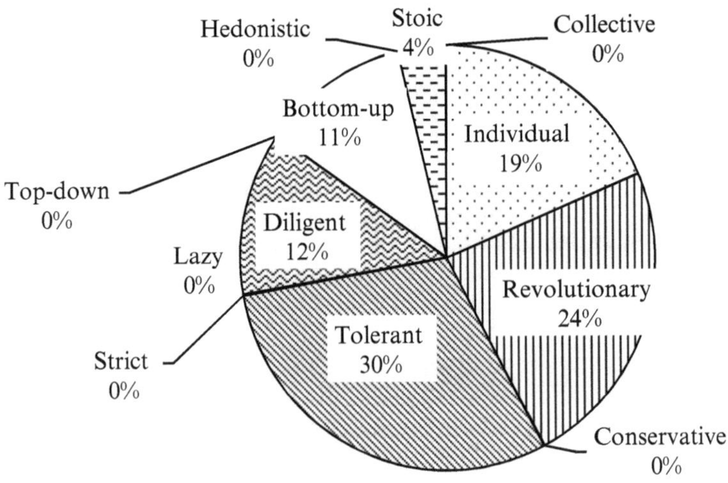

Fig. 8.9 Composition of the second strongest nation (No. 69)

8.5 Conclusion

In this chapter, we have discussed the possibility of deploying an agent-based model with adequate complexity in international political studies from the viewpoint of the methodology of politics. The sample model in this chapter demonstrated the basic

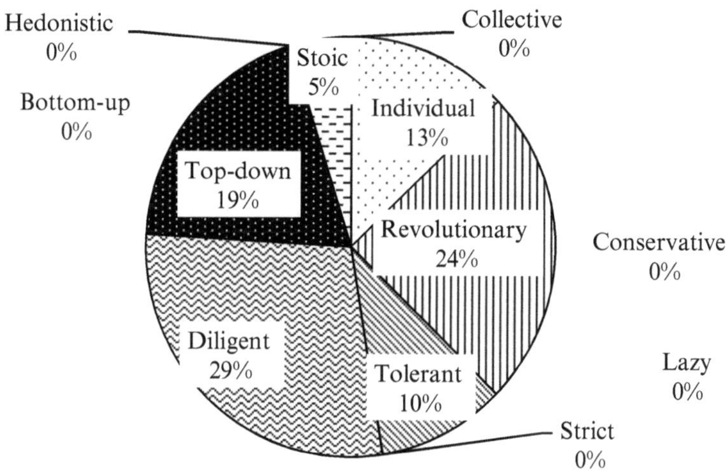

Fig. 8.10 Composition of a low-power nation (No. 30)

concept and does not have any theoretical foundations. Therefore, it should be noted that the results do not have any political implications. However, we were successful in demonstrating the process of "cultivating" national agents.

Political scientists are not able to "cultivate" observation objects in a laboratory, such as those that can be undertaken in biology. Also, it may not be useful to social scientists to realize an agent as complicated as an observation object because the results that emerge from their interactions are more complicated in comparison to those in the reality. It has been highlighted that the problem with international politics is that it does not have a general theory that was constructed deductively. This lack of a general theory means that although a current situation can be explained in a retrospective manner, there is no method to predict what will happen in the future from the viewpoint of the modern methodology of science. If political studies are a branch of history, this feature will not create any challenge. However, if we accept that social studies are a branch of political science and its focus is policy-making, prediction along with deductive science is required.

Fortunately, there is a wealth of research in cultural studies, history, and folklore that is the foundation and wellspring of existing political studies. Even if each study focuses on individual and path-dependent objects, we can create a deductive model of politics as an integrated science through computer simulation when we identify logical relationships between each factor. If we are successful in elucidating the pattern of the results of the simulations, it will be possible to establish a general theory of politics. The concept of "cultivating" agents, which has been demonstrated in this chapter, is an effective method for political science, which could deal with a multilayered problem.

References

Camerer C, Lowenstein G, Prelec D (2005) Neuroeconomics: how neuroscience can inform economics. J Econ Lit XLIII:9–64
Fearon JD (1994) Domestic political audiences and the escalation of international disputes. Am Polit Sci Rev 88(3):577–592
Hayek F (1973) Law, legislation and liberty, vol 1. Routledge, London
Kamiya M (2009) "POST9.11 NO KOKUSAISEIJI NI OKERU POWER," (Power in international politics Post-9.11). Kokusai Mondai (Int Aff) 586:29–39
Lawson T (1997) Economics and reality. Routledge, London
Marshall A (1890) Principles of economics. Macmillan, London
Nye J (2009) Soft power: the means to success in world politics. Public Affairs, New York
Popper KR (1972) Objective knowledge. The Clarendon Press, Oxford
Schultz KA (1999) Do democratic institutions constrain or inform? Contrasting two institutional perspectives on democracy and war. Int Organ 53:233–266
Smith VL (1976) Experimental economics: induced value theory. Am Econ Rev 72:923–955
Van Evera S (1997) Guide to methods for students of political science. Cornell University Press, New York
Van Evera S (1999) Causes of war: power and the roots of conflict. Cornell University Press, New York

Chapter 9
Considering Provision of Global Public Goods with Community Task Game: A Multi-agent Simulation Analysis

Takashi Hashimoto and Hiroaki Yamada

Abstract The provision of public goods is often problematic both in the international society and in local communities because it is hard to establish a government that forces its constituents to conform to a shared rule in both types of society. In this chapter, we employ a multi-agent simulation to analyze the issue of providing global public goods (GPGs), since multi-agent simulation is a useful tool to model and analyze complex phenomena including international political situations consisting of heterogeneous individuals with the complex and dynamic relationships among them. The situation of provision of a GPG is modeled with a Community Task Game, which is an extension of public goods game. We introduce two internal states of agents; one is self-efficacy, an agent's self-recognition of its ability to successfully perform a task; and the other is subjective norm, an agent's own understanding about others' desire for the agent to perform a task. Based on the simulation analysis about the effects of these two variables on the provision of GPGs, we show that the former works to maintain one's intention to continue participating in GPG provision activities and the latter to promote agents' intentions to participate. This means that two internal states synergistically function to provide GPGs. Further analysis shows that a possible intervention for GPG provision is to encourage country groups with neutral attitudes and relatively strong mutual relationships to participate in a GPG provision activity. We also discuss the development of the present model to incorporate heterogeneities, to measure the dynamics of the international political situation, and to consider countries' various recognition of the game situation.

Keywords Global public goods (GPGs) · Multi-agent simulation · Self-efficacy · Subjective norm · Community task game

T. Hashimoto (✉) · H. Yamada
School of Knowledge Science, Japan Advanced Institute of Science and Technology, Ishikawa, Japan
e-mail: hash@jaist.ac.jp

M. Tadokoro et al. (eds.), *Emerging Risks in a World of Heterogeneity*, Evolutionary Economics and Social Complexity Science 10,
https://doi.org/10.1007/978-981-10-7968-9_9

9.1 Introduction

As a society, we often require not only goods that can be traded in the marketplace but also public goods. A clean environment and safe local areas are examples of public goods. If a local or national government has the power to force its constituents to conform to a rule, the government may be able to provide public goods using tax money collected from the constituents or may impose a penalty for uncooperative behavior. A local community, however, where community order is formed and maintained by the members of the community themselves or is self-organized endogenously, may have difficulty establishing a mechanism that forces members to comply with rules and imposes strict penalties when such rules are violated. In such a case, the cooperative activities of community members are necessary for the stable provision of public goods.

This situation, where it is a challenge to establish a mechanism to force all constituents to conform to a rule and where community order is maintained by community members, is similar to the international community. This is because, based on the status quo, a "world government" has not yet been realized and international society is a form of anarchy. Order in the international society is maintained through the provision of global public goods (GPGs). Kaul and Mendoza (2003) provide a useful definition for a GPG as follows: "[A] good qualifies as being globally public when it benefits more than one group of countries and does not discriminate against any population group or generation." A more strict definition by Kaul et al. (1999) states that GPGs are "goods whose benefits extend to all countries, people, and generations." Examples of GPGs are world peace, free trade, scientific knowledge, and the prevention of global warming. Financial stability can also be seen as a type of GPG as we experienced with the bankruptcy of Lehman Brothers in 2008 (Shirakawa 2012). The bankruptcy had an influence not only on the direct stakeholders of Lehman Brothers such as shareholders, employers, and employees, but it also had a significant influence on the rest of the world. GPGs are not only institutions but also natural entities such as the atmosphere and the ozone layer. In order to provide various GPGs, the cooperation of many countries is essential. The report entitled International Cooperation in the National Interest (2006) defines GPGs as follows:

> [GPGs are] issues that are broadly conceived as important to the international community, that for the most part cannot or will not be adequately addressed by individual countries acting alone and that are defined through a broad international consensus or a legitimate process of decision-making.

A public good is theoretically characterized by two features: non-excludability and non-rivalry. Non-excludability means that when a good is provided by one individual, the good must be available to all others. This feature seems to give some individuals the incentives of free ride because the good is available for all individuals without effort once it has been provided. The safety of seaborne trade routes is one example, where all countries can utilize the routes even if a country does not send its navy or coast guard to patrol the routes and sea areas. Non-rivalry indicates that the availability of the good to all is not reduced when a good is consumed by one individual.

In this paper, we consider a situation where the cost of providing a GPG is shared by all participants and where there is a threshold to the provision of the GPG. For example, world or regional peace cannot be established through the efforts of one or a few countries. A framework of common defense and alliance reduces the costs incurred by each country, and we may be able to establish peace when a sufficient number of countries make cooperative efforts.

Ledyard (1995) summarized that a linear symmetric variable contribution environment and a linear symmetric threshold environment are simple representative models for the problem of the provision of public goods. In the former model, the benefits of a public good increase linearly with the number of cooperators. In the latter, a public good is provided when the number of cooperators exceeds a certain threshold, that is, a provision point, and the benefits of the public good do not depend on the number of cooperators. The payoff for noncooperators is higher at a fixed value than that of cooperators in both models. Thus, both are non-excludable and non-rivalry models and result in an increase in free riders. By combining these two models to address the above-referenced issues, the Community Task Game (Yamada and Hashimoto 2015; Yamada 2016) was introduced as an extension of step-level public goods games (Rapoport 1985). In the Community Task Game, all cooperators share the cost of providing a public good. Therefore, the cost in the payoff function is modeled as inversely proportional to the number of cooperators, which is different from the linear symmetric variable contribution environment where the payoff is linearly proportional to the number of cooperators. The benefits of the public good are constant, as in both of the other models, but the difference in the payoff between the cooperator and the noncooperator is not a fixed value; rather, it depends on the number of cooperators.

As we can see from the name, the Community Task Game was introduced to tackle community activity issues not international political problems (Yamada 2016). Under a sovereign state system, each country has its own sovereignty and all countries are basically equal irrespective of their size and power. We can regard each country as an individual actor. The mechanism of providing a public good through community activities, where the compelling force for members of society is weak, may provide useful knowledge and insight that we can apply to the provision of GPGs. The international system is changing from a situation where a unique superpower, the USA, maintains GPGs through significant effort to a multipolarized system where China and India have risen, Russia is revived, the UK leaves the EU, the EU takes its own path separate from the USA, and other countries in the Association of Southeast Asian Nations (ASEAN) and in Central and South America continue to develop. We believe that discovering how to allow more countries to participate in GPG provisional activities and how to balance costs and benefits as a stakeholder in the international community through an analysis of the Community Task Game will contribute to actualizing peace and stability in the world.

We claim that an effective means in treating complex systems, including international political dynamics, is constructive approach (Hashimoto et al. 2008). In constructive approach we try to abstract an objective system/phenomenon and construct it in operationalized systems using artificial systems such as computer simulations, human experiments, and robotic experiments. By using such artificial media, we can operate conditions relatively freely, observe the behavior of the systems precisely, and analyze objectively, often numerically. Adopting the constructive approach, we conducted the analysis of the Community Task Game using a multi-agent simulation that considered each country to be an agent. Because the Community Task Game provides agents with an incentive to be a free rider, as in other public game issues, the provision of public goods cannot be successful if all agents play the game selfishly. In their multi-agent analysis of the Community Task Game, Yamada and Hashimoto (2015) introduced a mechanism that may contribute to success. The mechanism assumes that an individual's intention to cooperate or not to cooperate, that is, to participate or not participate in providing public goods, is determined by certain internal states: attitude toward the task (the game); subjective norms, which are the recognition of significant other participants' requests to cooperate; and self-efficacy, which is the individual's own confidence in completing the task (Bandura 1977). The subjective norm is each individual's own recognition of social conduct about what should be or should not be done, while social norms are usually considered as collective representations of acceptable and unacceptable behavior in a society. The subjective norms may differ according to individuals because they are subjective and internal understandings of social states from the individuals' surroundings. These internal states change according to the individual's behavior, the outcome of the task, and significant others' behaviors. This mechanism was validated by Ajzen's (1991) theory of planned behavior. We use this method of analysis in the present study.

This paper is organized as follows. We define the Community Task Game in Sect. 9.2 and describe the agent model for our analysis using a multi-agent simulation in Sect. 9.3. In Sect. 9.4, we analyze the effects of self-efficacy and subjective norms on the provision of GPGs. It will be shown that both have the effect of positive feedback and contribute jointly to the provision of GPGs. In Sect. 9.5, we discuss the possibility of an institutional design for GPG provision, the significance of self-efficacy, and possible extensions to incorporate heterogeneity in the model. Section 9.6 delivers the summary and conclusion.

9.2 Community Task Game

The features of the Community Task Game are as follows:

- Non-rivalrous and non-excludable, which result in free riders.

- When the number of participants is larger than a certain value, the task succeeds and all agents benefit.
- The greater the number of participants, the lesser the cost to participate.

If we suppose N agents, then the payoff matrix of the Community Task Game can be defined as illustrated in Table 9.1 below.

In Table 9.1, $\alpha_1 N$ is the number of agents to achieve the task, the cost function is

$$\text{Cost} = -\frac{Cr}{n},$$

and the benefit function is

$$\text{Benefit} = \frac{Cr}{\alpha_2 N},$$

where C is the total cost to achieve the task, r is the value of the public goods, and N is the total number of agents. All parameters take positive values.

When the number of participants is greater than $\alpha_1 N$, the task is achieved (success), and all agents benefit from the success. The state of the participant can be divided into two categories, with actual benefit and without actual benefit, although the payoff function is the same. When the number of participants becomes greater than $\alpha_2 N$, the total benefit exceeds the cost (Cost + Benefit > 0), and the participants make actual gains. This structure is summarized in Table 9.2 and an example of the payoff function is depicted in Fig. 9.1.

Table 9.1 Payoff matrix of the Community Task Game

	The number of participants	
	$0 \leq n < \alpha_1 N$	$\alpha_1 N \leq n \leq N$
Participate (cooperate)	Cost	Cost + Benefit
Do not participate (defect)	0	Benefit

Table 9.2 Structure of the Community Task Game

Number of participants (n)	Payoff for participant	Payoff for nonparticipant	State of task
$0 \leq n < \alpha_1 N$	Cost	0	Failure
$\alpha_1 N \leq n < \alpha_2 N$	Cost + Benefit <0	Benefit	Success but no actual benefit for contributors
$\alpha_2 N \leq n \leq N$	Cost + Benefit ≧0	Benefit	Success with actual benefit for contributors

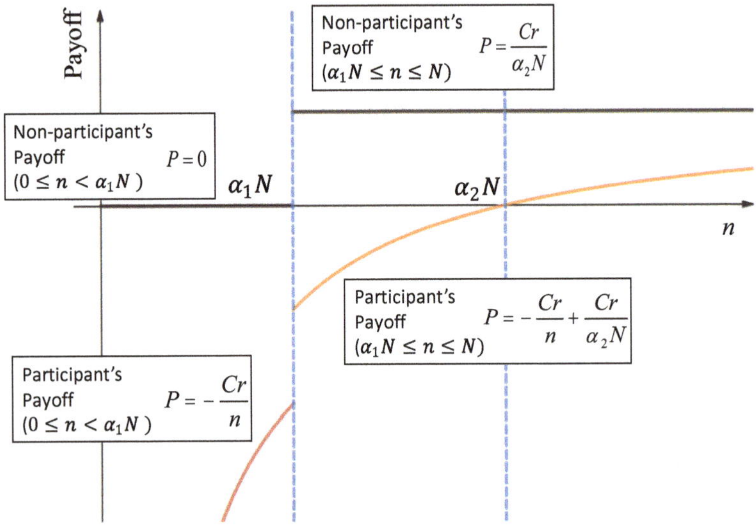

Fig. 9.1 Payoff function of the Community Task Game

9.3 Multi-agent Model for the Community Task Game

In this section, we describe the agent model for the Community Task Game. We use the theory of planned behavior (Ajzen 1991) as the basis for the agent's behavior and decision-making. This theory supposes three internal states (beliefs) in each agent: attitude, self-efficacy, and subjective norms. The self-efficacy plays an important role in this study, and we will discuss this concept later in more detail. Attitude is the preference to participate in the task and the expectation of an outcome. We represent attitude by the variable A ranging between -1 (negative attitude) and 1 (positive attitude). Self-efficacy is the belief in one's own ability to complete the task and is designated by the variable E, also ranging from -1 (negative belief) to 1 (positive belief). Subjective norms represent one's own understanding about the social appropriateness of participating in the task, denoted by S and ranging from -1 (inappropriate) to 1 (appropriate). This is interpreted as pressure from the international community.

It is considered that each agent's intention to participate in the task is represented by a weighted combination of these three beliefs. Here, we approximate this factor using a linear combination as the simplest form:

$$I_i^t = w_A A_i^t + w_E E_i^t + w_S S_i^t,$$

where i is the index of an agent, t is the index of a time step in repeated interactions, and $w_A \geq 0$, $w_E \geq 0$, and $w_S \geq 0$ ($w_A + w_E + w_S = 1$) are parameters to determine the relative strength of the effects on decision-making from the internal states of attitude, self-efficacy, and subjective norms, respectively. Although the weights are generally considered to be agent-specific and to change through interactions with other agents, the surrounding environment, and the agent's own internal situation, we use the same fixed parameter values for all agents for simplicity. If I_i^t is greater than or equal to zero, the i-th agent participates in the task at the time step t:

$$B_i^t = \begin{cases} -1 \text{ (means nonparticipation)}, & I_i^t < 0 \\ 1 \text{ (means participation)}, & I_i^t \geq 0 \end{cases}.$$

As shown in Table 9.1, the success or failure of the task at the time step t depends on the number (or ratio) of the participants at that time, namely, n^t:

$$\text{task}^t = \begin{cases} \text{failure}, & n^t < \alpha_1 N \\ \text{success}, & n^t \geq \alpha_1 N. \end{cases}$$

The internal states of the agents change according to their behaviors and the associated outcomes. We define that attitude of the i-th agent directly depends on its payoff, P_i^t, because it relates to participation and the associated outcome:

$$A_i^{t+1} = \begin{cases} A_i^t - P_i^t, & B_i^t = -1 \\ A_i^t + P_i^t, & B_i^t = 1. \end{cases}$$

Self-efficacy is based on the success or failure of the task, because it reflects the agent's belief about its ability to complete the task. Concretely, self-efficacy increases when the agent participates and succeeds in the task and decreases when the task fails (Bandura 1997). If the agent does not participate, self-efficacy does not change.

$$E_i^{t+1} = \begin{cases} E_i^t - \gamma, & B_i^t = 1 \text{ and task}^t = \text{failure} \\ E_i^t + \gamma, & B_i^t = 1 \text{ and task}^t = \text{success}, \\ E_i^t, & B_i^t = -1 \end{cases}$$

where γ is the unit of change in self-efficacy due to one's success/failure experience. Because the subjective norm is one's understanding of the social state, the behavior of other agents influences the subjective norm:

$$S_i^{t+1} = (1 - \varepsilon)S_i^t + \frac{\varepsilon}{M} \sum_j^{\text{All neighbor of } i} B_j^t,$$

where ε is the susceptibility of the subjective norm and M is the number of surrounding agents. Although susceptibility is, in reality, an agent-dependent variable, we approximate it to the common value for simplicity. The values A_i^t, E_i^t and S_i^t are bounded between -1 and 1.

We also introduce a spatial structure. This structure is not limited to a geographical space but is considered a relational space. In the following simulations, we use a regular two-dimensional lattice ($\sqrt{\mathrm{N}} \times \sqrt{N}$) with periodic boundaries and Moor neighbors ($M = 8$).

9.4 Simulation Results

We analyze the multi-agent model for the Community Task Game using computer simulations. In the simulations, the agents are engaged in the Community Task Game repeatedly. The parameter settings throughout this paper are $N = 100$, $w_E = w_S = 0.333$, $\alpha_1 = 0.333$, $\alpha_2 = 0.667$, $r = 1$, $C = 1$.

9.4.1 *Four Cases*

In order to understand the effects of self-efficacy and subjective norms in the provision of GPGs, we compare four settings:

(a) Where neither self-efficacy nor a subjective norm is introduced (only attitude)
(b) Where self-efficacy is introduced (attitude + self-efficacy)
(c) Where a subjective norm is introduced (attitude + subjective norm)
(d) Where both self-efficacy and a subjective norm are introduced (attitude + self-efficacy + subjective norm)

Setting (a) is the basis of all the other settings. The initial values of attitude, A_i^0, are distributed with a truncated normal distribution bounded between -1 and 1. The mean and variance are parameters. Here, we investigate the response to the mean but use a fixed variance of 0.3. The initial values of the other two internal states are 0 ($E_i^0 = S_i^0 = 0$) for all i. In Setting (a), the two states stay as 0 (no self-efficacy and no subjective norms) because the parameters for changing the two states are also 0 ($\gamma = 0$, $\varepsilon = 0$). In Setting (b), only the parameter for changing self-efficacy is $\gamma = 0.05$, and in Setting (c), only the parameter for changing the subjective norm is $\varepsilon = 0.5$. Both are used in Setting (d) ($\gamma = 0.05$, $\varepsilon = 0.5$).

9.4.2 *Dynamics of the Participants*

Figure 9.2 shows the typical dynamics of the number of participants in the four settings with a mean initial attitude of 0.03. The dashed lines correspond to $\alpha_1 N$ (lower line) and $\alpha_2 N$ (upper line). We found four dynamics:

(i) Immediate failure
(ii) Temporal formation
(iii) Establishment with partial participation

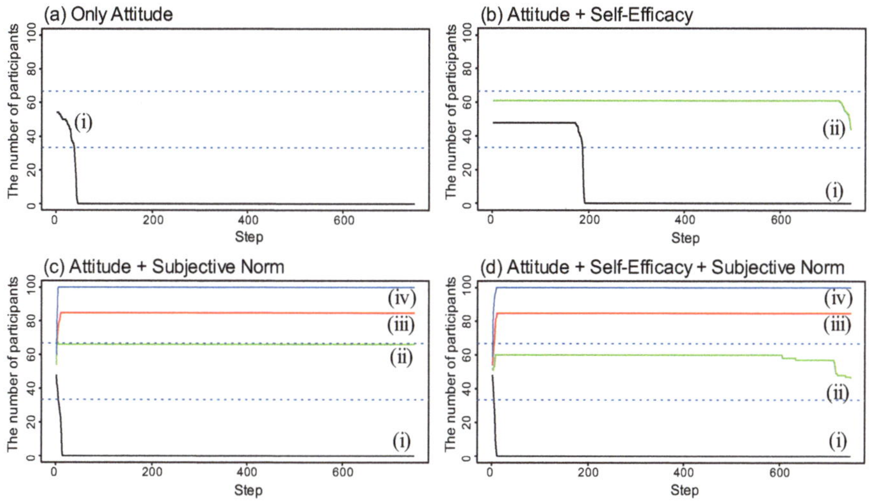

Fig. 9.2 Typical dynamics of the number of participants in the four settings. Notes: The x-axis is the step; the y-axis is the number of participants. We find four cases: (i) immediate failure, (ii) temporal formation, (iii) establishment with partial participation, and (iv) establishment with full participation. The mean of A_i^0 is 0.05, and all $E_i^0 = 0$ and $S_i^0 = 0$ for all four settings: (**a**) only attitude ($\gamma = 0$, $\varepsilon = 0$), (**b**) attitude + self-efficacy ($\gamma = 0.05$, $\varepsilon = 0$), (**c**) attitude + subjective norm ($\gamma = 0$, $\varepsilon = 0.5$), and (**d**) attitude + self-efficacy + subjective norm ($\gamma = 0.05$, $\varepsilon = 0.5$)

(iv) Establishment with full participation

In the graphs in Fig. 9.2c, d, all four dynamics can be seen. In any case, the number of participants increases only at the very beginning and eventually falls or is maintained. The number of participants drops early on unless there are at least some participants at the initial state (Case (i)). If the number of participants is just below a value of $\alpha_2 N$, it is often maintained for a long period of time. This is evident in Case (iii). We considered a state to be a temporal formation if the number of participants was $0 < n < \alpha_2 N$ at the 750th step in the present simulation. As shown in Fig. 9.1, when the number of participants is just below $n = \alpha_2 N$, which is a bifurcation point, the payoff for all participants takes a very small negative value. The closer to the left of the bifurcation point, the smaller the negative value of the payoff, and, thanks to the effect of self-efficacy, as will be described below, the number of participants is maintained for a very long period of time. In a longer period, however, some agents turn to nonparticipation due to the diversity of the A_i^0 distribution because the payoff is actually negative. Then, participation cannot be maintained and, finally, the task of the society becomes a failure (total nonparticipation).

In Fig. 9.2c, although Case (ii) remains at the 750th step, it was actually confirmed that this collapses to a state of nonparticipation over a long period. If $n \geq \alpha_2 N$, then the payoff of all agents, both participants and nonparticipants, is a positive value. Thus, the GPG can be provided. Partial or full participation, that is, Cases (iii) and (iv), respectively, depend on a spatial configuration of participants at the initial state.

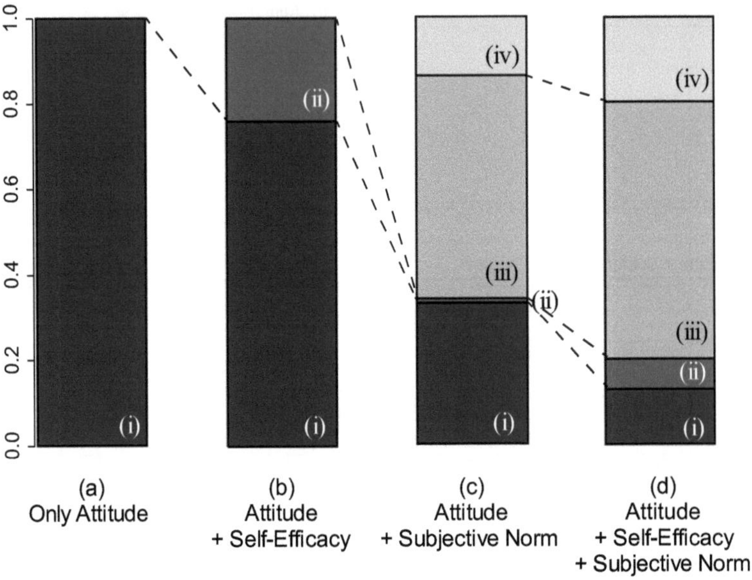

Fig. 9.3 The ratio of the four dynamics in the four settings (100 samples). Notes: The y-axis is the cumulative ratio of four dynamics: (i) immediate failure, (ii) temporal formation, (iii) establishment with partial participation, and (iv) establishment with full participation. The four shades of gray indicate dynamics (i) to (iv) from dark to light, respectively. The mean of A_i^0 is 0.05; all $E_i^0 = 0$ and $S_i^0 = 0$ for all four settings: (**a**) only attitude ($\gamma = 0$, $\varepsilon = 0$), (**b**) attitude + self-efficacy ($\gamma = 0.05$, $\varepsilon = 0$), (**c**) attitude + subjective norm ($\gamma = 0$, $\varepsilon = 0.5$), and (**d**) attitude + self-efficacy + subjective norm ($\gamma = 0.05$, $\varepsilon = 0.5$)

To summarize the above findings, only with attitude, Setting (a), does the number of participants at the initial state determine the final state. This is because self-efficacy and subjective norms do not change after the initial state. If more than $\alpha_2 N$ participate, the payoff of participants is positive and their attitude, A_i^t, increases. Then, participation is maintained at the initial number. Otherwise, A_i^t decreases to the minimum value and the state falls to nonparticipation.

Using the setting that introduces attitude only, Setting (a), as the basis, let us look at the effects of self-efficacy and subjective norms. The self-efficacy, E_i^t, of an agent does not change unless the agent participates and self-efficacy does not increase unless the task is successful. Thus, as can be seen in Fig. 9.2b, self-efficacy does not seem to contribute to increasing the number of participants. In Fig. 9.3, which consists of stacked charts that indicate the volumes of the four cases (in 100 samples), we can see that the volume of Case (ii), temporal formation, increases in Fig. 9.3b from the values in Fig. 9.3a. Thus, we consider one effect of self-efficacy is that it helps maintain participation as seen in Fig. 9.2a, b. This works to maintain rather than increase the motivation of participations only when the number of participants exceeds $\alpha_1 N$. Therefore, the participant dynamics stays in a temporal formation, $\alpha_1 N < n^t < \alpha_2 N$, and finally falls to non-establishment.

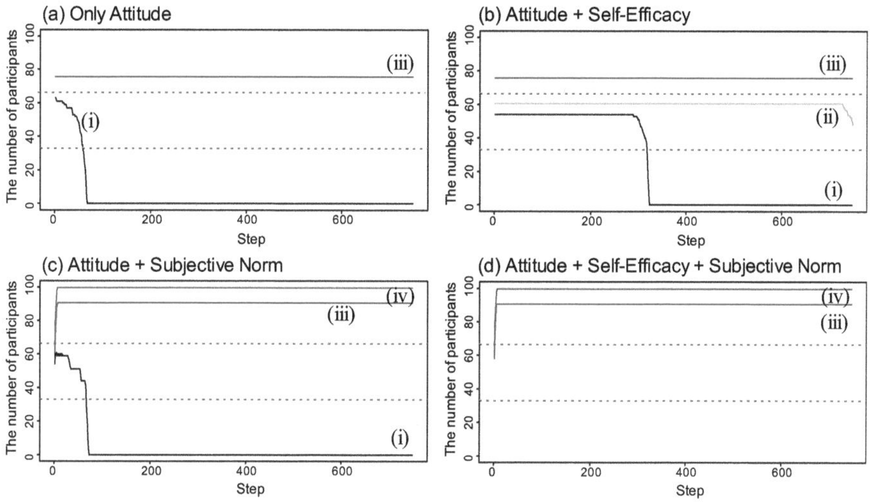

Fig. 9.4 Typical dynamics of the number of participants in the four settings. Notes: The x-axis is the step; the y-axis is the number of participants. We find four dynamics: (i) immediate failure, (ii) temporal formation, (iii) establishment with partial participation, and (iv) establishment with full participation. The mean of A_i^0 is 0.12, and all $E_i^0 = 0$ and $S_i^0 = 0$ for all four settings: (**a**) Only attitude ($\gamma = 0$, $\varepsilon = 0$), (**b**) attitude + self-efficacy ($\gamma = 0.05$, $\varepsilon = 0$), (**c**) attitude + subjective norm ($\gamma = 0$, $\varepsilon = 0.5$), and (**d**) attitude + self-efficacy + subjective norm ($\gamma = 0.05$, $\varepsilon = 0.5$)

Different from self-efficacy, the subjective norm works to turn nonparticipants into participants during the initial period. Even though the number of total participants is not large, a subjective norm can promote participation if a sufficient number participates in the local space because the number changes depending on the ratio of participation in the local space of each agent.

Comparing Fig. 9.3c, d gives an insight that self-efficacy and subjective norms have a positive feedback effect. The establishment volume in Fig. 9.3d (for both partial participation, Case (iii), and full participation, Case (iv)) is larger than in Fig. 9.3c. This is especially true for partial participation gains. This means that the likelihood of not falling after a period of maintenance but exceeding the upper threshold, $\alpha_2 N$, and realizing a state where all agents experience a positive payoff increases more in Setting (d) than in Setting (c). The process is as follows. During the initial period, some agents which became participants under the influence of subjective norms maintain their participation as a result of the effects of self-efficacy, the subjective norms function to recruit new participants before the number of participants falls, and, then, the self-efficacy of the new participants works to maintain their intention to participate.

The synergetic effect between self-efficacy and subjective norms is clearly confirmed by comparing Figs. 9.2 and 9.3 with Figs. 9.4 and 9.5, where the mean initial attitude was 0.12. In Fig. 9.4a, the initial number of participants exceeds $\alpha_2 N$ and Case (iii) is realized, where stable participation is maintained. Because the initial states completely determine the final state when there are no effects from the subjective norm, the volume of Case (iii), establishment with partial participation,

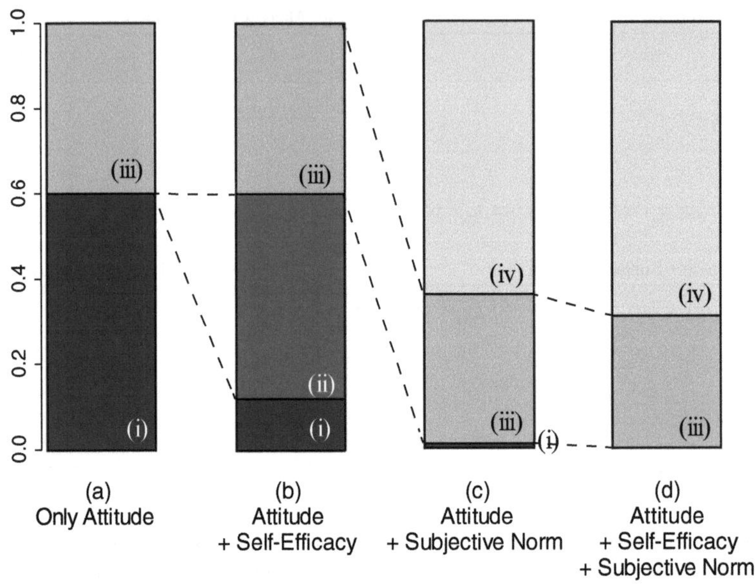

Fig. 9.5 The ratio of the four dynamics in the four settings (100 samples). Notes: The y-axis is the cumulative ratio of the four dynamics: (i) immediate failure, (ii) temporal formation, (iii) establishment with partial participation, and (iv) establishment with full participation. The four shades of gray indicate Case (i) to Case (iv) from dark to light, respectively. The mean of $A_i^0 = 0.12$; all $E_i^0 = 0$ and $S_i^0 = 0$ for all four settings: (**a**) only attitude ($\gamma = 0$, $\varepsilon = 0$), (**b**) attitude + self-efficacy ($\gamma = 0.05$, $\varepsilon = 0$), (**c**) attitude + subjective norm ($\gamma = 0$, $\varepsilon = 0.5$), and (**d**) attitude + self-efficacy + subjective norm ($\gamma = 0.05$, $\varepsilon = 0.5$)

does not change, as seen in Fig. 9.5a, b. Similar to Fig. 9.3b, self-efficacy has the effect of maintaining participation, and the provision of public goods is also maintained for a certain period (Fig. 9.4b) in the region where the number of participants is near $\alpha_2 N$ and the dynamic of Case (ii), temporal formation, is possible.

However, in the case of Figs. 9.4c and 9.5c, attitude + subjective norm, the number of participants increases at the beginning but soon falls and no such dynamic occurs with self-efficacy, as seen in Figs. 9.4d and 9.5d. We can infer that the positive feedback works, i.e., subjective norms function to recruit participants, self-efficacy functions to maintain the participation, and then the subjective norms function to reinforce the number of participants maintained through the self-efficacy. As a result, in the case of this initial distribution, where the mean of A_i^0 is 0.12, and $E_i^0 = S_i^0 = 0$ for all agents, non-establishment diminishes (Fig. 9.5d).

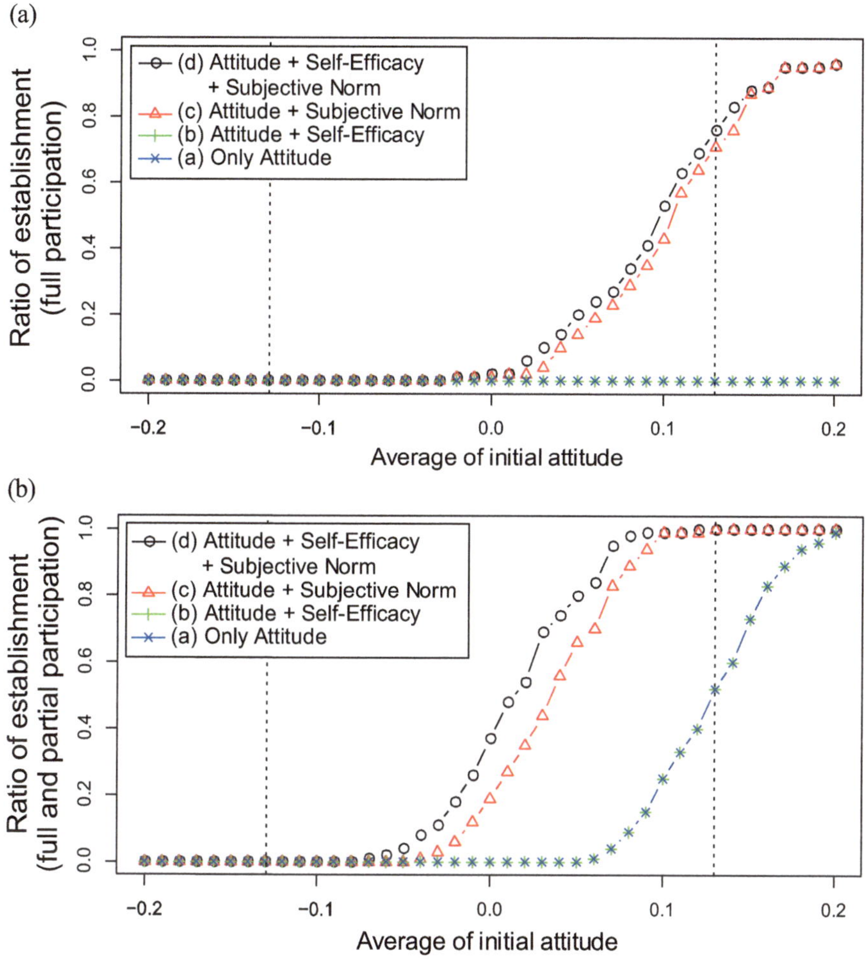

Fig. 9.6 The proportion of establishment with full participation (**a**) and partial and full participation (**b**) in 100 samples for the four settings: **a** only attitude ($\gamma = 0$, $\varepsilon = 0$), **b** attitude + self-efficacy ($\gamma = 0.05$, $\varepsilon = 0$), **c** attitude + subjective norm ($\gamma = 0$, $\varepsilon = 0.5$), and **d** attitude + self-efficacy + subjective norm ($\gamma = 0.05$, $\varepsilon = 0.5$). (Notes: The x-axis is the mean of the initial distribution of attitude (A^0). The variance of the initial distribution is 0.3. The other two internal states are $E_i^0 = S_i^0 = 0$ for all agents. The dashed vertical lines indicate the mean attitude corresponding to situations where the expectation value of the number of initial participants is $\alpha_1 N$ (left) and $\alpha_2 N$ (right), respectively)

9.4.3 Effects of Self-Efficacy and Subjective Norms

We examined the effects of self-efficacy and subjective norms at the broader initial distribution of attitude. Figure 9.6a shows the ratio of the Case (iv) dynamic, establishment with full participation, and Fig. 9.6b shows the ratios of Case (iii) and Case (iv), i.e., establishment with full or partial participation for the four settings (a–d). The initial value of attitude, A_i^0, is determined by normal distributions with various means and a fixed variance of 0.3. Both Case (iii) and Case (iv) can be considered as succeeding in providing GPGs. As the lines for Setting (a), only attitude, and setting (b), attitude + self-efficacy, overlap completely in Fig. 9.6a, b, we confirmed that self-efficacy alone did not affect the provision of a GPG. In the case of partial participation (Fig. 9.6b), GPG is provided for $n^0 \geq \alpha_2 N$ at the initial state and the curves are the accumulated normal distribution.

The effect of the subjective norm, which is exhibited by the difference between Setting (a), only attitude, and setting (c), attitude + subjective norm, depends on the initial distributions. For full participation (Fig. 9.6a), the effect develops linearly, and the mean of the initial attitude increases until approximately 0.18 when the mean value is positive. If we include partial participation in establishment, as in Fig. 9.6b, the subjective norm functions to establish a GPG even in the case of a small negative mean value for initial attitude, where more than half of the agents do not participate at the initial state. In a region where participants more than $\alpha_2 N$, appear as the initial distribution, partial establishment is possible in both Setting (a), only attitude, and Setting (b), attitude + self-efficacy. Therefore, when the expectation value of the number of initial participants is more than $\alpha_2 N$, that is, the right region of the right dashed line in Fig. 9.6b, a GPG is always provided, thanks to the effects of the subjective norm.

The most remarkable point of the synergy effect of self-efficacy and subjective norms, which can be seen as the difference between Setting (c), attitude + subjective norm, and Setting (d), attitude + self-efficacy + subjective norm, is found approximately where the mean of initial attitude is −0.05. This is where the conditions for establishing a GPG are quite harsh because the number of initial participants is very limited (Fig. 9.6b). In this region, the effects of both factors make the provision of GPGs possible, though subjective norms alone are not sufficient. Overall, the synergy effect works for full participation (Fig. 9.6a) when subjective norms have had their effect. For partial participation, it works more efficiently than for full participation until the mean of the initial attitude is 0.8, which exhibits a ceiling effect (Fig. 9.6b).

9.5 Discussion

9.5.1 Suggested Policy to Establish and Maintain International Order

The mechanism where positive feedback between subjective norms and self-efficacy facilitates the provision of GPGs gives us a clue for developing a policy to establish and maintain international order. A precise analysis of the Community Task Game shows that a promising measure to increase the number of participants is to enhance the successful experiences of closely related agents having neutral attitudes (Yamada

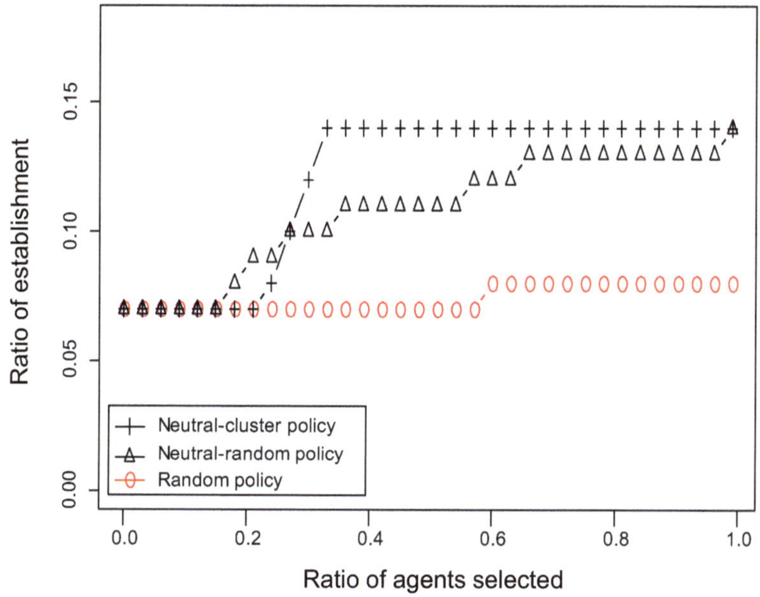

Fig. 9.7 The effects of three different policies for selecting agents whose success experiences are enhanced: neutral-cluster (+), neutral-random (△), and random (○). Notes: The x-axis is the ratio of agents selected; the y-axis is the ratio of establishment (100 samples). The mean of A_i^0 is 0, and E_i^0 and S_i^0 are 0 for all agents

and Hashimoto 2014; Yamada 2016).[1] When an agent participates in the provision of a GPG, if the attitude is not sufficiently high at the onset, then the agent may not be able to maintain participation, even though the provisional activity is successful. Therefore, it is important to select agents whose attitudes are neutral, that is, around $A_i = 0$, so that they can continue to participate and experience at least one or two successes. Further, forming a local cluster of participants, i.e., agents which are closely related, can boost the effects of subjective norms.

Figure 9.7 illustrates the results of an experiment that examined the effects of this policy. Three policies were compared:

- Neutral-cluster policy: Selecting neutral agents with close relationships (located in neighboring sites)
- Neutral-random policy: Selecting neutral agents randomly
- Random policy: Selecting agents randomly from all agents

Neutral agents refer to those with attitudes in the middle third range of all agents at the initial stage. This means that agents' attitudes are near 0, and the initial distribution of attitude is a normal distribution with the mean 0 in this experiment.

[1] Although the agent model (Yamada and Hashimoto 2014; Yamada 2016) is more complicated than described herein, the system's behavior is basically the same.

The ratio of agents selected according to the three policies is a control parameter. In this experiment, only the agents selected changed their self-efficacy, namely, to $\gamma = 0.05$, during the initial five steps and the other agents remained in $\gamma = 0$. We used Setting (d), attitude + self-efficacy + subjective norm, that is, $\varepsilon = 0.5$. The results show that the neutral-cluster policy promoted the possibility of provisioning GPGs by intervention to a lower number of agents than the other two policies.

In the present model, the self-efficacy of agents increases only when they participate and experience success in the task. Therefore, there is no self-efficacy effect on agents which do not participate. If we have the means, such as international negotiation or pressure, to encourage agents to participate in a provisioning activity of GPG, it is better to approach a group of agents with neutral attitudes and to let them participate in a relatively easy-to-achieve task. This is what the experiment's results suggest.

9.5.2 Possibility for the Provision of GPGs Through Means Other Than Participation by Most Agents

In this study, we presented two stable states. The first involves a number of agents greater than the threshold, which is a criterion for all agents who participate in order to obtain positive benefits, and the other is a state where no agents participate. Is there any other possible state that can stabilize society? Figure 9.8 illustrates such a case where a stable state is realized through agent participation at 40%. The spatial structure is indicated in Fig. 9.8b. Here, we find two clusters completely separated into participation and nonparticipation.

Because the number of participants is smaller than the upper threshold of $\alpha_2 N$, the payoff for participants is always negative, and their attitudes continue to decrease to the minimum. On the other hand, the task succeeds and the participants' self-efficacy is strengthened to the maximum, and the number of participants is larger than the lower threshold of $\alpha_1 N$. Their subjective norms are also kept at a high level because surrounding agents other than those at the edge of the participant cluster are all participants. For agents at the edge of the cluster, the surrounding five agents participate and subjective norms at a certain level work to maintain a balance between increase and decrease. Due to meeting this special condition, the effects of subjective norms maintain participation and create a stable state overall, even when the participants' payoff is negative and attitudes are at their lowest. Although this atypical case is a special situation that occurred only under specific parameters and in a two-dimensional space with periodic boundaries and a Moore neighbor, it suggests there is a possibility that the entire structure can become stable by maintaining a block of participants with strong relationships (a delicate balance may be possible in any relationship topology, as in the Cold War structure).

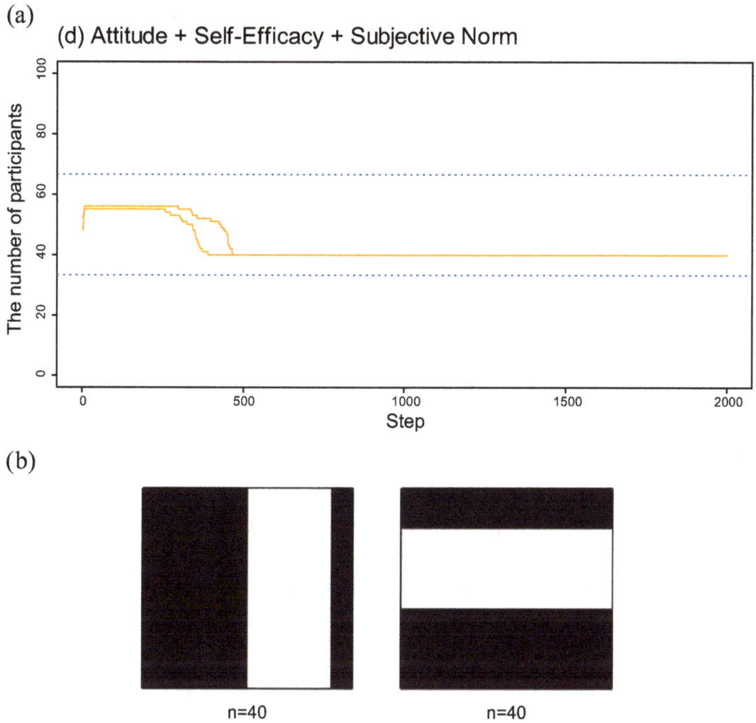

Fig. 9.8 Atypical stable state (Notes: **a** is an example of the dynamics in an atypical stable state. The x-axis is the step, and the y-axis is the number of participants. **b** Is an example of the spatial structure of an atypical stable state. White indicates participants. The mean of A_i^0 is 0 and $E_i^0 = S_i^0 =$ 0 for all agents. The graph in **a** shows the results of longer steps than shown in Figs. 9.2 and 9.4, and it was confirmed that this state did not change in a much longer simulation, that is, this is really a stable state)

9.5.3 Self-Efficacy

We adopt the theory of planned behavior (Ajzen 1991) as our model for individuals. Among the three components of individuals, attitude, subjective norms, and self-efficacy, it is thought that the latter is the most problematic in an international political analysis because the attitudes of different individuals are common to any issue, as is the case in countries, and norms are considered a relevant subject in international regime theory (Krasner 1983). Self-efficacy is a psychological conception related to individual emotion, which represents an individual's belief in his or her own ability to succeed in performing a task. We would like to apply this concept to the behavior and decision-making of a country or a nation state. How can this be accomplished? A country consists of a people. Because what benefits the country basically benefits people in the country, what is considered a benefit to the country is affected by the emotional judgment of people in a democratic country. A democratic political system does not mean that a country's policies are always determined though rational deliberation and careful consultation. Rather, political movements and the outcomes of elections and referendums are often dependent on emotional judgment, as can be seen in the results of the US presidential election and the referendum on Brexit in 2016 and in the rise of ultraconservatism in Europe. Under a dictatorship or an oligarchy system, the emotions of the dictator or a small group of decision makers reflect the policies of the country.

As stated above, self-efficacy reflects an individual's belief in the ability to successfully perform a task. If a people of a county believe in the success of an international activity, including war, the country may engage in the activity. There is a positive emotional cycle that is present in developing or even defeated countries that play certain roles in the international society following development or restoration. Their peoples feel that development is really taking place; they come to acknowledge their own roles in the international society; and they continue to develop. This was seen, for example, in Japan and Germany after World War II and throughout Asian countries in the late twentieth century. Thus, we assert that applying the self-efficacy argument to countries as agents is not necessarily irrelevant.

From this discussion it is naturally thought that self-efficacy constitutes nationalism in part. It should be noted that rising nationalism does not mean to contribute for GPG provision since self-efficacy is just a part of nationalism. Further, what incorporated in our model is the self-efficacy about GPG provision activities, not general self-efficacy.

9.5.4 *Introducion of Heterogeneity*

The purpose of this study is to understand the mechanisms underlying the provision of GPGs by assessing basic properties of the Community Task Game and the agent model through analyzing self-efficacy and subjective norms. Therefore, we used basic and homogeneous settings for the agents. We can introduce various heterogeneities into the present model as follows, while using the findings in this paper as a basis.

9.5.4.1 Initial Values

We used a normal distribution for attitude and zeros for self-efficacy and subjective norms as the initial values for all agents. However, naturally, these internal states actually depend on current internal and surrounding situations as well as the history of each country.

9.5.4.2 Parameters

The important parameters for decision-making are the weights of the internal states, w_A, w_E, and w_S. Uniform values were used in the analysis in the present paper. Here, uniform means the same value for all agents and virtually the same values for all three parameters. The most important factors in decision-making, of course, differ among countries. To understand the mechanism underlying participation in the provision of GPGs, we analyzed the effects of the distributions of these parameter values. To consider actual policy, they should be set according to an actual assessment.

9.5.4.3 Decision-Making and Adaptation

Moreover, the functions to combine factors may be more complicated than our linear combination, and they may differ among countries. The functions used to change the internal states, that is, adaptation to the situation, may also be more complicated than simple up/down equations for attitude and self-efficacy and combining the average values for subjective norms. Yamada and Hashimoto (2014) used nonlinear functions. We confirmed that the basic behaviors were not so different from the range of the present parameters and the initial value settings.

9.5.4.4 Actions

The agents' actions are also uniform: they either participate or they do not. Further, the effect of (non-)participation on GPG is the same. In reality, each country has its own ability of invest in GPGs. In order to incorporate the diversity of investment abilities, i.e., national power, the decision of each country is not merely whether or not to participate but to determine the amount of investment. A payoff function must also be developed to be dependent on the total investment amount.

9.5.4.5 Relations

Although relationships among agents are presently modeled using a regular network, this is also not realistic. The network may be a small word and might be scale-free. The behavior of the previous model (Yamada and Hashimoto 2014) for complex networks was analyzed by Komura et al. (2016). For developing a policy analysis on more realistic relationships among countries, we can refer to their results as a foundation but their analysis is not thorough and is not from the viewpoint of the provision of GPGs.

9.5.5 Further Possible Extensions

Even if all of these heterogeneities were introduced, the model still has a radical and somewhat old-fashioned simplification of the actual situations of international politics. Concerning agents, non-state actors, including enterprises, nongovernmental organizations, and groups of sovereign nations such as the EU and ASEAN, may have different modes of decision-making from the modes assumed in the present model. Modeling situations using only one game is another simplification but it is an abstraction in order to capture the essential mechanism underlying GPG provision. In actuality, games involving goals other than the provision of GPGs, both competitive and cooperative, are played in the domains of economics, politics, military affairs, and culture. Even if we limit the range of interest to the domain of GPG provision, it is reasonable to consider various other games concurrently, such as those involving global warming, other environmental issues, rules for commerce, freedom of navigation, global peace, and scientific research. Further, the importance of such games will change with time and that change depends on the actions and outcomes of the games.

The situation where there are multiple games and both actors' strategies and the importance of each game changes according to the outcomes of all the games simultaneously being played is known as the institutional ecosystem (Nishibe 2010). In this framework, the games represent institutions externally given, equilibria of games are institutions internally formed, and the interactions among actors and among games are considered, figuratively speaking, to represent an ecosystem. The ecosystem is mathematically modeled and analyzed using the rule ecosystem dynamics (Hashimoto and Nishibe 2017). It is reasonable to consider the dynamics of international political situations, including the provision of GPGs, as an institutional ecosystem and to develop a model for analysis using the framework of rule ecosystem dynamics.

The perceptions of the game situations, namely, which games each country believes it is playing, may differ. We may have to consider the different recognitions of games between, for example, a hegemon and other countries, between Western democratic countries and rising nondemocratic countries such as China, and among developing countries in various areas. This perspective has not yet been addressed in either the present model or the institutional ecosystem framework. When we consider payoff function as representing a strict von Neumann–Morgenstern-type utility, each actor makes decisions based on internal utility, and the perception of the situation is considered to be subjective. When the adaptation of each country's strategy is taken into account, we must be aware of the subjectivity and objectivity of utilities. If we adopt some form of replicator dynamics in which strategies change according to different payoffs, for example, imitating that strategy used by an agent that received a higher payoff effectively means that payoff is objectively comparable even though it is considered a subjective utility.

9.6 Conclusion

In this paper, the issue of providing GPGs was analyzed using a multi-agent simulation of the Community Task Game, which is a model used to consider the provision of public goods in community activities. In this simulation, we stressed two internal states of agents, self-efficacy and subjective norms, and investigated the effects of these two variables on the provision of GPGs. Self-efficacy is an agent's self-recognition of its ability to successfully perform a task, including GPG provision activities, and is considered to be a significant feature of a country that is an actor in international politics. A subjective norm is an agent's own recognition of its significant others' desire for the agent to perform a task. We found that self-efficacy alone did not increase agents' intentions to participate in GPG provision activities but it did work to maintain one's intention to continue participating. On the other hand, a subjective norm functions to promote agents' intentions to participate. It was shown that these two internal states had a synergetic effect on increasing the number of participants in the provision of GPGs. We conclude that political interventions to increase the number of participants is to make the self-efficacy of countries increase by encouraging country groups with neutral attitudes and relatively strong mutual relationships to participate in the provision of GPGs. Another way to stabilize GPG provisions, in addition to other than participation by almost all agents, is to create blocks of countries in which subjective norms and actions are common. Finally, for future development of the present work, we discuss three other possibilities: incorporating various heterogeneities into our model as extensions, measuring the dynamics of the international political situation as an institutional ecosystem, and considering countries' various recognition of the game situation.

Acknowledgments This work was partly supported by JSPS KAKENHI Grant Number JP25245027. This research progressed, in part, through discussions with Susumu Egashira and Eizo Akiyama. One of the present authors, T. Hashimoto, is especially grateful for their fruitful discussions. The authors are thankful for the valuable comments of Shigeto Kobayashi, Masayuki Tadokoro, Shigeru Fujimoto, Kazuya Yamamoto, and Makoto Sejima.

References

Ajzen I (1991) The theory of planned behavior. Organ Behav Hum Decis Process 50(2):179–211

Bandura A (1977) Self-efficacy: toward a unifying theory of behavioral change. Psychol Rev 84 (2):191–215

Bandura A (1997) Self-efficacy: the exercise of control. W.H. Freeman, New York

Hashimoto T, Nishibe M (2017) Theoretical model of institutional ecosystems and its economic implications. Evol Inst Econ Rev 14(1):1–27. https://doi.org/10.1007/s40844-017-0071-8

International Task Force on Global Public Goods (2006) Meeting global challenges: international cooperation in the National Interest. Final report. International Task Force on Public Goods, Stockholm

Kaul I, Mendoza RU (2003) Advancing the concept of public goods. In: Kaul I, Conceicao P, Le Goulven K, Mendoza RU (eds) Providing global public goods: managing globalization. Oxford University Press, Oxford

Kaul I, Grunberg I, Stern MA (1999) Defining global public goods. In: Kaul I, Grunberg I, Stern MA (eds) Global public goods: international cooperation in the 21st century. Oxford University Press, New York

Komura K, Mutoh A, Matsui T, Moriyama K, Inuzuka N (2016) Community activity models with network structure (in Japanese). Trans Math Model Appl 9(3):15–23

Krasner SD (ed) (1983) International regimes. Cornell University Press, Ithaca

Ledyard JO (1995) Public goods: a survey of experimental research. In: Kagel JH, Roth AE (eds) The handbook of experimental economics. Princeton, Princeton University Press, pp 111–194

Nishibe M (2010) Institutional ecosystem, four kinds of policies: classification by inner and outer institution. (in Japanese). In: Egashira S, Sawabe N, Hashimoto T, Nishibe M, Yoshida M (eds) Evolutionary economics: its foundation. Nihon Keizai Hyoron Sha, Tokyo, pp 241–250

Rapoport A (1985) Provision of public goods and the MCS experimental paradigm. Am Polit Sci Rev 79(1):148–155

Shirakawa M (2012) International financial stability as a public good. Keynote address at a high-level seminar co-hosted by the Bank of Japan and the International Monetary Fund (IMF) in Tokyo

Takashi H, Sato T, Nakatsuka M, Fujimoto M (2008) Evolutionary constructive approach for studying dynamic complex systems. In: Petrone G, Cammarata G (eds) Recent advances in modeling and simulation. I-Tech Education and Publishing, Aarhus, pp 111–136

Yamada H (2016) Study on mechanism of spontaneous formation and maintenance of local community and its design (in Japanese). Ph.D. dissertation, School of Knowledge Science, Japan Advanced Institute of Science and Technology

Yamada H, Hashimoto T (2015) Formation and expansion of community activity driven by subjective norm and self-efficacy (in Japanese). Trans Jpn Soc Artif Intell 30(2):491–497. https://doi.org/10.1527/tjsai.30.491

MIX
Papier aus verantwortungsvollen Quellen
Paper from responsible sources
FSC® C105338

If you have any concerns about our products,
you can contact us on
ProductSafety@springernature.com

In case Publisher is established outside the EU,
the EU authorized representative is:
Springer Nature Customer Service Center GmbH
Europaplatz 3, 69115 Heidelberg, Germany

Printed by Libri Plureos GmbH
in Hamburg, Germany